BARE BONES

BARE BONES

—┼—

Conversations on Terror with STEPHEN KING

—┼—

Tim Underwood and Chuck Miller,
editors

McGRAW-HILL BOOK COMPANY

New York St. Louis San Francisco Auckland
Bogotá Hamburg London Madrid Mexico Milan
Montreal New Delhi Panama Paris São Paulo
Singapore Sydney Tokyo Toronto

1 2 3 4 5 6 7 8 9 DOC DOC 8 9 2 1 0 9 8

ISBN 0-07-065759-9

LIBRARY OF CONGRESS CATALOGING-IN-PUBLICATION DATA

King, Stephen, 1947–
   Bare bones.

   1. King, Stephen, 1947– —Interviews. 2. Novelists, American—20th century—Interviews. 3. Horror tales—Authorship. I. Underwood, Tim. II. Miller, Chuck, 1952—
PS3561.I483Z465 1987 813'.54 87–31078
ISBN 0–07–065759–9

Book design by Kathryn Parise

ACKNOWLEDGMENTS

Chapter One: "Skeletons in the Closet"

"An Evening with Stephen King at the Billerica, Massachusetts Public Library." Copyright © 1983 by Colony Communications, Inc. All rights reserved. Reprinted by permission.

"Playboy Interview: Stephen King." Published in U.S. *Playboy*, June 1983. Reprinted by Special Permission of *Playboy* magazine. Copyright © 1983 by *Playboy*.

"Would You Buy a Haunted Car from This Man?" by Edwin Pouncey. Published in *Sounds* magazine, May 21, 1983. Copyright © 1983 by Spotlights Publications Ltd. All rights reserved. Reprinted by permission.

Chapter Two: "Building Nightmares"

"The Man Who Writes Nightmares" by Mel Allen. Published in *Yankee* magazine, March 1979. Copyright © 1979 by *Yankee* magazine. All rights reserved. Reprinted by permission.

"An Interview with Stephen King" by Joyce Lynch Dewes Moore. Published in *Mystery* magazine, March 1981. Copyright © by Joyce Lynch Dewes. All rights reserved. Reprinted by permission.

"An Interview with Stephen King" by Paul Janeczko. Published in *English Journal*, February 1980. Copyright © 1980 by the National Council of Teachers of English. All rights reserved. Reprinted by permission of the publisher and the author.

"Interview with Stephen King" by Charles L. Grant. Portions were published in *Monsterland Magazine*, May and June, 1985. Copyright © 1985 by Charles L. Grant. All rights reserved. Reprinted by permission.

"The King of Terror" by Keith Bellows. Published in *Sourcebook*, 1982. Copyright © 1982 by 13-30 Corporation. All rights reserved. Reprinted by permission.

"He Brings Life to Dead Issues" by Christopher Evans. Published in *Minneapolis Star*, September 8, 1979. Copyright © 1979 by *Minneapolis Star*. All rights reserved. Reprinted by permission.

Chapter Three: "Terror Ink"

"Stephen King's Court of Horror" by Abe Peck from *Rolling Stone College Papers*, Winter 1980 by Straight Arrow Publishers, Inc. Copyright © 1980. All rights reserved. Reprinted by permission.

"Interview with Stephen King" by Michael Kilgore. Portions published in *The Tampa Tribune*, August 31, 1980. Copyright © 1986 by Michael Kilgore. All rights reserved. Reprinted by permission.

"Interview with Stephen King" by Mat Schaffer. Broadcast by WBCN-FM Radio's *Boston Sunday Review*, October 31, 1983. Copyright © 1983 by Mat Schaffer. All rights reserved. Reprinted by permission.

"The Night Shifter," extracted from an interview with Stephen King by Stephen Jones. Published in *Fantasy Media*, March 1979, Volume One, Number One. Copyright © 1979 by Stephen Jones. All rights reserved. Reprinted by permission.

"Shine of the Times," an interview with Stephen King by Marty Ketchum, Pat Cadigan, and Lewis Shiner. Published in *Shayol*, Summer 1979, Volume One, Number Three. Copyright © 1979 by Flight Unlimited, Inc. All rights reserved. Reprinted by permission.

"Dear Walden People" by Stephen King. Published in Waldenbooks *Book Notes*, August 1983. Copyright © 1983 by Walden Book Company, Inc. All rights reserved. Reprinted by permission.

Chapter Four: "Hollywood Horrors"

"Flix" by Bhob Stewart. Published in *Heavy Metal*, January, February, and March 1980. Copyright © 1980 by Bhob Stewart. All rights reserved. Reprinted by permission.

"The Dark Beyond the Door: Walking (Nervously) into Stephen King's World" by Freff. Interview originally published in *Tomb of Dracula*, Issues No. 4 and 5. Copyright © 1980 Marvel Comics Group. All rights reserved. Reprinted by permission.

"Topic: Horrors!" by Craig Modderno. Published in *USA Today*, May 10, 1985. Copyright © 1985 *USA Today*. All rights reserved. Reprinted by permission.

"Interview with Stephen King" by Tim Hewitt. Portions published in *Cinefantastique*, Volume 15, Number 2. Magazine copyright © 1985 by Frederick S. Clarke. Book rights retained by Tim Hewitt. All rights reserved. Reprinted by permission.

Chapter Five: "Partners in Fear"

Portions of "Three Interviews with Stephen King and Peter Straub" first appeared in very different form in the following publications: Interview 1 in the *Springfield Morning Union*, October 31, 1979, and in *Fangoria* #6, June 1980. Interview 2 in the *Valley Advocate*, April 8, 1981, and May 27, 1981. Interview 3 in the *Valley Advocate*, October 31, 1984, and in *Fangoria* #42, February 1985, and #43, March 1985. Interview 3 Copyright © 1984 by Stanley Wiater and Roger Anker. Copyright reassigned to Stanley Wiater, and reprinted by permission of the author. All rights reserved and copyright © 1985 by Stanley Wiater.

Chapter Six: "Dancing in the Dark"

"Penthouse Interview: Stephen King" by Bob Spitz. Published in *Penthouse* magazine, April 1982. Copyright © 1982 by Bob Spitz and reprinted with permission of Penthouse International, Ltd. All rights reserved.

Chapter Seven: "The Bad Seed"

CONTENTS

EDITORS' NOTE

This series of interviews was conducted from 1979 through 1987. Textual inconsistencies are inherent in such material and due to copyright restrictions there is occasional duplication of content.

CHAPTER ONE

—✦—

SKELETONS IN THE CLOSET

—✦—

I worry about airplanes. I can remember being on a transcontinental flight and getting to the halfway point—and I thought, what if somebody said, "I need a pillow," and the stewardess opened the overhead rack and all these rats came out into her face, and she started to scream, and the rats were biting off her nose.

An Evening at the Billerica Library

Okay. I'm going to talk for a while. I used to be a high school teacher and high school teachers are sort of like Pavlov's dogs. Pavlov's dogs were taught to salivate at the sound of a bell, and high school teachers are taught to drop their mouths open and begin to work at the sound of a bell for about forty minutes, then another bell rings and they shut up and go away. So even though it's been a while since I've taught high school, I can tell pretty well when about forty minutes has past. I can't really lecture—I'm not good at that—and I can't speak with any sense from prepared notes.

About the most I can do is chautauqua, a fine old word that means you babble on for a little while about the thing that you do and then you sit down and let people get on to the serious drinking. I usually try to dispose of a lot of the questions that are asked—the common ones—in the course of my little chautauqua, or whatever you call it. Of all the questions I'm asked, the most difficult is, "How does it feel to be famous?" Since I'm not, that question always catches me with a feeling of surrealism.

The idea of fame. You know, I've got three kids and I've changed all their diapers in the middle of the night, and when it's two o'clock in the morning and you're changing something that's sort of special delivery with one eye open and one eye shut you don't *feel* famous. And I live in

1

Bangor, Maine, which is not a town calculated to make anybody feel famous. The only claim to fame is a big plastic statue of Paul Bunyan. You just live there and you keep your head down.

What I do is write stories and that seems very natural to me. I think it was two years ago—my youngest son was about six and I was thirty-four—I was ready to go on a promotional tour for *Firestarter*, and my wife asked him, "Owen, do you know where Daddy's going?" and he said "Yes, he's going off to be Stephen King." Which is what happens to me. But every now and then this thing hits you—that you are somebody who's known, let's say, beyond your own street. That maybe somebody is thinking about you at night besides your kids. Or hopefully, lying there, getting scared stiff in their beds. Every now and then it hits you that you're somebody.

But God always gets you: there's always a kicker to it. I remember the first time that I saw somebody that wasn't somebody that I knew actually reading one of my own books. I was on a plane coming from Colorado and going into New York. I'm not a good flier. Being in an airplane scares me because it's a long way down and if the engines stop, you die, that's all. You're dead, goodbye, you're dead. The air was very turbulent that day, and any civilized man's response to that is to get drunk very quickly. So I had two or three gin and tonics.

This was just after *Carrie* had come out in paperback. Now in hardcover, the original press run from Doubleday was 5,000 copies, which meant that a lot of my relatives read it, and a few other people, but I never saw anybody with the hardcover copy. There was this lady in first class on this airplane, and I was drunk, and she was sitting there and reading this book with my name across the front. I thought, okay, I'm getting up and walking in this turbulent plane because I have to go to that room at the front of the plane, and when I get back I'm going to ask that woman how she likes the book and when she tells me she likes it I'm going to sign it for her. I'm going to say I wrote that book, and if I have to show her my driver's license to prove it, I will. So I went up to the little room and I came back and I said, "How do you like that book?" and she said, "I think it's *shitty*." And so I said, "Okay, I won't get that one," and sat back down.

There was another time—I have a beard in the wintertime and I shave it off when the Red Sox start what they call playing baseball—I was in a hot dog joint in New York City. This was around the time of *The Shin-*

ing and I was just sitting there reading a book, eating a hot dog at the counter. I looked up and there happened to be one of these little square places, a pass-through for food where you can look into the kitchen. There was a cook back there, a guy in whites, who was looking at me and as soon as he saw me looking at him he started twirling the dogs and doing the french fries and everything. So I read my book some more and then I looked up a while later and he was looking at me again and I thought to myself, I've been *recognized*. It was sort of a golden moment. I was recognized. And a little while later the guy came out around the door that said "Employees Only" and he wiped his hands on his white apron and walked up to me and said, "Are you somebody?" And I said, "Yeah, everybody's somebody," and he said, "Yeah, I know they are, but you're *somebody*." And I said, "Yeah, sort of." And he said, "Are you Francis Ford Coppola?" And I said, "Yeah, I am." So he asked me for an autograph and I signed it Francis Ford Coppola. That was bad. God always gets you for that.

People also ask, "Why do you write that stuff?" That's one that always comes up. The first reason is because I'm warped, of course. A lot of people are afraid to say that, but I'm not. I have a friend named Robert Bloch, who wrote the novel *Psycho*, on which Hitchcock's film was based, and he would always say in answer to that question, "Actually, I have the heart of a small boy. I keep it in a jar on my desk."

Another reason that I've always written horror is because it's a kind of psychological protection. It's like drawing a magic circle around myself and my family. My mother always used to say, "If you think the worst, it can't come true." I know that's only a superstition, but I've always believed that if you think the very worst, then, no matter how bad things get (and in my heart I've always been convinced that they can get pretty bad), they'll never get as bad as *that*. If you write a novel where the bogeyman gets somebody else's children, maybe they'll never get your own children.

When people ask that question, "Why do you write this stuff?" they're talking about the real horror. They're talking about *The Shining*, where the little boy goes in the bathroom and pushes back the curtain and there's a dead lady in the tub and she comes out to get him. They're talking about vampires and things like that. But for me, writing is like a little hole in reality that you can go through and you can get out and you can be someplace else for a while. I live a very ordinary life. I have the children, and I have the wife—except for this thing that I do, this glitch, it's a very ordinary life.

I still remember the one moment that stood out for me, when I was a kid reading fiction. There's a book by C. S. Lewis called *The Lion, the Witch and the Wardrobe*. (Wardrobe is an Englishism for closet.) It's one of the Narnia stories. In the story, the kids are playing hide-and-go-seek and I was familiar with that game. This girl, Lucy, goes into a closet, and it seems to her to be very deep, a *very* deep closet. She's pushing through the coats—you know that dry smell of mothballs and that sort of slick feel of fur coats—and she looks down and the boards are gone and it's white down there, and she reaches down and touches it and it's cold. That minute, when the boards turned to snow, I thought, that's it, that's what I want to do. It's got to be something like that. That point when the writer or the filmmaker is able to take the reader over that line, to me, is a fine thing. For me it's always a fine place to go.

The other thing is, I really like to scare people. I really enjoy that. After *'Salem's Lot* was published, one lady sent me a letter and said, "You know, you ought to be ashamed of yourself. I'm sending this book back to you. You really frightened me. I couldn't sleep for three nights after I read this." I wrote her back and said, "So what. You bought it, I didn't buy it for you. I'm *glad* you were awake for three nights. I wish it had been six nights." The trick is to be able to get the reader's confidence. I'm not really interested in killing somebody in the first paragraph of a novel. I want to be your friend. I want to come up to you and put my arm around you and say, "Hey, you want to see something? It's *great!* Wait till you *see* it! You'll *really* like this thing." Then I get them really interested and lead them up the street and take 'em around the corner and into the alley where there's this awful thing, and keep them there until they're *screaming!* It's just fun. I know how sadistic that must sound, but you have to tell the truth.

The question that goes along with this, of course, is why do people read that stuff? Why do people want to go see those movies? And the answer that we all shy away from—but it's true—is that they're just as warped as I am. Not quite, but almost. You know, there was a reporter who caught me at the fourth World Fantasy Convention in Baltimore. It was before the banquet at which I had to make a speech and I was nervous, as I'm nervous every time I have to stand up before a bunch of people and talk. He said, "What do you think of your fans?" and I said, "Well, they're sort of like me. They're sort of warped—that's why they like this stuff." So the story came out in the newspaper, "King says his fans are warped"—which is true, but I had also said to this guy that I think you have to have a few warps in your record in order to survive life as we know it today.

I think, more seriously, they also like it because of what's between the lines. People read between the lines. Any piece of horror fiction, whether it's in the form of a novel or a movie, has subtext. There are things in between those lines that are full of tension. In other words, horror fiction, fantasy fiction, imaginative fiction is like a dream.

The Freudians say that our dreams are symbolic. They may or may not be, but a lot of the frights, a lot of the nightmares that we get in books and in movies really are symbolic. It may be talking about a vampire, it may be talking about a werewolf... but underneath or between the lines, in the tension, where the fear is, there's something else going on altogether. I know that, for instance, in my novel 'Salem's Lot, the thing that really scared me was not vampires, but the town in the daytime, the town that was empty, knowing that there were things in closets, that there were people tucked under beds, under the concrete pilings of all those trailers. And all the time I was writing that, the Watergate hearings were pouring out of the TV. There were people saying "at that point in time." They were saying, "I can't recall." There was money showing up in bags. Howard Baker kept asking, "What I want to know is, what did you know and when did you know it?" That line haunts me, it stays in my mind. It may be *the* classic line of the twentieth century: what did he know and when did he know it. During that time I was thinking about secrets, things that have been hidden and were being dragged out into the light. It shows a little bit in the book, although I think that most books should be written and read for fun.

You see these subtexts everywhere but I think they're the most fun, really, in the movies. In the fifties there was a spate of horror movies in the United States that were about giant bugs. There were giant bugs everywhere in the fifties. There was a movie called *Them!* where there were giant ants in the storm drains in Los Angeles. And there was one called *Tarantula*, where Leo G. Carroll had taken this little tarantula and had grown it very big; in one place it's sort of crawling up Route 66 and one of the jet pilots that shoots it is Clint Eastwood, in his first screen role. But you don't care about Clint, you care about that big spider. There was *The Beginning of the End*, where giant grasshoppers took over Chicago. They got rid of the giant grasshoppers by recording the mating call of the wild grasshopper; they took a bunch of boats out on Lake Michigan and put it through loudspeakers and all those grasshoppers came off the buildings and went into the lake and drowned—'cause sex always gets you in the end.

There were a whole bunch of those films, but I think that my personal favorite is the all-time classic movie, *The Deadly Mantis*. It starred William Hopper, who used to play Paul Drake on the old *Perry Mason* show. This picture featured a gigantic praying mantis inside a cake of ice which actually ends up hopping around in New York City. At one point it knocks over a city bus and you can see the word "Tonka" written across the bottom of that bus. It's one of those moments when you know why you kept going to the movies all those years. It's so great.

But the *cause* of the horror in all those movies was always the same thing. It was radiation. The films would often start with news footage of bombs being exploded on Bikini Atoll or the Mojave Desert. The old scientist at the end of *Them!* says, "We've opened a door that we can never close and there's a white light behind that door." Again and again, these huge bugs would come down on our cities and stomp them flat in a fairly clear symbolic representation of what a real nuclear weapon would do to a real city. It was always a city being destroyed and it was always radiation that caused it.

This was about the time that people first began to realize that our friendly atom wasn't going to be old friendly Redi-Kilowatt after all. Fallout radiation was showing up in cow's milk and then in mother's milk. Nasty old strontium 90. But there was never a film producer in the fifties, in the days when American International was making pictures in seven days for $40,000, who said, "This is a burning social issue." Instead, they said, "We've got to make some bucks. What's a good idea? What's going to scare people?" And what they came up with was a kind of Rorschach, which they knew was going to scare people.

A few years ago, Jane Fonda produced and starred in a movie called *The China Syndrome*, which featured this same big-bug fear. She and her people said to themselves, "We've got a point to make here. Let's scare people and see if we can't get them to reconsider this business before something terrible really happens." But six years before that, a couple of drive-in entrepreneurs from Connecticut had made a picture called *The Horror of Party Beach*, which is an awful movie, a dreadful movie. But it begins with radiation waste being dumped in Long Island Sound, and then these bones of dead sailors sink down there—are you getting this?—and they sort of come back to life and get the girls at the slumber party. It's marvelous. It made a lot of money and it scared a lot of people. It's dreadful, but it combined the beach party movies and the horror movies into one film. The point is, when these two Connecticut drive-in entrepreneurs got together they didn't say, "Let's talk about nuclear wastes and nuclear dumping and what's happening to that stuff." They said, "Let's make a buck." What comes out is that subtext, that thing between the lines, which is another way of saying, "What scares you? What scares me? Let's talk about our nightmares."

The same thing is true with the original version of *The Thing*, which appeared back in Joe McCarthy's time. Everybody was afraid of the Reds. There was supposed to be a Red under every bed; everybody was afraid of the fifth column. There was a show with Richard Carlson on TV at that time called *I Led Three Lives*, where he made it clear that every librarian, every college dean...they were all commies. They were working for *those guys*. So the army, in the original Howard Hawks version of *The Thing*, finds a monster in an ice cube—he's always in an ice cube—I always think of those novelties with the fly in the ice cube—so they find this creature and thaw it out. They all want to kill it, they all know it's evil—except for the scientist, who's one of these fellows who wants to lie down with the bad guys, someone who's soft, you know, and intellectual, who doesn't realize that the army has the best answer to these things, which is, get rid of them quick. And the scientist says, "I think we can learn a lot from this creature. Let's talk to him." But of course he gets killed and then Kenneth Tobey fries the thing on an electric sidewalk and that's the end of that creature and it's a victory for America.

About twenty-five years later, a few years ago, along comes John Carpenter and remakes *The Thing*. (A lot of critics didn't care for the movie but I thought it was a marvelous remake.) Times have changed. Richard Carlson's *I Led Three Lives* is no longer on the tube. People are not so concerned with a Red under every bed as they are about other things. When you say to people, "What are you afraid of, what scares you?"

they'll list a number of things. One of the things that very obviously scares a lot of people is cancer. We live in a society with an information over-load, information comes in from everywhere, it pours in—the last two or three years, especially. Cigarettes are no good for you, they're going to pollute your lungs, you're going to get lung cancer, have heart attacks. Lung cancer scares people. Don't drink too much coffee because you'll get stomach cancer, gall bladder cancer. Don't eat too much meat—bowel cancer, uh-oh. Don't breathe too much air, because hydrocarbons do all sorts of things. We've got PVC brain cancer, the stuff that's in animal feed now supposedly can give you cancer. Cancer is everywhere. It's all around us. So Carpenter's version of *The Thing* focuses on *mutation*.

In the late seventies and early eighties, we see a spate of what I think of as tumor movies, where there are things inside that come out and they look real bad. I mean they don't look like anything that you'd have at your supper table. The example that everybody remembers is *Alien*, where there was a fellow—and this really does happen at dinner, it's sort of the ultimate affront—who begins to say, "I don't feel well, my stomach's up-set," and this *thing* sort of rips its way out of his stomach and goes scur-rying off. That seems to me to be a very clear tumor imagery. The same thing exists in John Carpenter's remake of *The Thing*, where again we're seeing things that are growing inside.

A lot of Canadian filmmaker David Cronenberg's work focuses on this idea, that things are *growing* inside of you. Cronenberg studied for and got a degree in medicine; cancer is one of the things that he's frankly very worried about, and it shows in his work. Time and time again in his films, people are actually incubating parasites inside their bodies. There's another movie called *The Beast Within* that expresses the same idea.

One more thing and then we'll go on. Probably the most famous hor-ror movie of the last twenty-five years is *The Exorcist*, which drew a tre-mendous audience. Everybody's talked about the Catholic thing, a lot of people supposedly came to see it because of that religious infusion—the idea that here was a story of good and evil with religious overtones. But don't forget that at this time the youth quake of the sixties was going on. Kids were coming home and saying the president of the United States was a war criminal; they were also coming home and saying a lot of words at the supper table that they never learned from their parents. (Well, may-be they did, but maybe their parents didn't know they were listening.) Parents were finding things in bureau drawers that didn't look like Herbert

Tareytons. And in the midst of all this comes the story of this pretty little fourteen-year-old girl, Regan, who turns into a harridan: her hair is dirty, her face is covered with terrible sores, she's swearing at her mother and at the priest and saying all these nasty words. All of a sudden all those harried parents understood what had happened to their children, who had grown their hair long and had thrown away their bras. The devil did it! The devil was in them, and it was very comforting to understand that what happened to their children wasn't their fault.

People like this "religious" interpretation because it confirms their normative values. Horror fiction has always had a reputation as an outlaw genre. It's thought of as kind of nasty, and when people see you reading *'Salem's Lot* or something similar, there's a little bit of an attitude that you must be strange or warped. And of course a guy like me, who actually *writes* it, is like the geek in the circus. The geek was the guy who supposedly bit the head off a live chicken and ate it. (How was your supper tonight, by the way?)

But horror fiction is really as Republican as a banker in a three-piece suit. The story is always the same in terms of its development. There's an incursion into taboo lands, there's a place where you shouldn't go, but you do, the same way that your mother would tell you that the freak tent is a place you shouldn't go, but you do. And the same thing happens inside: you look at the guy with three eyes, or you look at the fat lady, or you look at the skeleton man or Mr. Electrical or whoever it happens to be. And when you come out, well, you say, "Hey, I'm not so bad. I'm all right. A lot better than I thought." It has that effect of reconfirming values, of reconfirming self-image and our good feelings about ourselves.

One small example that I love—there was a movie in 1957 called *I Was a Teenage Frankenstein*. In this one the great-grandson of Dr. Frankenstein is living in this small Hollywood suburb and he's on a very busy corner where teenage hot-rodders get killed roughly every four or five hours...there's always this scream of tires and another one of those terrible boys from Hollywood High bites the dust. Although this guy lives in L.A., he has alligators down below his house. There seems to be some sort of a Jacuzzi down there that's full of alligators and there's also a trap door. What he's doing is, he's taking these dead hot-rodders into his house and chopping off the parts of their bodies that are usable and sewing them together to make the ultimate sort of James Dean/*High School Confidential!* thing and when he's done—the last hot-rodder has obviously hit the street on his face—he's created the worst kid you knew in high school, with a face that looks like Mount Vesuvius. It makes this Frankenstein fellow look like Robert Redford in comparison.

Of course, much of the movie audience, much of the impact audience, are teenagers who don't feel good about themselves a lot of the time, who feel confused, who look in the mirror and instead of seeing somebody who's perhaps better than they really are (which we tend to do as we get older, I think), they see somebody who's much, much worse. They think, "How can I go to school? I look awful. I've got zits on my face. I'm ugly. I don't have any friends. Nobody likes me." So for them, the horror movie or the horror story has a reconfirming value, where they can see themselves again in a valuable way, as part of the mainstream, part of what we call the norm. They feel better about themselves, and for that reason the experience is probably valuable. It's also reactionary, it resists any kind of change. In these movies things should never change. Boris Karloff and Elsa Lanchester are never allowed to get married because, well, think of the kids. You wouldn't want them on your street. So they always end up getting burned to death or they end up going around and around on a windmill, or something terrible happens to them. An electrocution, anything, just get rid of them.

Last reason for reading horror: it's a rehearsal for death. It's a way to get ready. People say there's nothing sure but death and taxes. But that's not really true. There's really only death, you know. Death is the biggie. Two hundred years from now, none of us are going to be here. We're all going to be someplace else. Maybe a better place, maybe a worse place; it may be sort of like New Jersey, but someplace else. The same thing can be said of rabbits and mice and dogs, but we're in a very uncomfortable position: we're the only creatures—at least as far as we know, though it may be true of dolphins and whales and a few other mammals that have very big brains—who are able to contemplate our own end. We know it's going to happen. The electric train goes around and around and it goes under and around the tunnels and over the scenic mountains, but in the end it always goes off the end of the table. Crash.

We have to do something about this awareness. That we can deal at all with our daily lives without going insane is one of the best proofs of the godhead that I know. Somehow we're going about living, and most of us are being good to our friends and our relatives, and we help the old lady across the street instead of pushing her into the gutter. And at the same time we know that sooner or later it's going to end. My favorite deathbed story is Oscar Wilde, who had been in a coma for three days and was obviously sinking and nobody expected him to come to. But he was contrary to the end, and he came to and he looked around himself and said, "Either that wallpaper goes or I go." And he went. The wallpaper stayed.

In that way, the horror story or the horror movie is a little bit like the amusement park ride. When there's a double bill at the drive-in, it turns into an amusement park for teenagers—and sometimes the amusement is not always on the screen. I think of teenagers because in spite of their self-image problems, they feel healthy, they feel good inside themselves. Those bones are easy inside the arms, the heart feels good inside the chest. They're not people who lie there at night and say, "I've got to sleep on the right side because if I sleep on the left I'm going to wear it out faster." That happens later on. Teenagers feel healthy and they can cope with, let's say, the rides in the amusement park that mimic violent death, things like the parachute drop where you get to experience your own plane crash, the bumper cars where you get to have a harmless head-on collision, and so on.

The same thing is true of the horror movie. You very rarely see old people on their golden-agers passes lurching out of theaters playing *Zombie* and *I Eat Your Skin*, because they don't need that experience. They know. They don't need to rehearse death. They've seen their friends go, they've seen their relatives go. They're the ones who sleep on their right side, they feel the arthritis. They know the pain, they live with the pain, and they don't need to rehearse it because it's there. The rest of us sometimes do.

I also think that some of horror's current popularity has to do with the failure of religion. My wife is a fallen-away Catholic and I'm a fallen-away Methodist. As a result, while we both keep in our hearts a sort of realization of God, the idea that God must be part of a rational world, I must say that our children are much more familiar with Ronald McDonald than they are with, let's say, Jesus or Peter or Paul or any of those people. They can tell you about the Burger King or the Easter Bunny but some of this other stuff they're not too cool on. Horror fiction, supernatural horror fiction, suggests that we go on.

All those supernatural possibilities are there. Good or bad, black or white, they suggest that we go on. I started off saying that I write horror because I'm warped and the people who read it read it because they're warped, but I also said I write it because it's a trip. It's like what Rod Serling used to say: "There's a signpost up ahead. Next stop, the Twilight Zone." Every now and then people need to go there. You have to have a little insanity in your life, in your conscious life as well as your unconscious or dreaming life.

People ask what scares me. Everything scares me. Bugs are bad. Bugs are *real* bad. Sometimes I think about taking a bite into a great big hoagie, you know, and...full of bugs. Imagine that. Isn't that awful? Elevators. Getting stuck in elevators. Having that door just open on a blank wall. Especially if it's full and you can't even really take a breath. Airplanes. The dark is a big one. I don't like the dark. Dark rooms—I always leave a light on in the bathroom when I'm in a hotel and I always say to myself, well, this is because if I have to get up in the night and go to the bathroom I don't want to stumble over the cable that goes to the TV. But really it's so the thing under the bed can't get out and get me. I know it isn't there and I know that as long as there's some light in the room it can't come out. Because that's like kryptonite, the thing under the bed, it can't come out without following certain rules.

I always leave the light on when I leave the hotel room because I think about coming into a strange room and feeling for the light switch and having a hand close over mine and put it on the switch. We can laugh about these things and have a good time now because the lights are on and we're all together. But later on, sooner or later, everybody's alone. It's like keeping your feet under the covers when you're in bed, because when you're a kid you understand that if you let them dangle out— *phfoof*—you're down under there and you can't ever come out again.

Just about everything frightens me, in one way or another. I can see something frightening in most things. And I think about getting all of this out—you know, there are people who are full of fear in our society who pay psychiatrists $75 or $80 an hour and it's not even a full hour, it's about fifty minutes. And I get rid of all of this stuff by writing and people pay me. It's great. I love it.

Last of all, people ask, "Where do you get your ideas?" That's the toughest one. Usually what I say is Utica, I get my ideas in Utica. There's no satisfactory way to answer that question, but you can answer it individually and say this idea came from here, this idea came from there. With *'Salem's Lot*, I was teaching *Dracula* in high school; I taught it three or four times, and every time I taught it I got more interested in what a really strong novel it was. We were talking about it with a friend one night at supper and I said, "This is the magic question. What would happen if Dracula came back today?" And my wife said, "Well, he'd land at Port Authority in New York and get run over by a taxicab and that'd be the end of him." And then this friend of mine said, "But suppose he came back to a little town somewhere inland in Maine. You know, you go through some of those little towns and everybody could be dead and you'd never know it."

Anyway, every now and then before I fell asleep, after I'd made sure my feet were under the covers, this idea would rise back up and I'd think about it for a while and then put it away, and finally the story kind of crystallized and I had to write it.

Now, some months ago my youngest boy, the one who says Daddy's going off to be Stephen King, said, "I've got one problem with kindergarten." And I said, "What's that?" And he said, "I'm embarrassed about going to the basement." And at first I thought he meant the basement. I couldn't imagine why they were sending kindergarten kids down to the school basement. Then this sort of ancient memory from grammar school came up in my mind and I thought, he means the bathroom, because that's what we always used to say, "Can I go to the basement." Okay.

He said, "We have to raise our hands to go to the basement, and everybody knows that I have to go pee-pee." So I immediately set out to say, "Well, listen, don't be embarrassed about this, Owen. This is perfectly okay." Then I shut my mouth because I remembered that I had been terribly embarrassed about that as well. So I said something that I hoped was comforting, and a little story came out of it, which was, I think, a direct response to that question. I began to play with the idea of mean old teachers who make you raise your hands in front of all these little kids and they all laugh when you're walking out of the room because they *know* what you're going to do. They know it.

This became the story *Here There Be Tigers*, which was for my little boy. But it's also for anybody else who wants it or needs it or anybody else who ever sat there in school and suffered 'cause you didn't want to admit in front of everybody else that you had to do those things.

Q: What is your favorite, your best novel? And how did you get all those cockroaches in the movie *Creepshow*?

KING: I don't go along with words like best or anything. I'm afraid to use those. The one that I think works the best is *Dead Zone*. It's the one that seems to me to be the most story. And as for the cockroaches in *Creepshow*, most of them were *cockroachus giganticus*, which grow in South America in caves that are full of bats, and they're actually cheaper than local bugs.

We mounted an expedition that became the cockroach trip. I didn't go on it, but I heard a wonderful story. They're cheaper because American cockroaches cost 50 cents apiece, from these supply houses. I know there are people who pay to get rid of them but it's the truth—50 cents apiece for American roaches, but down there you can get them free. You just have to sign a paper that says that you'll destroy them all when you come back into the country.

So they went down there, these fellows who've got a credit at the end of the movie, the roach wranglers, and they dealt with the roaches. They went down there, and these caves where the bats had been there for thousands of years are full of bat guano. And the roaches live in the guano. Billions of these gigantic cockroaches are living, if you can allow me to be crude for a minute, they're living in bat shit. The smell in those caves is really awful, and these guys wore wet suits and they wore skin divers' tanks and regulators. And they discovered they could fall flat in the guano—of course they were protected by their wet suits and they had the air—and the cockroaches were very frightened and they went into their little roachie houses or whatever. But after a while, since they just have little brains, they forget. They would come out and start to motorboat around. The roaches would be on the move and the guys would have to go all over the place to get them. Isn't that a wonderful story?

Also, they were easier to work with because they were big. I did an interview with these big roaches crawling all over me. It was for *Entertainment Tonight*, and I think I flubbed some of the questions. We sort of freoned the roaches. They lived in garbage cans, and they ate a mixture of Gainesmeal and bananas. The smell was terrible, but they had their own trailer and they were well treated. That's my bug story.

Q: Have you ever written anything really scary that kept you up all night?

KING: Yeah. Not very often though, because a lot of the time you feel like you've got it in the palm of your hand. In *'Salem's Lot*, Ben Mears has one of these globes that you shake up and it's full of snow. A lot of times the really scary stuff feels like that, to me. It feels like you've got it finally, whatever scared you real bad, you've got it in this thing and it's yours and it can't get out.

But sometimes I think it does get out. The worst one was the tub thing in *The Shining*, where the little boy goes in and discovers the dead woman and the dead woman gets out and chases him. It wasn't too bad when I wrote it; all at once it was there. It was one of those things that just happened. It was nothing that was planned to be in the book. It just happened. But on the rewrite, as I got closer to that point, I would say to myself, eight days to the tub, and then six days to the tub. And then one day it was *the tub today*. When I went down to the typewriter that day I felt frightened and my heart was beating too fast and I felt the way that you do when you have to make a big presentation, or when something's going to happen. And I was scared. I did the best job I could with it, but I was glad when it was over.

Pet Sematary was like that, the whole book was like that. Once I was on *Good Morning America* . . . I guess this goes back to what I was saying about how you never feel like a celebrity, and then all at once, you're on TV and you know that millions of people are watching you over their breakfast. I mean they're scarfing English muffins and eggs or whatever it is they scarf, bourbon and whatever. But they're looking at you; maybe with only half an eye, but they're looking at you. I was very frightened and this lady interviewed me, and she gave me a question that I've never been asked before. (This does happen, but for most questions a tape deck pops in your mind and you spiel off the answer.) She asked, "Have you ever written anything so frightening that you wouldn't publish it?" And I said, "I've written this novel called *Pet Sematary*." Well, obviously I published it, and on reconsideration I don't think it's possible to write in a book anything so frightening. Maybe something that's so gruesome that people wouldn't want to read it, but as far as actual fright goes, no, I don't think that in prose it's possible to do that. The only two things I ever read where the fright actually raised itself to uncomfortable levels were the end of *Lord of the Flies* and near the end of *Nineteen Eighty-four*. What I meant was that one part was so painful for me and such a hard thing to get through that I didn't want to work it over again, but I did. Why not?

Q: I've enjoyed everything of yours and I particularly like *The Stand*—

KING: Thank you. Randy Flagg, my man.

Q: It helps you look out for the evil people in the world. Throughout all your novels I had the feeling there were two characters who were closely associated with you personally: Carrie was one of them, and Harold in *The Stand* was another.

KING: Oh, Harold Water. Thanks. I've got some friends that'll be at your house tonight. They only come out after dark. What type is your blood?

Harold is based to a large extent on me, or on parts of me. Any character that any writer creates.... You try to get out, you look at people, and you try to feel for people a little bit and understand the way they think. But, Harold is a terrible loner, and he's somebody who feels totally rejected by everybody around him, and he feels fat and ugly and unpleasant most of the time. He has other bad habits that I won't go into. And sometimes I used to feel rejected and unpleasant. I can remember that from high school. And of course Harold is sort of a frustrated writer. But on the whole, if there was a Harold aspect to my own character, it was fairly small because most of the time I felt much sunnier. I never felt resentful and I certainly never felt that the people around me didn't appreciate my great and blazing talent, because there were times when I thought that if I had a great and blazing talent, it was probably for picking my nose in study hall.

But there's a little bit of Carrie White in me too. I've seen high school society from two perspectives, as has any high school teacher. You see it once from the classroom, where the rubber bands fly around, and you see it again from behind the desk. You see high school society.

I said that horror fiction was conservative and that it appeals to teenagers—the two things go together because teenagers are the most conservative people in American society. You know, small children take it as a matter of course that things will change every day and grown-ups understand that things change sooner or later and their job is to keep them from changing as long as possible. It's only kids in high school who are convinced they're never going to change. There's always going to be a pep rally and there's always going to be a spectator bus, somewhere out there in their future.

In that light, social castes form that are almost as firmly set as the castes of society in India, where you've got the top people at the top. They're the guys—generally, it's economically based—they're the kids who had braces and orthodontics, so their teeth don't look all yucky when they smile. They're into Clearasil and the National Honor Society and things like that. And then you've got your middle-class kids, who just sort of hang around their lockers and say, "Hey, how are you, man?" like that. And then there are always two or three who are just hanging out. There's a guy in *Christine* who's sort of a form of that.

But I was never really that way. There were a couple of girls I knew, who formed facets of Carrie White's character. I think girls are always much more vicious about this, much more aware of it than boys are, but boys do a good job when they get going.

Q: *The Body* seemed so real. Did that story really happen to you?

KING: No. But again, this goes back to "Where do you get your ideas?" I had a roommate in college, George McCloud, to whom this story is dedicated. He grew up in a little, what I'd call upscale, trendy community; a place like Westin, Massachusetts, where all the girls wear A-line skirts and cardigans and that kind of thing. He said he'd never seen a dead animal. Where he lived there was a street-cleaning team, and if there were sparrows or wood-chucks or anything that got plastered in the road, they were sort of scraped up before little kids whose minds could be warped were up and outside.

One day at their summer camp, or whatever it was, a story circulated that a dog had been hit by a train and the dead body was on the tracks. These guys are saying, "And you should see it, man, it's all swelled up and its guts are falling out and it's *real* dead. I mean it's just as dead as you ever dreamed of anything being dead." And you could see it your-self just walk down these tracks and take a look at it, which they did. George said, "Someday I'd like to write a story about that," but he never did. He's running a restaurant now, a great restaurant.

So about five years ago I went to him and said, "I took your idea and I wrote a story about these kids who walk down a railroad track to find the body of a boy." I didn't think anybody would be too interested in going to look at the body of a dog. I took the main character and I took a lot of the things that I had felt when I was a kid and put them into that character, Gordon McChance. But John Irving also says, never believe a writer when he seems to be offering you autobiography, because we all lie. We all edit it and we say, well, this is what happened, but that doesn't make a good story, so I'll change it. So it's mostly a lie.

Q: In *Cujo* it surprised me when the little boy died. Did you know you were going to kill him?

KING: No, but I got mad. When I was talking about fears, you know, I was talking about the bogeyman and all those things—those are real fears with me. They're not anything that's ruling my life, but one of the things that really does frighten me is the idea of coming in some night to check on my kids—you know, you go around at night and check on them—and finding one of them dead.

A lot of people say, well, it must be great to have an imagination, you know, a really good imagination. Look at you, you've made a lot of money and it's fantastic. If you want to fly first class, you can fly first class, and all the rest of it. But other things come up. It isn't just the idea that you might find your kid dead. It comes in Technicolor. You see the swelled neck and the staring eyes and the rest of it. I've been drawn back to the idea, again and again, that if you write it, if this is the worst thing that you can think of, and you write it down, then it'll be all right.

There's a boy in 'Salem's Lot who gets away. His name is Mark Petrie and he and the writer, Ben Mears, get away. There's a little boy in The Shining, Danny Torrance, who also gets away. I think most of the times the kids get away. But we also know as adults, as thinking rational people, that sometimes they don't. There are crib deaths, there are kids who are abused and get killed that way. I didn't know that the kid in Cujo was going to die until he died. He wasn't supposed to die. He was just gone. His mother tried to give him respiration, and the kid just wouldn't come back.

Q: How do you regiment your time, with your writing? And how do you write, at a typewriter or a word processor or longhand?

KING: Whatever it is I'm working on, that's the most important or the most serious, I work on in the morning. I worked with Peter Straub on The Talisman, and we used word processors for that. I have a Wang—I think Wang rules this part of Massachusetts—he has an IBM. The Wang is by far superior to the IBM. Cheaper, too. So when I worked on that, I worked with a word processor. But it's tough. I don't like it in a way, because it's more like being a spectator. Once the stuff is out, there's that screen and it's very handy but it's also strange. I write every morning from eight until eleven, or from eight until ten-thirty if I'm not hung over and if I'm having a good day. Then at night, after everybody's in bed, sometimes I'll play with something. I'll have an idea, I'll push it around a little and have a little fun with it. So I usually work on two things at one time. If one of them blows up, it doesn't matter.

Q: If you personally had lived through some real-life horror, if you had experienced Hiroshima or the bombing of Dresden or Vietnam, would you still write about horror?

KING: I think so, yes. I forgot to mention when I was talking about subtext and about the bug movies that the very people who actually *felt* the atomic bomb were the first ones to create an atomic monster out of their—and I'm convinced of this, really—out of their national nightmares.

The Japanese in 1954 released a movie called *Godzilla*. Godzilla is a creature which comes to the surface because of atomic testing. He has atomic halitosis; he goes huuuuh and blows up whole cities. We're treated to a very long, sort of surreal destruction of Tokyo, and the results at the end look very much as though a nuclear weapon had been at work. It's all in flames and there are a lot of people dead. It seems to me that this is an effort by the Japanese to work this thing out. So to answer your question, I think if you have it, it works whether you want it to work or not.

Q: I find that very hard to believe. I went through World War II and I find it very hard to write about.

KING: Yeah, but the same thing is true of a lot of World War II writers like Leon Uris and Norman Mailer. Leon Uris wrote *Battle Cry*, Mailer was—

Q: But those people didn't go through what they wrote about.

KING: Oh yes. Mailer was on that island that he wrote about in *The Naked and the Dead*. When Herman Wouk wrote *The Caine Mutiny*, he wrote about the very experience that he underwent. He was on a mine-sweeper in the South Pacific. These things are conscious efforts to deal with what they've been through. I think this is true of a lot of horror fiction as well.

Q: Is *The Stand* going to be a motion picture?

KING: Yes. I've got to work on the screenplay some more and then it's going to be a motion picture. Should be pretty good. Robert Duvall might play Randy Flagg.

Q: We all aspire to do something different. You do what you do very well. But twenty years from now what do you expect from Stephen King?

KING: I don't know. 'Cause I just go day by day. I love to write. But there are other things. I'd like to be a pro bowler. And also I'd like to be Smokey Robinson. You know I'd love to be able to jive, to be Ike Turner or somebody like that. Everybody has those things. If I'm alive in twenty years, I suppose I'll still be writing things, unless I go dry, which I guess is always a possibility. If that happened I'd like to be able to accept it with grace and not stick a gun in my mouth the way that Hemingway did.

Q: Do you think your books are hard to bring to the screen?

KING: I thought the film treatment of *Carrie* was great. I really liked it because the novel is the novel of a very young man. I think the first draft of *Carrie* was done when I was about twenty-two, and at the time it was very sobersided. I was maybe too close to the subject, and De Palma's film is kind of light and frothy and he gets you at the end when you think it's over, and you're ready to go out.

In your mind you have a guard, when you go to see horror movies. You're prepared to be scared, and you're also prepared to laugh. Immediately. You know the reaction in a horror movie is always aauugghh! And then everybody laughs and goes, "I was just kidding. I wasn't really frightened. I screamed that way to scare you, darling." Those are the only two verbalizations usually that we make in movies—either to scream or to laugh—because those two reactions are rather close. Most things we laugh at are things that are really horrible, when you think about them. It's funny and you don't scream, as long as it's not you. If it's somebody else you can laugh.

With *The Shining* I have more problems. I have my days when I think that I gave Kubrick a live grenade which he heroically threw his body on.

Q: What about machines? Do they hold some fascination for you?

KING: I'm scared by machines. Machines frighten me because I don't know how they work in a lot of cases. And I'm fascinated by them because they do so much of my work. I was the kind of kid who had a bad year when I was four because I couldn't figure out if that light in the refrigerator was still on when the door was shut. I had to get that into my head.

Machines frighten me, and of course on a turnpike you get one of those ten-wheelers in front of you, and one behind you, and one that's going by in the passing lane, and you say your rosary. They look big and you can't see who's in them. I'm always convinced that the flatbed trucks, the big ones that have these tarpaulins over whatever's on the back of them...could be alien communicators or disruptors. For a long time I've been curious whether or not there are outbreaks of violence wherever a lot of these things are seen, because maybe aliens turn these things on and make people crazy.

Machines make me nervous. They just make me nervous. Because I live in a world that's surrounded by them. It's impossible to get away from them.

Q: How many stories did you write before you came up with a story you thought was good enough for publication? And how did you go about finding someone to publish it?

KING: I started to submit when I was twelve, and obviously at that time they weren't good enough, and I suppose in my heart of hearts I knew it. But you have to start sooner or later, you have to dig in. My career was more fortunate than a lot of people's. I published first when I was eighteen. I wrote a really terrible story called *The Glass Door*, which was published in a pulp magazine called *Startling Mystery Stories* and I got a check for $35 for that. Before that I picked up about sixty rejection slips. A lot of guys pick up 400, 500, or something like that. I wrote, I think, maybe four or five novels, one of them very long, before I wrote a saleable novel. I still have those things piled up, and they're the kind of things you look at when you've had a few beers or something, and you say that's not too bad, but if you read it when you're sober you say ouch. I still say ouch about *Carrie* a little bit, but she was good to me, that girl.

Q: Did you submit your work to as many different places as you could find?

KING: No, I didn't. I think if you want to do this you've got to look at yourself as somebody who's entering a jungle environment where a lot of people will simply eat your stories up. There's that famous story about a guy who picked up about 600 rejection slips and became totally paranoid that nobody was reading his stories, so he put a little dab of glue between pages nine and ten and sent it off. The story came back, "Sorry, this does not suit our needs," or something, and the guy turned to pages nine and ten and sure enough they were still glued together, and he wrote the editor an angry letter and said, "You didn't read my story. Pages nine and ten, I glued them together, and they're still glued together." And the editor said, "I only had to read to page five to know how bad it was."

I was with Doubleday in the beginning. I went to them because at that time they were a book mill, they published like 500 novels per year, and I thought, they've got to want novels more than anybody else because they publish more novels than anybody else, so I went to them. If you want to write, you have to read the market. You can't send a *True Romance* story to *Fantasy & Science Fiction* because they're not going to read it. You can't send a western to *Fantasy & Science Fiction* because they're not going to read it. You can't mention things such as childbirth or menstruation or the death of children in magazines like *McCalls* or *Good Housekeeping*, because they deny that those things exist. At least in their fiction, you know. You can read articles about all sorts of interesting things like that in their columns, but their fiction is still going to be about the nice young couple that moves into town, and how the welcome wagon lady came and said, "You ought to sell Tupperware," and it changed this woman's life. In a large sense this is still the women's magazine market. So you have to read the markets and send your stories to places where they might be reasonably bought.

Q: What does Stephen King do when he wants to get away from the success and the books and the movies and everything else? Who would Stephen King like to be other than Stephen King?

KING: Oh, I don't know. I wouldn't want to be Carl Yastremski, but I'd like to be some young guy. I'd like to be somebody like Wade Boggs. That'd be great. Not to be clumsy and big and run slow and all that. When I want to get away, I like to play baseball and softball. I like to play the guitar. I used to be in a group when I was in high school. I never had any talent, but still. . . . The cat leaves the room when I pick up the guitar, but I play anyway. So I do those things and I just sort of hang out.

Q: Are you going to write a sequel to *Firestarter?*"

KING: I really don't want to. James Clavell said one time that the novel ends when you don't know what comes next. At the end of that book, there's a little girl who walks into the editorial offices of a magazine, and she says "I want to tell you a story," and I didn't know after that what happened next, so I just wrote The End.

I have these wild moments. Charlie McGee, who was the little girl in that book, is pyrokinetic, which means she can light fires by thinking about them. I wrote about another kid, Danny Torrance, who had the ability to shine or read thoughts and sense the future. What if they met and got married and then went to live in 'Salem's Lot? That's about the closest that I've ever come. I rarely think about sequels because there are too many other sorts of new things.

Q: Who are the authors that you like to read?

KING: That's a hard question, because there are a lot of people that I like a lot. I like Evan Hunter, who also writes under the name Ed McBain. There's a writer from Massachusetts, George Higgins, that I like a lot. I think he's good. John D. MacDonald, who writes mysteries. There's a guy who writes paperback originals, horror stories, Michael McDowell. I like his work. I like Peter Straub's writing a lot or I wouldn't have worked with him.

Q: What about Robert Parker?

KING: I like Robert Parker very much, and I know him. He's a good guy.

Q: Might *The Stand* be your reflection of the future?

KING: *The Stand*, you know, is about this flu bug that takes over the world and kills almost everybody. I think that everybody has had those visions from time to time. There are a lot of writers who've written that end of the world novel. Anthony Burgess has one out now. And in 1909 there was a book by M. P. Shiel called *The Purple Cloud*, that was about the same thing. I read one in high school called *Earth Abides*.

I think that the actual impetus to write *The Stand* came from a chemical-biological spill in Utah. This stuff got loose that was like Agent Orange, except more deadly, and it killed a bunch of sheep because the wind happened to be blowing away from Salt Lake City and into the barrens. But on another day, if the wind had come from a different direction, it very well could have blown over Salt Lake City and things might have been entirely different.

I think a lot about our informational overload. And there's also the fact that there are more of us now than ever before, and as a result a communicable disease can be passed very rapidly, from just the flu bugs, the regular flu bugs that go around. At the time of *The Stand* I was interested in the fact that the flu virus changes—that's why you have to keep getting different flu boosters. It comes at you one way, and then it shifts its antigen and comes at you a different way, and your old flu shot doesn't do any good because this is the new and improved flu. So I sat down to write, and the book sort of galloped away from me on horses.

In the middle of writing it, news bulletins started coming from Philadelphia that all these legionnaires were dying and nobody knew what the disease was. I thought, awhh, I'm never going to get to publish this because everybody's going to be dead before it comes out. Luckily that didn't happen—but even as we sit here, something could be passing between us. There could be somebody here with typhoid or diptheria or almost anything. Even right now. I just thought you ought to have something to cheer you up, when you go home.

With Eric Norden[*]

PLAYBOY: The protagonist of 'Salem's Lot, a struggling young author with a resemblance to his creator, confesses at one point, "Sometimes when I'm lying in bed at night, I make up a *Playboy Interview* about me. Waste of time. They only do authors if their books are big on campus." Ten novels and several million dollars in the bank later, your books *are* big on campus and everywhere else. How does it feel?

KING: It feels great. I love it! And, sure, it's an ego boost to think that I'll be the subject of one of your interviews, with my name in black bold print and those three mug shots crawling along the bottom of the page on top of the quotes where I really fucked up and put my foot in my mouth. It's an honor to be in the stellar company of George Lincoln Rockwell and Albert Speer and James Earl Ray. What happened, couldn't you get Charles Manson?

PLAYBOY: We picked you as our scary guy for this year. The vote wasn't even close.

KING: OK, truce. Actually, I am pleased because when I was trying, without much apparent success, to make it as a writer I'd read your interviews and they always represented a visible symbol of achievement as well as celebrity. Like most writers, I dredge my memory for material, but I'm seldom really explicitly autobiographical. That passage you quote from 'Salem's Lot is an exception, and it reflects my state of mind in those days before I sold my first book, when nothing seemed to be going right. When I couldn't sleep, in that black hole of the night when all your doubts and fears and insecurities surge in at you, snarling, from the dark— what the Scandinavians call the wolf hour—I used to lie in bed alternately wondering if I shouldn't throw in the creative towel and spinning out masturbatory wish-fulfillment fantasies in which I was a successful and respected author. And that's where my imaginary *Playboy Interview* came in. I'd picture myself calm and composed, magisterial, responding with lucidly reasoned answers to the toughest questions, bouncing brilliant aperçus off the walls like tennis balls. Now that you're here, I'll probably do nothing but spew out incoherencies! But I suppose it was good therapy. It got me through the night.

PLAYBOY: How you got through your nights is going to be a major topic of this interview. Were you intrigued by ghost stories as a child?

KING: Ghoulies and ghosties and things that go bump in the night—you name 'em, I loved 'em! Some of the best yarns in those days were spun by my Uncle Clayton, a great old character who had never lost his childlike sense of wonder. Uncle Clayt would cock his hunting cap back on his mane of white hair, roll a Bugler cigarette with one liver-spotted hand, light up with a Diamond match he'd scratch on the sole of his boot, and launch into great stories, not only about ghosts but about local legends and scandals, family goings-on, the exploits of Paul Bunyan, everything under the sun. I'd listen spellbound to that slow down-East drawl of his on the porch of a summer night, and I'd be in another world. A better world, maybe.

PLAYBOY: Did such stories trigger your initial interest in the supernatural?

KING: No, that goes back as far as I can remember. But Uncle Clayt was a great spinner of tales. He was an original, Clayt. He could "line" bees, you know. That's a quirky rural talent that enables you to trail a honeybee all the way from a flower back to its hive—for miles, sometimes, through woods and brambles and bogs, but he never lost one. I sometimes wonder if more than good eyesight was involved. Uncle Clayt had another talent, too: he was a dowser. He could find water with an old piece of forked wood. How and why I'm not sure, but he did it.

PLAYBOY: Did you really believe that old wives' tale?

KING: Well, wrapping an infected wound in a poultice of moldy bread was an old wives' tale, too, and it antedated penicillin by the odd thousand years. But, yeah, I was skeptical about dowsing at first, until I actually saw it and experienced it—when Uncle Clayt defied all the experts and found a well in our own front yard.

PLAYBOY: Are you sure you just didn't succumb to the power of suggestion?

KING: Sure, that's one explanation, or maybe rationalization, but I tend to doubt it. I was bone-skeptical. I think it's far more likely that there's a perfectly logical and nonsupernatural explanation for dowsing—merely one science doesn't' understand yet.

It's easy to scoff at such things, but don't forget Haldane's law, a maxim coined by the famous British scientist J. B. S. Haldane: "The universe is not only queerer than we suppose, but it is queerer than we *can* suppose."

PLAYBOY: Did you have any other psychic experiences as a child?

KING: Well, once again, I'm not even sure that the dowsing was psychic at all—at least, not in the way that term is bandied around today. Was it a psychic experience when people in the early eighteenth century saw stones falling from the sky? It certainly took the scientific establishment another fifty years to admit the existence of meteorites. But to answer your question, no, I never experienced anything else as a kid that smacks of the paranormal.

PLAYBOY: Didn't we read somewhere that your house—where this interview is taking place, incidentally—is haunted?

KING: Oh, sure, by the shade of an old man named Conquest, who shuffled off this mortal coil about four generations back. I've never seen the old duffer, but sometimes when I'm working late at night, I get a distinctly uneasy feeling that I'm not alone. I wish he'd show himself; maybe we could get in some cribbage. Nobody in my generation will play with me. By the way, he died in the parlor, the room we're in right now.

PLAYBOY: Thanks. Can we take it from your experiences with dowsing and such that you're a believer in extrasensory perception and in psychic phenomena in general?

KING: I wouldn't say I believe in them. The scientific verdict's still out on most of those things, and they're certainly nothing to accept as an article of faith. But I don't think we should dismiss them out of hand just because we can't as yet understand how and why they operate and according to what rules. There's a big and vital difference between the unexplained and the inexplicable, and we should keep that in mind when discussing so-called psychic phenomena. Actually, I prefer the term "wild talents," which was coined by the science fiction writer Jack Vance.

But it's too bad that the orthodox scientific establishment isn't more open-minded on those questions, because they should be subjected to rigorous research and evaluation—if for no other reason than to prevent them from becoming the exclusive property of the kooks and cultists on the occult lunatic fringe.

There's a lot of evidence that both the American and Soviet governments take the subject a damn sight more seriously than they let on in public and are conducting top-priority studies to understand and isolate a whole range of esoteric phenomena, from levitation and Kirlian photography—a film process that reveals the human aura—to telepathy and teleportation and psychokinesis.

Sadly, and maybe ominously, neither side is pursuing the subject out of some objective search for scientific truth. What they're really interested in is its espionage and military potential, as in scrambling the brains of missile-silo operators or influencing the decisions of national leaders in a crisis. It's a shame, because what you're talking about here is unlocking the secrets of the human mind and exploring the inner frontier. That's the last thing that should be left in the hands of the CIA or the KGB.

PLAYBOY: Both *Carrie* and *Firestarter* deal with the wild talents of young girls on the threshold of adolescence. Were they fictional reworkings of the poltergeist theme, as popularized by Steven Spielberg's recent film *Poltergeist?*

KING: Not directly, though I suppose there's a similarity. Poltergeist activity is supposed to be a sudden manifestation of semihysterical psychic power in kids, generally girls who are just entering puberty. So in that sense, Carrie, in particular, could be said to be a kind of superpoltergeist. Again, I'm not saying there's anything objectively valid to the so-called poltergeist phenomenon, just that that's one of the explanations advanced for it. But I've never seriously researched the whole subject, and those cases I've read about seem surrounded by so much *National Enquirer*–style hype and sensationalism that I tend to suspend judgment. Charlie McGee, the girl in *Firestarter*, actually had a specific gift, if that's the word, that goes beyond the poltergeist phenomenon, though it's occasionally reported in conjunction with it. Charlie can start fires—she can burn up buildings or, if her back's against the wall, people.

On this whole subject of wild talents, it was fascinating to discover when researching *Firestarter* that there is a well-documented if totally baffling phenomenon called pyrokinesis, or spontaneous human combustion, in which a man or woman burns to a crisp in a fire that generates almost inconceivable temperatures—a fire that seems to come from *inside* the victim. There have been medically documented cases from all over the world in which a corpse has been found burned beyond recognition while the chair or the bed on which it was found wasn't even charred. Sometimes, the victims are actually reduced to ash, and I know from researching burial customs for a forthcoming book that the heat required to do that is tremendous. You can't even manage it in a crematorium, you know; which is why, after your body comes out of the blast furnace on the conveyor belt, there's a guy at the other end with a rake to pound up your bones before they pour you into the little urn that goes on the mantelpiece.

I remember a case reported in the press in the mid-sixties in which a kid was just lying on a beach when suddenly he burst into flames. His father dragged him into the water and dunked him, but he continued to burn *underwater*, as if he'd been hit by a white-phosphorus bomb. The kid died, and the father had to go into the hospital with third-degree burns on his arms.

There's a lot of mystery in the world, a lot of dark, shadowy corners we haven't explored yet. We shouldn't be too smug about dismissing out of hand everything we can't understand. The dark can have *teeth*, man!

PLAYBOY: The dark has also been very lucrative for you. Aside from the phenomenal sales of the books themselves, *'Salem's Lot* was sold to television as a miniseries, and *Carrie* and *The Shining* have been made into feature films. Were you pleased with the results?

KING: Well, considering the limitations of TV, *'Salem's Lot* could have turned out a lot worse than it did. The two-part TV special was directed by Tobe Hooper of *Texas Chainsaw Massacre* fame, and outside of a few boners—such as making my vampire Barlow look exactly like the cadaverously inhuman night stalker in the famous German silent film *Nosferatu*—he did a pretty good job. I breathed a hearty sigh of relief, however, when some plans to turn it into a network series fell apart, because today's television is just too institutionally fainthearted and unimaginative to handle real horror.

Brian De Palma's *Carrie* was terrific. He handled the material deftly and artistically and got a fine performance out of Sissy Spacek. In many ways, the film is far more stylish than my book, which I still think is a gripping read but is impeded by a certain heaviness, a Sturm und Drang quality that's absent from the film. Stanley Kubrick's version of *The Shining* is a lot tougher for me to evaluate, because I'm still profoundly ambivalent about the whole thing. I'd admired Kubrick for a long time and had great expectations for the project, but I was deeply disappointed in the end result. Parts of the film are chilling, charged with a relentlessly claustrophobic terror, but others fall flat.

I think there are two basic problems with the movie. First, Kubrick is a very cold man—pragmatic and rational—and he had great difficulty conceiving, even academically, of a supernatural world. He used to make transatlantic calls to me from England at odd hours of the day and night, and I remember once he rang up and asked, "Do you believe in God?" I thought a minute and said, "Yeah, I think so." Kubrick replied, "No, I don't think there is a God," and hung up. Not that religion has to be involved in horror, but a visceral skeptic such as Kubrick just couldn't grasp the sheer inhuman evil of the Overlook Hotel. So he looked, instead, for evil in the characters and made the film into a domestic tragedy with only vaguely supernatural overtones. That was the basic flaw: because he couldn't believe, he couldn't make the film believable to others.

The second problem was in characterization and casting. Jack Nicholson, though a fine actor, was all wrong for the part. His last big role had been in *One Flew Over the Cuckoo's Nest,* and between that and his manic grin, the audience automatically identified him as a loony from the first scene. But the book is about Jack Torrance's gradual *descent* into madness through the malign influence of the Overlook, which is like a huge storage battery charged with an evil powerful enough to corrupt all those who come in contact with it. If the guy is nuts to begin with, then the entire tragedy of his downfall is wasted. For that reason, the film has no center and no heart, despite its brilliantly unnerving camera angles and dazzling use of the Steadicam. What's basically wrong with Kubrick's version of *The Shining* is that it's a film by a man who thinks too much and feels too little; and that's why, for all its virtuoso effects, it never gets you by the throat and hangs on the way real horror should.

I'd like to remake *The Shining* someday, maybe even direct it myself if anybody will give me enough rope to hang myself with.

PLAYBOY: In *The Stand,* which has become something of a cult object to many of your fans, a rapidly mutating flu virus accidentally released by the U.S. military wipes out nine-tenths of the world's population and sets the stage for an apocalyptic struggle between good and evil. That ultimate genocide was presaged on a more modest scale by *Carrie* and *Firestarter,* both of which conclude with the beleaguered heroines raining fiery death and destruction on their tormentors and innocent bystanders alike; by *'Salem's Lot,* in which you burn down the town at the end; and by the explosion and burning of the Overlook Hotel at the conclusion of *The Shining.* Is there a pyromaniac or a mad bomber inside you screaming to get out?

KING: There sure is, and that destructive side of me has a great outlet in my books. Jesus. I *love* to burn things up—on paper, at least. I don't think arson would be half as much fun in real life as it is in fiction. One of my favorite moments in all my work comes in the middle of *The Stand*, when one of my villains, the Trashcan Man, sets all these oil-refinery holding tanks on fire and they go off like bombs. It's as if the night sky had been set ablaze. God, that was a gas! It's the werewolf in me, I guess, but I love fire, I love destruction. It's great and it's black and it's exciting. When I write scenes like that, I feel like Samson pulling down the temple on top of everybody's head.

The Stand was particularly fulfilling, because there I got a chance to scrub the whole human race and, man, it was fun! Sitting at the typewriter, I felt just like Alexander lifting his sword over the Gordian knot and snarling, "Fuck unraveling it; I'll do it *my* way!" Much of the compulsive, driven feeling I had while I worked on *The Stand* came from the vicarious thrill of imagining an entire entrenched social order destroyed in one stroke. That's the mad-bomber side of my character, I suppose.

But the ending of the book reflects what I hope is another, more constructive aspect. After all the annihilation and suffering and despair, *The Stand* is inherently optimistic in that it depicts a gradual reassertion of humane values as mankind picks itself out of the ashes and ultimately restores the moral and ecological balance. Despite all the grisly scenes, the book is also a testament to the enduring human values of courage, kindness, friendship, and love, and at the end it echoes Camus' remark: "Happiness, too, is inevitable."

PLAYBOY: There must have been a time, before all this wealth and fame, when happiness didn't seem inevitable to you. How rough were the early days?

KING: Well, let's just say that, like most overnight successes, I've had to pay my dues. When I got out of college in the early seventies with a degree in English and a teaching certificate, I found there was a glut on the teaching market, and I went to work pumping gas in a filling station and later on pressing sheets in an industrial laundry for $60 a week. We were as poor as church mice, with two small kids, and needless to say, it wasn't easy to make ends meet on that salary. My wife went to work as a waitress in a local Dunkin' Donuts and came home every night smelling like a cruller. Nice aroma at first, you know, all fresh and sugary, but it got pretty goddamned cloying after a while—I haven't been able to look a doughnut in the face ever since.

Anyway, in the fall of 1971, I finally got a job as an English instructor at Hampden Academy, just across the Penobscot River from Bangor, but it paid only $6,400 a year, barely more than I had been earning before. In fact, I had to go back and moonlight in the laundry just to keep our heads above water. We were living in a trailer on top of a bleak, snow-swept hillside in Hermon, Maine, which, if not the asshole of the universe, is at least within farting distance of it. I'd come home exhausted from school and squat in the trailer's furnace room, with Tabby's little Olivetti portable perched on a child's desk I had to balance on my knees, and try to hammer out some scintillating prose.

That was where I wrote 'Salem's Lot, actually. It was my second published book, but the bulk of the writing was completed before Carrie was even accepted by Doubleday. And believe me, after a day of teaching and then coming home and watching Tabby gamely juggle her way through a mountain of unpaid bills, it was a positive pleasure to squeeze into that cramped furnace room and do battle with a horde of blood-thirsty vampires. Compared with our creditors, they were a fuckin' relief!

PLAYBOY: Were you selling any of your work at that time?

KING: Yes, but only short stories, and only to the smaller-circulation men's magazines, such as Cavalier and Dude. The money was useful, God knows, but if you know that particular market, you know there wasn't much of it. Anyway, the payment for my stories wasn't enough to keep us out of the red, and I was getting nowhere with my longer work. I'd written several novels, ranging from awful to mediocre to passable, but all had been rejected, even though I was beginning to get some encouragement from a wonderful editor at Doubleday named Bill Thompson. But as gratifying as his support was, I couldn't bank it. My kids were wearing hand-me-downs from friends and relatives, our old rattletrap 1965 Buick Special was rapidly self-destructing and we finally had to ask Ma Bell to remove our phone.

On top of everything else, I was fucking up personally. I wish I could say today that I bravely shook my fist in the face of adversity and carried on undaunted, but I can't. I copped out to self-pity and anxiety and started drinking far too much and frittering money away on poker and bumper pool. You know the scene: it's Friday night and you cash your pay check in the bar and start knocking them down, and before you know what's happened, you've pissed away half the food budget for that week.

PLAYBOY: How did your marriage stand up under those strains?

KING: Well, it was touch and go for a while there, and things could get pretty tense at home. It was a vicious circle: The more miserable and inadequate I felt about what I saw as my failure as a writer, the more I'd try to escape into a bottle, which would only exacerbate the domestic stress and make me even more depressed. Tabby was steamed about the booze, of course, but she told me she understood that the reason I drank too much was that I felt it was never going to happen, that I was never going to be a writer of any consequence. And, of course, I feared she was right. I'd lie awake at night seeing myself at fifty, my hair graying, my jowls thickening, a network of whiskey-ruptured capillaries spiderwebbing across my nose—"drinker's tattoos," we call them in Maine—with a dusty trunkful of unpublished novels rotting in the basement, teaching high school English for the rest of my life and getting off what few literary rocks I had left by advising the student newspaper or maybe teaching a creative-writing course. Yechh! Even though I was only in my mid-twenties and rationally realized that there was still plenty of time and opportunity ahead, that pressure to break through in my work was building into a kind of psychic crescendo, and when it appeared to be thwarted, I felt desperately depressed, cornered. I felt trapped in a suicidal rat race, with no way out of the maze.

PLAYBOY: Did you ever seriously contemplate suicide?

KING: Oh, no, never; that phrase was just metaphorical overkill. I have my share of human weaknesses, but I'm also bone-stubborn. Maybe that's a Maine trait; I don't know. Anyway, wasn't it Mencken who said that suicide is a belated acquiescence in the opinion of your wife's relatives? But what did worry me was the effect all that was having on my marriage. Hell, we were already on marshy ground in those days, and I feared that the quicksand was just around the bend.

I loved my wife and kids, but as the pressure mounted, I was beginning to have ambivalent feelings about them, too. On the one hand, I wanted nothing more than to provide for them and protect them—but at the same time, unprepared as I was for the rigors of fatherhood, I was also experiencing a range of nasty emotions from resentment to anger to occasional outright hate, even surges of mental violence that, thank God, I was able to suppress. I'd wander around the crummy little living room of our trailer at three o'clock on a cold winter's morning with my teething nine-month-old son Joe slung over my shoulder, more often than not spitting up all over my shirt, and I'd try to figure out how and why I'd ever committed myself to that particular lunatic asylum. All the claustrophobic fears would squeeze in on me then, and I'd wonder if it hadn't already all passed me by, if I weren't just chasing a fool's dream. A nocturnal snowmobile would whine in the dark distance, like an angry insect, and I'd say to myself, "Shit, King, face it; you're going to be teaching fuckin' high school kids for the rest of your life." I don't know what would have happened to my marriage and my sanity if it hadn't been for the totally unexpected news, in 1973, that Doubleday had accepted *Carrie*, which I had thought had very little chance of a sale.

PLAYBOY: What was more important to you—the money from *Carrie* or the fact that you had finally been recognized as a serious novelist?

KING: Both, actually, though I might question how serious a novelist Doubleday took me for. It wasn't about to promote *Carrie* as that year's answer to *Madame Bovary*, that's for sure. Even though there's a lot I still like and stand behind in the book, I'm the first to admit that it is often clumsy and artless. But both creatively and financially, *Carrie* was a kind of escape hatch for Tabby and me, and we were able to flee through it into a totally different existence. Hell, our lives changed so quickly that for more than a year afterward, we walked around with big, sappy grins on our faces, hardly daring to believe we were out of that trap for good. It was a great feeling of liberation, because at last I was free to quit teaching and fulfill what I believe is my only function in life: to write books. Good, bad, or indifferent books, that's for others to decide; for me, it's enough just to *write*. I'd been writing since I was twelve, seriously if pretty badly at first, and I sold *Carrie* when I was 26, so I'd had a relatively long apprenticeship. But that first hardcover sale sure tasted sweet!

PLAYBOY: As you've indicated, that compulsion to be a writer has been with you since you were a boy. Was it a means of escape from an unhappy childhood?

KING: Maybe, though it's generally impossible even to remember the feelings and motivations of childhood, much less to understand or rationally analyze them. Kids, thank God, are all deliciously, creatively crazy by our desiccated adult standards. But it's true that I was prey to a lot of conflicting emotions as a child. I had friends and all that, but I often felt unhappy and different, estranged from other kids my age. I was a fat kid—husky was the euphemism they used in the clothing store—and pretty poorly coordinated, always the last picked when we chose teams.

At times, particularly in my teens, I felt violent, as if I wanted to lash out at the world, but that rage I kept hidden. That was a secret place in myself I wouldn't reveal to anyone else. I guess part of it was that my brother and I had a pretty shirttail existence as kids. My father deserted us when I was two and David was four and left my mother without a dime. She was a wonderful lady, a very brave lady in that old-fashioned sense, and went to work to support us, generally at menial jobs because of her lack of any professional training. After my father did his moonlight flit, she became a rolling stone, following the jobs around the country. We traveled across New England and the Midwest, one low-paying job following another. She worked as a laundry presser and a doughnut maker—like my wife, twenty years later—as a housekeeper, a store clerk; you name it, she did it.

PLAYBOY: Did living on the edge of poverty leave any lasting scars?

KING: No, and I didn't think of it in terms of poverty, either then or now. Ours wasn't a life of unremitting misery by any means, and we never missed a meal, even though prime sirloin was rarely on our plates. Finally, when I was about ten, we moved back to Maine, to the little town of Durham.

For ten years, we lived a virtual barter existence, practically never seeing any hard cash. If we needed food, relatives would bring a bag of groceries; if we needed clothes, there'd always be hand-me-downs. Believe me, I was never on the best-dressed list at school! And the well dried up in the summer, so we had to use the outhouse. There was no bath or shower, either, and in those icy Maine winters, we'd walk half a mile or so to my Aunt Ethelyn's for a hot bath. Shit, coming home through the snow, we'd steam! So, yeah, I guess in many ways it was a hard-scrabble existence but not an impoverished one in the most important sense of the word. Thanks to my mother, the one thing that was never in short supply, corny as it may sound to say it, was love. And in that sense, I was a hell of a lot less deprived than countless children of middle-class or wealthy families, whose parents have time for everything but their kids.

PLAYBOY: Has your father ever contacted you in the years since he walked out, out of either guilt or—in view of your new-found wealth—greed?

KING: No, though I suspect the latter would be his more likely motivation. Actually, it was a classic desertion, not even a note of explanation or justification left behind. He said, *literally*, that he was going out to the grocery store for a pack of cigarettes, and he didn't take any of his things with him. That was in 1949, and none of us have heard of the bastard since.

PLAYBOY: Now that you're a multimillionaire with more resources at your command than your mother could have dreamed of, have you ever considered launching your own investigation to track down your father or, at least, to determine whether he's alive or dead?

KING: The idea has crossed my mind now and then over the years, but something always holds me back. Superstition, I guess, like the old saw about letting sleeping dogs lie. To tell the truth, I don't know how I'd react if I ever did find him and we came face to face. But even if I ever did decide to launch an investigation, I don't think anything would come of it, because I'm pretty sure my father's dead.

PLAYBOY: Why?

KING: From everything I've learned about my father, he would have burned himself out by now. He liked to drink and carouse a lot. In fact, from what my mother hinted, I think he was in trouble with the law on more than one occasion. He used aliases often enough—he was born Donald Spansky in Peru, Indiana, then called himself Pollack and finally changed his name legally to King.

He'd started out as an Electrolux salesman in the Midwest, but I think he blotted his copybook somewhere along the way. As my mother once told me, he was the only man on the sales force who regularly demonstrated vacuum cleaners to pretty young widows at two o'clock in the morning. He was quite a ladies' man, according to my mother, and I apparently have a beautiful bastard half-sister in Brazil. In any case, he was a man with an itchy foot, a travelin' man, as the song says. I think trouble came easy to him.

PLAYBOY: So you're not exactly eager to be taken for a chip off the old block?

KING: Let's hope heredity takes second place to environment in my case. From what I'm told, my father certainly beat the hell out of me in the Lothario department, where I'm monotonously monogamous, though I do have a weakness for booze that I try to control, and I love fast cars and motorcycles. I certainly don't share his wanderlust, which is one among many reasons that I've remained in Maine, even though I now have the financial freedom to live anywhere in the world. Oddly enough, the only point of similarity may be our literary tastes. My father had a secret love for science fiction and horror tales, and he tried to write them himself, submitting stories to the major men's magazines of his day, such as *Blue-book* and *Argosy*. None of the stories sold and none survives.

PLAYBOY: A scrapbook of your vanished father's personal effects is prominent in the study of your summer house. Doesn't that preservation of the memorabilia of a man you never knew suggest that you're still mentally gnawing at the wound?

KING: No, the wound itself has healed, but that doesn't preclude an interest in how and why it was inflicted. And that, I think, is a far cry from picking at some psychic scab. Anyway, the scrapbook you mention isn't some kind of secret shrine to his memory, just a handful of souvenirs: a couple of old dog-eared postcards he'd sent my mother from various ports of call, mainly in Latin America; a few photographs of different ships on which he'd sailed; a faded and rather idealized sketch from a Mexican marketplace. Just the odds and ends he'd left behind, like the corpse in the E. C. horror comics of the fifties—God, I loved those mothers!— who comes back from a watery grave to wreak revenge on the wife and boyfriend who did him in but phones first and whispers, "I'm coming; I'd be there sooner but little bits of me keep falling off along the way."

Well, the little bits of my father that fell off along the way are preserved in that scrapbook, like a time capsule. It all cuts off in 1949, when he took a powder on us. Sometimes, I'll leaf through the pages and it reminds me of a chilly autumn day in the fifties when my brother and I discovered several spools of old movie film my father had taken. He was an avid photography buff, apparently, but we'd never seen much of his handiwork beyond a few snapshots. My mother had stowed the film away in my aunt and uncle's attic. So here you have these two kids—I must have been around eight and David ten—struggling to operate this old dinosaur of a movie projector we had managed to rent.

When we finally got it working, the stuff was pretty disappointing at first—a lot of strange faces and exotic scenes but no signs of the old man. And then, after we'd gone through a couple of reels of film, David jumped up and said, "That's him! That's our father!" He'd handed the camera to one of his buddies and there he was, lounging against a ship's rail, a choppy sea in the background. My old man. David remembered him, but it was a stranger's face to me. By the look of the sea, he was probably somewhere on the North Atlantic, so the film must have been taken during the war. He raised his hand and smiled, unwittingly waving at sons who weren't born yet. Hi, Dad, don't forget to write.

PLAYBOY: Considering what you write about, have you ever thought of going to a seance or of finding some other supernatural way to communicate with him?

KING: Are you kidding? I've never even attended a seance. Jesus, no! Precisely because I know a little bit about the subject, that's the last thing I'd ever do. You couldn't drag me to one of those things, and the same thing goes for a Ouija board. All that shit—stay away from it! Sure, I know most mediums are fakes and phonies and con artists, the worst kind of human vultures, preying on human suffering and loss and loneliness. But if there *are* things floating around out there—disembodied entities, spirit demons, call them what you will—then it's the height of folly to invite them to use you as a channel into this world. Because they might like what they found, man, and they might decide to stay!

PLAYBOY: Is your fear of seances an isolated phenomenon, or are you superstitious about other aspects of the so-called supernatural?

KING: Oh, sure, I'm very superstitious by nature. I mean, part of my mind, the rational part, will say, "Come on, man, this is all self-indulgent bullshit," but the other part, the part as old as the first caveman cowering by his fire as something huge and hungry howls in the night, says, "Yeah, maybe so, but why take a chance?" That's why I observe all the old folk superstitions: I don't walk under ladders; I'm scared shitless I'll get seven years' bad luck if I break a mirror; I try to stay home cowering under the covers on Friday the thirteenth. God, once I had to fly on Friday the thirteenth—I had no choice—and while the ground crew didn't exactly have to carry me onto the plane kicking and screaming, it was still no picnic. It didn't help that I'm afraid of flying, either. I guess I hate surrendering control over my life to some faceless pilot who could have been secretly boozing it up all afternoon or who has an embolism in his cranium, like an invisible time bomb. But I have a thing about the number 13 in general; it never fails to trace that old icy finger up and down my spine. When I'm writing, I'll never stop work if the page number is 13 or a multiple of 13; I'll just keep on typing till I get to a safe number.

PLAYBOY: Are you afraid of the dark?

KING: Of course. Isn't everybody? Actually, I can't understand my own family sometimes. I won't sleep without a light on in the room and, needless to say, I'm very careful to see that the blankets are tucked tight under my legs so that I won't wake up in the middle of the night with a clammy hand clutching my ankle. But when Tabby and I were first married, it was summer and she'd be sleeping starkers and I'd be lying there with the sheets pulled up to my eyes and she'd say, "Why are you sleeping in that crazy way?" And I tried to explain that it was just safer that way, but I'm not sure she really understood. And now she's done something else I'm not very happy with: she's added this big fluffy flounce around the bottom of our double bed, which means that before you go to sleep, when you want to check what's hiding under there, you have to flip up that flounce and poke your nose right in. And it's too *close*, man; something could claw your face right off before you spotted it. But Tabby just doesn't appreciate my point of view.

PLAYBOY: Have you ever considered probing under the bed with a broom handle?

KING: Naw, man, that would be pussy. I mean, sometimes we have houseguests staying overnight. How would it look if the next morning, they said, "Gee, we were going to the bathroom last night and we saw Steve on his hands and knees, sticking a broom handle under his bed"? It might tarnish the image. But it's not only Tabby who doesn't understand; I'm disturbed by the attitude of my kids, too. I mean I suffer a bit from insomnia, and every night, I'll check them in their beds to see that they're still breathing, and my two oldest, Naomi and Joe, will always tell me, "Be sure to turn off the light and close the door when you leave, Daddy." Turn off the light! Close the door! How can they face it? I mean, my God, *anything* could be in their room, crouched inside their closet, coiled under their bed, just waiting to slither out, pounce on them and sink its talons into them! Those things can't stand the light, you know, but the darkness is *dangerous!* But try telling that to my kids. I hope there's nothing wrong with them. God knows, when I was their age, I just knew that the bogeyman was waiting for me. Maybe he still is.

PLAYBOY: What, besides your own imagination, scares you?

KING: A movie I'll certainly never forget is *Earth vs. the Flying Saucers*, starring Hugh Marlowe, which was basically a horror flick masquerading as science fiction. It was October 1957, I'd just turned ten and I was watching it in the old Stratford Theater in downtown Stratford, Connecticut—one of those quarter-a-shot Saturday-afternoon matinees for kids. The film was pretty standard stuff, about an invasion of Earth by this deadly race of aliens from a dying planet; but towards the end—just when it was reaching the good part, with Washington in flames and the final, cataclysmic interstellar battle about to be joined—the screen suddenly went dead. Well, kids started to clap and hoot, thinking the projectionist had made a mistake or the reel had broken, but then, all of a sudden, the theater lights went on full strength, which really surprised everybody, because nothing like that had ever happened before in the middle of a movie. And then the theater manager came striding down the center aisle, looking pale, and he mounted the stage and said, in a trembling voice, "I want to tell you that the Russians have put a space satellite into orbit around Earth. They call it Sputnik." Or *Spootnik*, as he pronounced it.

There was a long, hushed pause as this crowd of fifties kids in cuffed jeans, with crewcuts or ducktails or ponytails, struggled to absorb all that; and then, suddenly, one voice, near tears but also charged with terrible anger, shrilled through the stunned silence: "Oh, go show the movie, you liar!" And after a few minutes, the film came back on, but I just sat there, frozen to my seat, because I knew the manager wasn't lying.

That was a terrifying knowledge for a member of that entire generation of war babies brought up on *Captain Video* and *Terry and the Pirates* and *Combat Casey* comic books, reared smug in the myth of America's military invincibility and moral supremacy, convinced we were the good guys and God was with us all the way. I immediately made the connection between the film we were seeing and the fact that the Russians had a space satellite circling the heavens, loaded, for all I knew, with H-bombs to rain down on our unsuspecting heads. And at that moment, the fears of fictional horror vividly intersected with the reality of potential nuclear holocaust; a transition from fantasy to a real world suddenly became far more ominous and threatening. And as I sat there, the film concluded with the voices of the malignant invading saucerians echoing from the screen in a final threat: "Look to your skies. . . . A warning will come from your skies. . . . Look to your skies. . . ." I still find it impossible to convey, even to my own kids, how terribly frightened and alone and depressed I felt at that moment.

PLAYBOY: Kids do, as you say, have active imaginations, but wasn't yours unhealthily overheated?

KING: I think most kids share some of my morbid preoccupations, and there's probably something missing in those who don't. It's all a matter of degree, I guess. An active imagination has always been part of the baggage I've carried with me, and when you're a kid, it can sometimes exact a pretty grueling toll. But many of the fears I had to learn to cope with had nothing to do with the supernatural. They stemmed from the same day-to-day anxieties and insecurities a lot of children have to come to terms with. For example, when I was growing up, I'd think a lot of what would happen if my mother died and I were left an orphan. Now, a kid with relatively little imagination, the kind with a great future in computer programming or the chamber of commerce, will say to himself, "So what, she's not dead, she's not even sick, so forget it." But with the kind of imagination I had, you couldn't switch off the images once you'd triggered them, so I'd see my mother laid out in a white-silk-lined mahogany coffin with brass handles, her dead face blank and waxen; I'd hear the organ dirges in the background; and then I'd see myself being dragged off to some Dickensian workhouse by a terrible old lady in black.

But what really scared me most about the prospect of my mother's death was not being shipped off to some institution, rough as that would have been. I was afraid it would drive me crazy.

PLAYBOY: Did you have any doubts about your sanity?

KING: I didn't trust it, that's for sure. One of my big fears as I was growing up was that I was going to go insane, particularly after I saw that harrowing film *The Snake Pit*, with Olivia de Havilland, on TV. There were all those lunatics in a state mental institution tormenting themselves with their delusions and psychoses and being tormented, in turn, by their sadistic keepers, and I had very little trouble imagining myself in their midst. In the years since, I've learned what a tough, resilient organ the human brain is and how much psychic hammering it can withstand, but in those days, I was sure that you just went crazy all at once; you'd be walking down the street and—*pffft!*—you'd suddenly think you were a chicken or start chopping up the neighborhood kids with garden shears. So, for a long time, I was very much afraid of going nuts.

PLAYBOY: Is there any history of insanity in your family?

KING: Oh, we had a ripe crop of eccentrics, to say the least, on my father's side. I can recall my Aunt Betty, who my mother always said was a schizophrenic and who apparently ended her life in a loony bin. Then there was my father's mother, Granny Spansky, whom David and I got to know when we were living in the Midwest. She was a big, heavy-set woman who alternately fascinated and repelled me. I can still see her cackling like an old witch through toothless gums while she'd fry an entire loaf of bread in bacon drippings on an antique range and then gobble it down, chortling, "My, that's *crisp!*"

PLAYBOY: What other fears haunted you in your childhood?

KING: Well, I was terrified and fascinated by death—death in general and my own in particular—probably as a result of listening to all those radio shows as a kid and watching some pretty violent TV shows, such as *Peter Gunn* and *Highway Patrol*, in which death came cheap and fast. I was absolutely convinced that I'd never live to reach twenty. I envisioned myself walking home one night along a dark, deserted street and somebody or something would jump out of the bushes and that would be it. So death as a concept and the people who dealt out death intrigued me.

I remember I compiled an entire scrapbook on Charlie Starkweather, the fifties mass murderer who cut a bloody swath through the Midwest with his girlfriend. God, I had a hard time hiding that from my mother. Starkweather killed nine or ten people in cold blood, and I used to clip and paste every news item I could find on him, and then I'd sit trying to unravel the inner horror behind that ordinary face. I knew I was looking at big-time sociopathic evil, not the neat little Agatha Christie–style villain but something wilder and darker and unchained. I wavered between attraction and repulsion, maybe because I realized the face in the photograph could be my own.

PLAYBOY: Once again, those aren't the musings of your typical Little Leaguer. Weren't you worried even then that there might be something abnormal about your obsession?

KING: Obsession is too strong a word. It was more like trying to figure out a puzzle, because I wanted to know why somebody could do the things Starkweather did. I suppose I wanted to decipher the unspeakable, just as people try to make sense out of Auschwitz or Jonestown. I certainly didn't find evil seductive in any sick way—that would be pathological—but I did find it compelling. And I think most people do, or the bookstores wouldn't still be filled with biographies of Adolf Hitler more than thirty-five years after World War II. The fascination of the abomination, as Conrad called it.

PLAYBOY: Have the fears and insecurities that plagued you in childhood persisted into adult life?

KING: Some of the old faithful night sweats are still with me, such as my fear of darkness, but some of the others I've just exchanged for a new set. I mean, you just can't stick with yesterday's fears forever, right? Let's see, now, updated phobias. OK, I have a fear of choking, maybe because the night my mother died of cancer—practically the same minute, actually— my son had a terrible choking fit in his bed at home. He was turning blue when Tabby finally forced out the obstruction. And I can see that happening to me at the dinner table, and everybody panics and forgets the Heimlich maneuver and I'm polished off by half a Big Mac. What else? I don't like bugs in general, though I came to terms with the 30,000 cockroaches in our film *Creepshow*. But I just can't take spiders! No way— particularly those big hairy ones that look like furry basketballs with legs, the ones that are hiding inside a bunch of bananas, waiting to jump out at you. Jesus, those things petrify me.

PLAYBOY: Since you've mentioned *Creepshow*, which you wrote and starred in, this may be the time to ask you why it bombed so badly at the box office.

KING: We don't know that it did, because the gross receipts from around the country aren't all in and tabulated yet. It had a fantastic first couple of weeks and since then has done badly in some places and quite well in others. But I think the critical drubbing it got might have driven some adults away, though a lot of teenagers have flocked to see the film. I ex- pected bad reviews, of course, because *Creepshow* is based on the horror– comic book traditions of the fifties, not a send-up at all but a recreation. And if the mainstream critics had understood and appreciated that, I'd have known right off that we'd failed miserably in what we were trying to do. Of course, a few big-name critics, such as Rex Reed, did love the film, but that's because they were brought up on those comics and re- member them with affection.

PLAYBOY: Even Reed was less than overwhelmed by the bravura of your performance, writing, "King looks and acts exactly like an overweight Li'l Abner." Unjust?

KING: No, right on the mark, because that's the kind of local yokel I was supposed to be depicting, and Romero told me to play it "as broad as a freeway." Of course, my wife claims it was perfect typecasting, but I'll just let that one pass.

PLAYBOY: Back to what still petrifies you—besides bombing at the box of- fice. What's your darkest fear?

KING: I guess that one of my children will die. I don't think I could handle that. There are a lot of other things, too: the fear that something will go wrong with my marriage; that the world will blunder into war; shit, I'm not even happy about entropy. But those are all wolf-hour thoughts, the ones that come when you can't sleep and you're tossing and turning and it becomes quite possible to convince yourself that you have cancer or a brain tumor or, if you're sleeping on your left side and can hear your heart pounding, that you're on the verge of a fatal coronary. And sometimes, particularly if you're overworked, you can lie there in the dark and imagine that you hear something downstairs. And then, if you really strain, you can hear noises coming *up* the stairs. And then, Jesus, *they're here*, they're in the bedroom! All those dark night thoughts, you know—the stuff that pleasant dreams are made of.

PLAYBOY: You've mentioned your insomnia, and throughout this interview, you've been popping Excedrin like jelly beans. Do you also suffer from persistent headaches?

KING: Yes, I have very bad ones. They come and go, but when they hit, they're rough. Excedrin helps, but when they're really out of control, all I can do is go upstairs and lie in the dark till they go away. Sooner or later, they do, all at once, and I can function again. From what I've read in the medical literature, they're not traditional migraines but "stressaches" that hit me at points of tension or overwork.

PLAYBOY: You consume even more beer than Excedrin; and you've revealed that you once had a drinking problem. Do you smoke grass as well?

KING: No, I prefer hard drugs. Or I used to, anyway; I haven't done anything heavy in years. Grass doesn't give me a particularly great high; I'll get a little giggly, but I always feel ill afterward. But I was in college during the late sixties. Even at the University of Maine, it was no big deal to get hold of drugs. I did a lot of LSD and peyote and mescaline, more than sixty trips in all. I'd never proselytize for acid or any other hallucinogen, because there are good-trip personalities and bad-trip personalities, and the latter category of people can be seriously damaged emotionally. If you've got the wrong physiological or mental make-up, dropping acid can be like playing Russian roulette with a loaded .45 automatic. But I've got to say that for me, the results were generally beneficial. I never had a trip that I didn't come out of feeling as though I'd had a brain purgative; it was sort of like a psychic dump truck emptying all the accumulated garbage out of my head. And at that particular time, I needed that kind of mental enema.

PLAYBOY: Did your experience with hallucinogens have any effect on your writing later on?

KING: None at all. Acid is just a chemical illusion, a game you play with your brain. It's totally meaningless in terms of a genuine expansion of consciousness. So I've never bought the argument of Aldous Huxley that hallucinogens open the doors to perception. That's mystical self-indulgence, the kind of bullshit Timothy Leary used to preach.

PLAYBOY: Are you afraid of writer's block?

KING: Yes, it's one of my greatest fears. You know, earlier, we were discussing my childhood fear of death, but that's something with which I've pretty much come to terms. I mean, I can comprehend both intellectually and emotionally that a day will come when I'll have terminal lung cancer or I'll be climbing a flight of stairs and suddenly feel an icy pain run down my arm before the hammer stroke hits the left side of my chest and I topple down the stairs dead. I'd feel a little surprised, a little regretful, but I'd also know that it was something I'd courted a long time and it had finally decided to marry me. On the other hand, the one thing I cannot comprehend or come to terms with is just drying up as a writer.

Writing is necessary for my sanity. As a writer, I can externalize my fears and insecurities and night terrors on paper, which is what people pay shrinks a small fortune to do. In my case, they pay me for psychoanalyzing myself in print. And in the process, I'm able to "write myself sane," as that fine poet Anne Sexton put it. It's an old technique of therapists, you know: get the patient to write out his demons. A Freudian exorcism. But all the violent energies I have—and there are a lot of them—I can vomit out onto paper. All the rage and hate and frustration, all that's dangerous and sick and foul within me, I'm able to spew into my work. There are guys in padded cells all around the world who aren't so lucky.

PLAYBOY: What do you think you'd be today without your writing talent?

KING: It's hard to say. Maybe I'd be a mildly embittered high school English teacher going through the motions till the day I could collect my pension and fade away into the twilight years. On the other hand, I might very well have ended up there in the Texas tower with Charlie Whitman, working out my demons with a high-powered telescopic rifle instead of a word processor. I mean, I *know* that guy Whitman. My writing has kept me out of that tower.

PLAYBOY: You've been candid in discussing your innermost fears and insecurities, but the one area we haven't touched upon is sexual. Do you have any hang-ups there?

KING: Well, I think I have pretty normal sexual appetites, whatever the word normal means in these swinging times. I mean, I'm not into sheep or enemas or multiple amputees or marshmallow worship or whatever the latest fad is. God, I was walking through a porn shop recently and saw a glossy magazine with a guy on the cover vomiting all over a naked girl. I mean, *chacun à son goût* and all that, but *yucchhh!* I'm not into the sadomasochism trip, either, on which your competitor *Penthouse* has built an entire empire. Hell, you can shoot a photo spread of a nude girl in a diamond-studded dog collar being dragged around on a leash by a guy in leather and jackboots, and despite all the artistic gloss and the gauzy lens and the pastel colors, it's still sleaze; it still reeks corruptingly of concentration-camp porn. There's a range of sexual variations that turn me on, but I'm afraid they're all boringly unkinky.

PLAYBOY: So there are no bogeymen hiding in your libido?

KING: No, not in that sense. The only sexual problem I've had was more functional. Some years ago, I suffered from periodic impotence, and that's no fun, believe me.

PLAYBOY: What brought it on?

KING: Well, I'm really not good enough at clinical introspection to say for sure. It wasn't a persistent problem. Drinking was partially responsible, I guess—what the English call the old brewer's droop. Henry Fielding points out that too much drink will cause a dulling of the sexual appetite in a dull man, so if that's the case, I'm dull, because if I knock them down too fast, I'm just too drunk to fuck. Booze may whet the desire, but it sure louses up the performance. Of course, part of it has to be psychological, because the surest way I know for a guy to become impotent is to say, "Oh, Christ, what if I'm impotent?" Fortunately, I haven't had any trouble with it for quite a while now. Oh, shit, why did I get onto this subject? Now I'll start thinking about it again!

PLAYBOY: Have you found that your sex appeal has increased along with your bank balance and celebrity status?

KING: Yeah, there are a lot of women who want to fuck fame or power or whatever it is. The entire groupie syndrome. Sometimes, the idea of an anonymous fuck *is* sort of appealing; you know, some gal comes up to you at an autograph signing in a bookstore and says, "Let's go to my place," and you're leaving town the next morning and part of you is tempted to say, "Yeah, let's; we'll pour Wesson Oil over each other and really screw our eyes out." But it's better not to start down that slippery slope—no reference to the Wesson Oil intended—and I haven't. My marriage is too important to me, and anyway, so much of my energy goes into writing that I don't really need to fool around.

PLAYBOY: Have you always been faithful to your wife?

KING: Yes, old-fashioned as it may sound, I have been. I know that's what you'd expect somebody to say in print, but it's still true. I'd never risk my wife's affection for some one-night stand. I'm too grateful for the unremitting commitment that she's made to me and the help she's given me in living and working the way I want to. She's a rose with thorns, too, and I've pricked myself on them many times in the past, so apart from anything else, I wouldn't *dare* cheat on her!

PLAYBOY: Did you feel at all threatened when your wife began to pursue her own writing career and published her first novel, *Small World?*

KING: I sure did. I felt jealous as hell. My reaction was like a kid's: I felt like saying, "Hey, these are *my* toys; you can't play with them." But that soon changed to pride when I read the final manuscript and found she'd turned out a damned fine piece of work. I knew she had it in her, because Tabby was a good poet and short-story writer when we started dating in my senior year at college, and she'd already won several prizes for her work. So I was able to come to terms with that childish possessiveness pretty quickly. Now, the first time she outsells me, that may be another story!

PLAYBOY: Why is explicit sex so consciously absent from your work? Are you uncomfortable with it?

KING: Well, Peter Straub says, "Stevie hasn't discovered sex," and I try to dispute him by pointing to my three kids, but I don't think he's convinced. Actually, I probably am uncomfortable with it, but that discomfort stems from a more general problem I have with creating believable romantic relationships. Without such strong relationships to build on, it's tough to create sexual scenes that have credibility and impact or advance the plot, and I'd just be dragging sex in arbitrarily and perfunctorily—you know, "Oh, hell, two chapters without a fuck scene; better slap one together." There is some explicit sex in *Cujo* and in my novella "Apt Pupil" in *Different Seasons*, in which the teenager, seduced by Nazi evil, fantasizes about killing a girl as he rapes her, electrocuting her slowly and savoring every spasm and scream until he coordinates his orgasm with her death throes. That was consonant with the kid's twisted character but about as far as I could ever go in the direction of S&M, because after a point, my mental circuit breakers just trip over.

PLAYBOY: Along with your difficulty in describing sexual scenes, you apparently also have a problem with women in your books. Critic Chelsea Quinn Yarbro wrote, "It is disheartening when a writer with so much talent and strength and vision is not able to develop a believable woman character between the ages of 17 and 60." Is that a fair criticism?

KING: Yes, unfortunately, I think it is probably the most justifiable of all those leveled at me. In fact, I'd extend her criticism to include my handling of black characters. Both Hallorann, the cook in *The Shining*, and Mother Abagail in *The Stand* are cardboard caricatures of superblack heroes, viewed through rose-tinted glasses of white-liberal guilt. And when I think I'm free of the charge that most male American writers depict women as either nebbishes or bitch-goddess destroyers, I create someone like Carrie—who starts out as a nebbish victim and then *becomes* a bitch goddess, destroying an entire town in an explosion of hormonal rage. I recognize the problems but can't yet rectify them.

PLAYBOY: Your work is also criticized for being overly derivative. In *Fear Itself*, a recent collection of critical essays on your novels, author Don Herron contends that "King seems content to rework well-worn material.... Rarely in King's stories are there supernatural creations that do not at least suggest earlier work in the genre [and] usually they are borrowed outright." Would you contest the point?

KING: No, I'd concede it freely. I've never considered myself a blazingly original writer in the sense of conceiving totally new and fresh plot ideas. Of course, in both genre and mainstream fiction, there aren't really too many of those left, anyway, and most writers are essentially reworking a few basic themes, whether it's the angst-ridden introspection and tiresome identity crises of the aesthetes, the sexual and domestic problems of the John Updike school of cock contemplators, or the traditional formulas of mystery and horror and science fiction. What I try to do—and on occasion, I hope, I succeed—is to pour new wine from old bottles. I'd never deny, though, that most of my books have been derivative to some extent, though a few of the short stories are fairly *sui generis*, and *Cujo* and *The Dead Zone* are both basically original conceptions. But *Carrie*, for example, derived to a considerable extent from a terrible grade-B movie called *The Brain From Planet Arous; The Shining* was influenced by Shirley Jackson's marvelous novel *The Haunting of Hill House; The Stand* owes a considerable debt to both George R. Stewart's *Earth Abides* and M. P. Shiel's *The Purple Cloud;* and *Firestarter* has numerous science fiction antecedents. *'Salem's Lot,* of course, was inspired by and bears a fully intentional similarity to the great classic of the field, Bram Stoker's *Dracula.* I've never made any secret of that.

PLAYBOY: You also seem intrigued by the phenomenon of Nazism and have written about it at length in both *Different Seasons* and *The Dead Zone,* which deals with the rise to power of an American Hitler and the desperate efforts of one man to stop him before it's too late.

KING: Well, the nature of evil is a natural preoccupation for any horror writer, and Nazism is probably the most dramatic incarnation of that evil. After all, what was the holocaust but the almost literal recreation of hell on earth, an assembly-line inferno replete with fiery furnaces and human demons pitchforking the dead into lime pits? Millions have also died in the gulag and in such places as Cambodia, of course, but the crimes of the Communists have resulted from the perversion of an essentially rational and Apollonian nineteenth-century philosophy, while Nazism was something new and twisted and, by its very nature, perverted. But when it exploded onto the German scene in the twenties, I can see how it exercised a dangerously compelling appeal. That werewolf in us is never far from the surface, and Hitler knew how to unleash and feed it. So, yes, if I had been in Germany in the early thirties, I suppose I might have been attracted to Nazism.

But I've got a pretty sure feeling that by 1935 or 1936, even before the concentration camps and the mass murders got going in earnest, I'd have recognized the nature of the beast, in myself as well as in the ideology, and would have gotten out. Of course, unless you're actually in a situation like that, you never know how you'd respond. But you can see echoes of the mad Dionysian engine that powered the Nazis all around you. I'm a big rock-and-roll fan, and rock has been an important influence on my life and work, but even there you can sometimes hear that beast rattling its chains and struggling to get loose. Nothing so dramatic as Altamont, either; just the kind of wild, frenzied mob emotions that can be generated when you get a couple of thousand people blasted out of their skulls on sound and dope in an auditorium.

I love Bruce Springsteen, and recently, my wife and I were at one of his concerts in Toronto, where he suddenly started pumping his arm straight out from his chest with a clenched fist, like a Fascist salute, and all the screaming fans in the audience followed suit, and for a discordant moment, we felt we were in Nuremberg. And there's obviously not the faintest hint of fascism or racism or violent nihilism in Springsteen, such as you'll find in some of the English punkers, but all at once, that mass hysteria you can get at rock concerts had coalesced into a dark and disturbing apparition. Of course, good, strong rock can evoke a powerhouse of emotional reaction, because by nature, it's go-for-broke stuff; it's anarchistic in the most attractive sense of the word; it's all about living fast, dying young, and making a handsome corpse. And horror is like that, too. Both go for the jugular, and if they work, both evoke primal archetypes.

PLAYBOY: You're universally identified as a horror writer; but shouldn't such books as *The Stand*, which is essentially a futuristic disaster novel, really be classified as science fiction?

KING: Yes, technically, you're right. In fact, the only books of mine that I consider pure unadulterated horror are *'Salem's Lot*, *The Shining*, and now *Christine*, because they all offer no rational explanation at all for the supernatural events that occur. *Carrie*, *The Dead Zone*, and *Firestarter*, on the other hand, are much more within the science fiction tradition, since they deal with the psionic wild talents we talked about before. *The Stand* actually has a foot in both camps, because in the second half of the book, the part that depicts the confrontation between the forces of darkness and the forces of light, there is a strong supernatural element. And *Cujo* is neither horror nor science fiction, though it is, I hope, horrifying. It's not always easy to categorize these things, of course, but basically, I do consider myself a horror writer, because I love to frighten people. Just as Garfield says, "Lasagna is my life," I can say, in all truth, that horror is mine. I'd write the stuff even if I weren't paid for it because I don't think there's anything sweeter on God's green earth than scaring the living shit out of people.

PLAYBOY: How far will you go to get the desired effect?

KING: As far as I have to, until the reader becomes convinced that he's in the hands of a genuine, gibbering, certifiable homicidal maniac. The genre exists on three basic levels, separate but independent, and each one a little bit cruder than the one before. There's terror on top, the finest emotion any writer can induce; then horror; and, on the very lowest level of all, the gag instinct of revulsion. Naturally, I'll try to terrify you first, and if that doesn't work, I'll try to horrify you, and if I can't make it there, I'll try to gross you out. I'm not proud; I'll give you a sandwich squirming with bugs or shove your hand into the maggot-churning innards of a long-dead woodchuck. I'll do anything it takes; I'll go to any lengths, I'll geek a rat if I have to—I've geeked plenty of them in my time. After all, as Oscar Wilde said, nothing succeeds like excess. So if somebody wakes up screaming because of what I wrote, I'm delighted. If he merely tosses his cookies, it's still a victory but on a lesser scale. I suppose the ultimate triumph would be to have somebody drop dead of a heart attack, literally scared to death. I'd say, "Gee, that's a shame," and I'd mean it, but part of me would be thinking, Jesus, that really *worked!*

PLAYBOY: Is there anywhere you'd draw the line—at necrophilia, say, or cannibalism or infanticide?

KING: I really can't think of any subject I wouldn't write about, though there are some things I probably couldn't handle. There *is* an infanticide scene in *'Salem's Lot*, in which the vampire sacrifices a baby, but it's only alluded to, not described in any detail, which I think heightens the obscenity of the act. As far as cannibalism goes, I have written a story about a kind of cannibalism. It's called "Survivor Type" and deals with a surgeon who's in a shipwreck and is washed up on a tiny, barren coral atoll in the South Pacific. To keep alive, he's forced to eat himself, one piece at a time. He records everything meticulously in his diary, and after amputating his foot, he writes, "I did everything according to Hoyle. I washed it before I ate it." People claim I've become such a brand name that I could sell my laundry list, but nobody would touch that story with a ten-foot pole, and it gathered dust in my file cabinet for five years before it was finally included in a recent anthology. I will admit that I've written some awful things, terrible things that have really bothered me. I'm thinking now mainly of my book *Pet Sematary*, and one particular scene in which a father exhumes his dead son. It's a few days after the boy has been killed in a traffic accident, and as the father sits in the deserted graveyard, cradling his son in his arms and weeping, the gas-bloated corpse explodes with disgusting belches and farts—a truly ghastly sound and smell that have been described to me in grim detail by mortuary workers and graveyard attendants. And that scene still bothers me, because as I wrote it—in fact, it almost wrote itself; my typewriter raced like automatic writing—I could see that graveyard and I could hear those awful sounds and smell that awful smell. I still can. *Brrr!* It was because of that kind of scene that Tabby didn't want me to publish the book.

PLAYBOY: Have you ever censored your own work because something was just too disgusting to publish?

KING: No. If I can get it down on paper without puking all over the word processor, then as far as I'm concerned, it's fit to see the light of day. I thought I'd made it clear that I'm not squeamish. I have no illusion about the horror genre, remember. It may be perfectly true that we're expanding the borders of wonder and nurturing a sense of awe about the mysteries of the universe and all that bullshit. But despite all the talk you'll hear from writers in this genre about horror's providing a socially and psychologically useful catharsis for people's fears and aggressions, the brutal fact of the matter is that we're still in the business of selling public executions.

Anyway, though I wouldn't censor myself, I *was* censored once. In the first draft of *'Salem's Lot*. I had a scene in which Jimmy Cody, the local doctor, is devoured in a boardinghouse basement by a horde of rats summoned from the town dump by the leader of the vampires. They swarm all over him like a writhing, furry carpet, biting and clawing, and when he tries to scream a warning to his companion upstairs, one of them scurries into his open mouth and squirms there as it gnaws out his tongue. I loved the scene, but my editor made it clear that *no way* would Doubleday publish something like that, and I came around eventually and impaled poor Jimmy on knives. But, shit, it just wasn't the same.

PLAYBOY: Are you ever worried about a mentally unstable reader's emulating your fictional violence in real life?

KING: Sure I am; it bothers me a lot, and I'd just be whistling past the graveyard if I said it didn't. And I'm afraid it might already have happened. In Florida last year, there was a homosexual-murder case in which a famous nutritionist known as the Junk-Food Doctor was killed in a particularly grisly way, tortured and then slowly suffocated while the murderers sat around eating fast food and watching him die. Afterward, they scrawled the word REDRUM, or murder spelled backward, on the walls, and, of course, that's a word I used in *The Shining*. Not only should the dumb bastards be fried or at least put away for life, but they should be sued for plagiarism, too!

There were two other cases in a similar vein. In Boston in 1977, a woman was killed by a young man who butchered her with a variety of kitchen implements, and the police speculated that he'd imitated the scene in the film version of *Carrie* in which Carrie kills her mother by literally nailing her to the kitchen wall with everything from a corkscrew to a potato peeler. And in Baltimore in 1980, a woman reading a book at a bus stop was the victim of an attempted mugging. She promptly whipped out a concealed knife and stabbed her assailant to death, and when reporters asked her afterward what she'd been reading, she proudly held up a copy of *The Stand*, which does not exactly exhort the good guys to turn the other cheek when the bad guys close in. So maybe there is a copycat syndrome at work here, as with the Tylenol poisonings.

But, on the other hand, those people would all be dead even if I'd never written a word. The murderers would still have murdered. So I think we should resist the tendency to kill the messenger for the message. Evil is basically stupid and unimaginative and doesn't need creative inspiration from me or anybody else. But despite knowing all that rationally, I have to admit that it is unsettling to feel that I could be linked in any way, however tenuous, to somebody else's murder. So if I sound defensive, it's because I am.

PLAYBOY: In a review of your work in *The New Republic*, novelist Michele Slung suggested that the grisly nature of your subject matter may lead some critics to underestimate your literary talents. According to Slung, "King has not been taken very seriously, if at all, by the critical establishment. [His] real stigma—the reason he is not perceived as being in competition with *real* writers—is that he has chosen to write about... things that go bump in the night." Do you think the critics have treated you unfairly?

KING: No, not in general. Most reviewers around the country have been kind to me, so I have no complaints on that score. But she has a point when she touches on the propensity of a small but influential element of the literary establishment to ghettoize horror and fantasy and instantly relegate them beyond the pale of so-called serious literature. I'm sure those critics' nineteenth-century precursors would have contemptuously dismissed Poe as the great American hack.

But the problem goes beyond my particular genre. That little elite, which is clustered in the literary magazines and book-review sections of influential newspapers and magazines on both coasts, assumes that *all* popular literature must also, by definition, be bad literature. Those criticisms are not really against bad writing; they're against an entire type of writing. *My* type of writing, as it turns out. Those avatars of high culture hold it almost as an article of religious faith that plot and story must be subordinated to style, whereas my deeply held conviction is that story must be paramount, because it defines the entire work of fiction. All other considerations are secondary—theme, mood, even characterization and language.

PLAYBOY: *Time* magazine, hardly a high-brow bastion, has condemned you as a master of "postliterate prose," and *The Village Voice* published a scathing attack illustrated by a caricature of you as a gross, bearded pig smirking over bags of money while a rat crunched adoringly on your shoulder. *The Voice* said, "If you value wit, intelligence or insight, even if you're willing to settle for the slightest hint of good writing, all King's books are dismissible."

KING: There's a political element in that *Voice* attack. You see, I view the world with what is essentially an old-fashioned frontier vision. I believe that people can master their own destiny and confront and overcome tremendous odds. I'm convinced that there exist absolute values of good and evil warring for supremacy in this universe—which is, of course, a basically religious viewpoint. And—what damns me even more in the eyes of the "enlightened" cognoscenti—I also believe that the traditional values of family, fidelity, and personal honor have not all drowned and dissolved in the trendy California hot tub of the "me" generation. That puts me at odds with what is essentially an urban and liberal sensibility that equates all change with progress and wants to destroy all conventions, in literature as well as in society. But I view that kind of cultural radical chic about as benignly as Tom Wolfe did in its earlier political manifestations, and *The Village Voice*, as a standard-bearer of left-liberal values, quite astutely detected that I was in some sense the enemy. People like me really do irritate people like them, you know. In effect, they're saying, "What right do you have to entertain people. This is a serious world with a lot of serious problems. Let's sit around and pick scabs; *that's* art."

The thrust of the criticism in the *Time* piece was a bit different. It basically attacked me for relying on imagery drawn from the movies and television, contending that that was somehow demeaning to literature and perhaps even heralded its imminent demise. But the fact is, I'm writing about a generation of people who have grown up under the influence of the icons of American popular culture, from Hollywood to McDonald's, and it would be ridiculous to pretend that such people sit around contemplating Proust all day. The *Time* critic should have addressed his complaint to Henry James, who observed eighty years ago that "a good ghost story must be connected at a hundred different points with the common objects of life."

PLAYBOY: John D. MacDonald, a big fan of yours, has predicted that "Stephen King is not going to restrict himself to his present field of interest." Is he right? And if so, where will you go in the future?

KING: Well, I've written so-called mainstream stories and even novels in the past, though the novels were pretty early, amateurish stuff. I'll write about anything that strikes my fancy, whether it's werewolves or baseball. Some people seem convinced that I see horror as nothing more than a formula for commercial success, a money machine whose handle I'm going to keep pulling for the rest of my life, while others suspect that the minute my bank balance reaches the right critical mass, I'm going to put all that childish nonsense behind me and try to write this generation's answer to *Brideshead Revisited*. But the fact is that money really has nothing to do with it one way or the other. I love writing the things I write, and I wouldn't and *couldn't* do anything else.

My kind of storytelling is in a long and time-honored tradition, dating back to the ancient Greek bards and the medieval minnesingers. In a way, people like me are the modern equivalent of the old Welsh sin eater, the wandering bard who would be called to the house when somebody was on his deathbed. The family would feed him their best food and drink, because while he was eating, he was also consuming all the sins of the dying person, so at the moment of death, his soul would fly to heaven untarnished, washed clean. And the sin eaters did that year after year, and everybody knew that while they'd die with full bellies, they were headed straight for hell.

So in that sense, I and my fellow horror writers are absorbing and defusing all your fears and anxieties and insecurities and taking them upon ourselves. We're sitting in the darkness beyond the flickering warmth of your fire, cackling into our caldrons and spinning out our spider webs of words, all the time sucking the sickness from your minds and spewing it out into the night.

PLAYBOY: You indicated earlier that you're a superstitious person. Do you ever fear that things are going just *too* well for you and that suddenly, some malign cosmic force is going to snatch it all away?

KING: I don't fear it, I *know* it. There's no way some disaster or illness or other cataclysmic affliction isn't already lurking in wait for me just down the road. Things never get better, you know; they only get worse. And as John Irving has pointed out, we are rewarded only moderately for being good, but our transgressions are penalized with absurd severity. I mean, take something petty, such as smoking. What a small pleasure that is: you settle down with a good book and a beer after dinner and fire up a cigarette and have a pleasantly relaxed ten minutes, and you're not hurting anybody else, at least so long as you don't blow your smoke in his face. But what punishment does God inflict for that trifling peccadillo? *Lung cancer, heart attack, stroke!* And if you're a woman and you smoke while you're pregnant, He'll make sure that you deliver a nice, healthy, dribbling baby Mongoloid. Come on, God, where's Your sense of proportion? But Job asked the same question 3,000 years ago, and Jehovah roared back from the whirlwind, "So where were you when I made the world?" In other words, "Shut up, fuck face, and take what I give you." And that's the only answer we'll ever get, so I know things are going to go bad. I just *know* it.

PLAYBOY: With anyone else, this final question would be a cliché. With you, it seems just right. What epitaph would you like on your gravestone?

KING: In my novella "The Breathing Method," in *Different Seasons*, I created a mysterious private club in an old brownstone on East 35th Street in Manhattan, in which an oddly matched group of men gathers periodically to trade tales of the uncanny. And there are many rooms upstairs, and when a new guest asks the exact number, the strange old butler tells him, "I don't know, sir, but you could get lost up there." That men's club really is a metaphor for the entire storytelling process. There are as many stories in me as there are rooms in that house, and I can easily lose myself in them. And at the club, whenever a tale is about to be told, a toast is raised first, echoing the words engraved on the keystone of the massive fireplace in the library: IT IS THE TALE, NOT HE WHO TELLS IT.

That's been a good guide to me in life, and I think it would make a good epitaph for my tombstone. Just that and no name.

With Edwin Pouncey

Q: What frightened you as a child?

KING: Monsters. Martians. Ray Bradbury Martians and H. G. Wells Martians. There was a series of comic books called *Classics Illustrated* and a lot of the classics they concentrated on were *Frankenstein, Dracula, Dr. Jekyll and Mr. Hyde,* that sort of thing and one that they did was H. G. Wells' *War of the Worlds,* where the Martians looked like these evil, intelligent squids and that frightened me very much.

Q: What do you think started your interest in that sort of stuff in the first place?

KING: I have no idea. I think it's innate, sort of bred in the bone the same way that a kid who has a tendency to diabetes doesn't know that; all he knows is that when he's very tired he wants something that's sugary.

There's no answer to that question, particularly not a Freudian or a Jungian one. I find these types of questions more interesting than the answers because they all presuppose the idea that there has to be some kind of unreconciled childhood conflict that's causing these stories, but it's not true, it's not true at all.

Q: How do you handle your own children's fears?

KING: One way is, I treat them and their fears the way that my mom treated mine, because my mom brought me up. I try to be sympathetic, I try to work them through it if there are things I can do that will make the thing easier.

Just lately my smallest son has got this horror of going to school on rainy days. I don't know what it is, something's obviously happened to him, they wouldn't let him into the building or something. He's only six and whatever it is right now is in his brain but he can't get it out of his mouth, it's too big. For now what I can do is keep him in the car on rainy days until the school bell rings and it's time for him to go in.

A psychiatrist would say, "Well, you're treating the symptom but you're not treating the cause," but I couldn't give a shit what the cause is. If keeping him in the car until the bell rings makes it better, then OK.

On the other hand I'm not above instilling certain fears in my children, if it will help me get my own way sometimes. For instance, my kids wanted to sit in the third row whenever we went to the movies and although it didn't bother them I'd spend three hours with these giant people looming over me like an avalanche.

So I finally told them that we couldn't do this anymore and they said, "Why not?" and I told them that the screen was a hole and they could fall into the movie and they'd never be able to get out. They looked at me in this uneasy way and said, "Naah, that's not true," and I said, "Sure it is. See those people in the background? You don't think they can pay that many people to be in the movie? Those are people that fell in and can't get out." Then they didn't want to sit in the front row anymore. I solved the problem. They became a little afraid but it's OK, it doesn't hurt a kid.

Q: Many of the first things you wrote were science fiction–based short stories. What were they about?

KING: A lot of those things were disguised horror stories. In fact, a lot of the novels I've written are really science fiction. *Firestarter, Carrie*, and *The Dead Zone* are all science fiction, in other words they are not novels about ghosts, vampires, or ghouls. But then again the idea of me writing hard science fiction, of doing an Arthur C. Clarke or a Larry Niven, is ludicrous. I got C's and D's in chemistry and physics.

Q: What do you think is the cause for the present fascination with both the science fiction and horror mediums?

KING: We live in a science fiction world and we live in a world that's full of horrible implications. We now have a disease called AIDS that causes a total immunological breakdown. It's a blood disease that sounds like something out of *The Stand*. A lot of people retreat into fantasy worlds because the real world is kind of a gruesome place.

People pick up *'Salem's Lot* and read about vampires. Vampires seem optimistic compared to Ronald Reagan, who is our American version of a vampire, of the living dead. I mean Reagan's real, he's a real person, but vampires look good next to him because you know that you can at least dismiss the vampires when the movie's over or when you close the book.

Q: How do you feel about the screen adaptations of your work?

KING: I'm happy with *Creepshow* because I was involved with the entire thing from beginning to end and the writing process was original.

I'm also pleased with Brian De Palma's *Carrie* and have a real fondness for what Tobe Hooper did with *Lot*. A guy called Paul Monash, who incidentally produced *Carrie*, wrote the screenplay for *'Salem's Lot* and it seemed to me that he was the only one (there were several scripts done) to solve the problems of adaptation.

Q: To return to *Creepshow*, whose idea was it to print the stories in the form of an E. C.-type horror comic?

KING: The comic, that was my idea. They wanted a novelization, they wanted to farm it out, and I told them I've never allowed anything to be novelized. I said that if we're going to do this then let's do it in the spirit of the movie itself, which is of the E. C. Comics, the horror pulps, let's go ahead and do a comic book.

So we hired a guy called Berni Wrightson to do the panels and I just did the continuity. It was kind of fun.

Q: You also worked with him on *Cycle of the Werewolf*, didn't you?

KING: That idea started as a calendar, with Berni doing the illustrations for twelve separate months but with some kind of continuity, as though it were a story.

I suggested the idea of a small town that would have an incursion, some sort of outside supernatural force: a werewolf. I liked that because werewolves are full-moon creatures, and every month there's a full moon. I thought here we can have twenty-three new and interesting murders, sort of like *Friday the 13th*—except that in itself seemed to be very shaky, like snuff stuff, set 'em up and knock 'em down like dominoes.

A story did develop out of it however, but the individual pieces were too long to do as a calendar, so now it's a book with the illustrations and the twelve months.

Q: How did you like playing Jordy Verrill in the film version of *Creepshow?*

KING: I didn't care for it that much. Near the end of "Jordy" I was in a chair for six hours a day getting this Astro-turf stuff put all over my body.

Tom Savini did the special effects and he made a mold of my tongue because one of the scenes calls for me to stick out my tongue and it's growing with this meteor fungus.

Tom had this pepperminty stuff and he slathered it onto my tongue with a stick and I had to sit there for ten minutes with my tongue out with about ten pounds hanging off it.

When it was done he had a perfect cast of my tongue with which he made four green latex tongues. They were like the gloves surgeons wear only you had to roll them on over your tongue. It was very realistic.

There was a shopping mall next door, and I went in there one day wearing this thing into some department store where this salesgirl came up and said, "Can I help you?" I stuck out my tongue and went "Bleeeahhh!!" and she went "Yaaaaahhhhhh!!" She went bullshit, called the mall cop and everything, but it was worth it, it was so funny. But that was the best fun as far as that thing goes.

Q: What other reactions do you get from the general public as a rule?

KING: There are people who write me letters that are almost religious. They've read everything and they're trying to relate things and they see themes and messages and the rest of it.

Then there are other people who write in letters to say, "Thanks for the entertainment, it took my mind off my job and the problems I was having with my wife," and I like that. I like the idea that you're building these little rooms where people can go for a while in order to get away into make-believe.

Also there are some critics who write reviews that say, "This stuff is crap." It may be "dangerous crap" or "pulp" to them, but on the whole I think as far as any judgment goes, the only thing that matters is what I think of it. I don't mean that in an egotistical way either.

There's a particularly prevalent view among the popular arts where people are a little unsure about what they're doing in terms of "real art," and that is the attitude, "I know what I'm doing, so fuck you!" and I don't buy that. What I do mean is that if you had to turn to look over your shoulder to say to some mythical authority figure, "Hey, am I doing OK?" you're not doing anything. You might as well forget it.

I like to feel that I give an honest deal for the dollar or pound. I mean shit, these guys are selling at $18.95 and I don't want anybody to go get that book and say, "Well, I got about $13.50 out of this, I want my change." What you'd like to hear is for some guy to go pay $18.95 for *Christine* and say, "Gee, I got $19.50's worth."

And there's also an element of sadism involved, I like the idea of somebody getting really scared and sleeping with the lights on and that sort of thing. I like the sensation of power involved.

Q: With *Christine*, was the idea to create a four-wheeled version of *The Shining*'s haunted Overlook Hotel?

KING: It's a haunted car and I think your idea is a lot closer to the truth than the people who say, "Well, this Roland LeBay has possessed the car," or that "The car is a rolling ghost of Roland LeBay," I don't think that's true at all.

I do think that if there is survival, if people really do remain after death, then what's going on there is that places absorb the emotions of those individuals who have been there.

In *The Yellow Wallpaper* by Charlotte Perkins Gilman, the new tenant of the house sees this greasy mark on the wallpaper where another woman's gone mad, walking around on her hands and knees for weeks on end with her head tipped against the wallpaper, so it's left that greasy mark. But it's left something far more sinister than that. It's left the spirit of madness.

That's what I feel is going on in *Christine*; there's a woman who commits suicide in the car and there's a little girl who chokes to death on a hamburger that she ate in the car, although she dies by the side of the road.

Q: So basically the car, Christine, is acting like a giant emotional video recorder?

KING: Yeah, just playing these things back.

There's also the car-as-vampire aspect. As it begins to feed on people, as it begins to do these terrible things, the odometer begins to run backward and the car begins to get younger. I was taken with this idea. It would be like a film running backward. If you see in a movie some guy's hat blowing off, you run the film backward and his hat will go Voop! back on his head. That was the kind of idea I had and it never really got across that much in the book.

Q: Who, if anybody, is the villain Roland LeBay based on?

KING: He's not anybody, the car had to have an owner. *Christine* started as a short story, and I wanted him to be funny in a twisted sort of way, but I think that all evil's funny. Ultimately, you get to the point where you just have to laugh because the whole thing gets so hollow.

It's like reading *The 120 Days of Sodom* by de Sade. After a while you say, "My God, all these people walking around with assholes down to their knees, what is this about?" and you just screech with laughter because that's all there is left to do.

LeBay started off to be a funny character to begin with, but he kind of grew in my mind after a while and I couldn't seem to keep him out of the book. Even after he died he kept coming back for one more curtain call, getting uglier and uglier all the time.

Q: Do you find a lot of your readers prefer the uglies to the victims in your books?

KING: Sure, we're fascinated with evil, we're human beings, that's all. I used to have a scrapbook as a kid with this picture of a famous mass murderer in it. When my mother found my scrapbook with pictures of Charles Starkweather, she said, "Good God, you're warped."

But I just wanted to see if I could figure out what he was up to. I mean, Jesus, it was a part of the world and he killed all those people, apparently for sport, and I wanted to understand it if I could. Of course there's a morbid side to it, and why shouldn't there be?

That's the sort of thing that most of us go around denying, saying things like, "I'm not interested in that, I read *The Guardian*" or "I'm not interested in that sort of stuff, I read Jane Austen."

But at home, under the bed, in the closet, behind the shoes, who knows what these people have hidden? Domination magazines? Pictures of people being spanked? They could be hoarding anything from sexual kinks to pictures of Hitler.

If a writer like me has any value at all, then I think what I'm supposed to say are things that other people either don't dare to say or find embarrassing. They say to themselves, "But if I say that, what will people think of me?"

That's why I think most people see horror writers as depraved individuals who are strange, weird, a little bit creepy, probably unlovely, somebody who would be clammy to touch.

Most of the ones I know are big, hale and hearty, cheerful, outgoing, friendly people, and I think one of the reasons they are is that you have to have a certain confidence in yourself to be able to create a human monster.

Those are things that a lot of us keep locked in the closets of our minds and if we let them out, we let them out when there's nobody around and our wives, husbands, or lovers are asleep.

Or, alternatively, you read a book and if somebody asks you what you're reading you can say, "Oh, this belongs to my kids, I just happened to pick it up."

Q: What frightens you now?

KING: I'm afraid that we're going to have nuclear meltdown. We're going to have a bad nuclear accident somewhere and we'll lose 40 to 50 percent of one of our states.

I'm afraid that right now there's some terrorist, maybe twenty-three or twenty-five years old, walking around with a very dirty suitcase-sized nuclear weapon.

Q: But basically, like the rest of humanity, you're scared of death?

KING: Oh yeah, I'm afraid of death.

CHAPTER TWO

— ✦ —

BUILDING NIGHTMARES

— ✦ —

I believe the success of these books says something rather wistful about the American reading and moviegoing public: we know about the nuclear bomb, about the nerve gas that can cause stereotoxic overload in seven seconds, but we still need to make believe about the troll under the bridge, the witch in the woods, and the unquiet spirits in the old hotel.

With Mel Allen

The tall man is leaning against his Scout, grappling with a handful of 800-page books and a pen, with hands that are slow to unlimber from the cold. The wind whips across the parking lot of the supermarket and finds the man where he stands pinned to his car in the school parking lot, writing inscriptions inside the books with the cautious rapidity of a man who wants to say something well, but who is getting colder by the minute.

His denim jacket is badly frayed, and there are holes in the sleeves. Years before, as a student at the University of Maine at Orono, his courtship with Tabitha Spruce, daughter of the owners of a Maine general store in nearby Milford, nearly stumbled over his personal dress code. Once, as a high school student in Lisbon, Maine, he was preening in front of a full-length mirror, trying to look like his friends. His mother, a tall, thin, but powerful woman who bequeathed her son her Irish blue eyes, threw him against a wall.

"Inside our clothes, we all stand naked," she thundered. "Don't ever forget it."

His shirt flaps loose in the back, and he wants to tuck it back into his jeans, but that would mean putting the books on the ground, so he fin-

*ishes his business with the pen and walks quickly past the football field
into a side door of the school.*

*The name of the school is Hampden Academy. It is a small public school
despite its highbrow name, located in Hampden, Maine, across the Penobscot
River from Bangor. He knows his way around, he thinks, until he opens the
door of what he remembers to be the teachers' room, and finds a startled photography student hanging prints to dry in the school's darkroom.*

*The tall man is confused and runs a hand through his thick black hair
that hangs to his left eyebrow, as it always has, except when it's groomed
by an expensive hairdresser for publicity photographs. The student stares
at the intruder, knowing he has seen that face somewhere. It is a striking
face, with or without the dark beard that appears and disappears each
year like autumn foliage. After writing 'Salem's Lot, the novel about vampires ravaging a small Maine town that increased his already considerable
fame and fortune twofold, the man remarked ruefully that, unlike his vampires, he, "unfortunately, could still see himself in the mirror."*

*He opens the doors, sees familiar faces, smiles, says hello, and by trial
and error finds the teachers' room that by twelve forty-five is deserted. A
place for a quick smoke. He has smoked since he was eighteen and now
says he's trying to quit, as he said the year before, and the year before
that. He fights his personal demons one by one, he says, and this one
clings to him like quicksand.*

*Others have described him as hyperkinetic, and he roams the small room
restlessly, taking in the titles of the paperbacks used in the English courses.
He picks up a well-worn copy of 'Salem's Lot. It is a cover that created a
sensation a few years ago with its single drop of crimson drooling from the
icy blue lips of a child.*

*For a moment, as Stephen King pauses outside the door, he realizes
that the circle has come around. For the next fifty minutes the world's
best-selling writer of the macabre will stand in a classroom at Hampden
Academy and talk about vampires, as he had eight years before. Eight
years filled with so many changes, they might well have been 800....*

KING: I was teaching *Dracula* here at Hampden Academy. I was also teaching Thornton Wilder's *Our Town* in freshman English. I was moved by
what he had to say about the town. The town is something that doesn't
change. People come and go but the town remains. I could really identify with the nature of a very small town.

I grew up in Durham, Maine, a really small town. I went to a one-room schoolhouse. I graduated at the top of my grammar class, but there were only three of us. We had an eight-party line. You could always count on the heavy breathing of the fat old lady up the street when you talked to your girlfriend on the phone. There was a lot to love in that town. But there was a lot of nastiness, too. I was thinking about *Dracula* a lot, I was thinking about *Our Town*.

It always seemed when I taught *Dracula* that Stoker wanted to make science and rationalism triumphant over superstition. But Stoker wrote his book at the turn of the century. I started mine when I'd seen all the flies on modern science. It doesn't look so great anymore when you can see spray cans dissipating the ozone layer and modern biology bringing us such neat things as nerve gas and the neutron bomb. So I said, I'll change things around. In my novel, superstition will triumph. In this day and age, compared to what is really there, superstition seems almost comforting.

There will always be a special cold place in my heart for *'Salem's Lot*. It seemed to capture some of the special things about living in a small town that I'd known all my life. It's funny, but after reading the book people will say to me, "You must really hate Maine." And I really like it here. The novel shows a lot of scars about the town. But so much of it is a love song to growing up in a small town.

So many things are dying in front of us—the small stores where the men hang out, the soda fountains, the party lines. Maybe it's just that when I wrote the book we were so poor and our trailer was little and cold and I could go back to my little furnace room where I wrote with a fourth-grade desk propped on my knees. And when I got excited it jiggled up and down as I hunched forward. Maybe that's why I like it so much. I could go down there and fight vampires whenever I wanted.

I was always interested in monsters. I read *Fate* magazine omnivorously. There are good psychological reasons for my attraction to horror stories as a kid. Without a father, I needed my own power trips. My alter ego as a child was Cannonball Cannon, a daredevil. Sometimes I went out west if I was unhappy, but most of the time I stayed home and did good deeds.

My nightmares as a kid were always inadequacy dreams. Dreams of standing up to salute the flag and having my pants fall down. Trying to get to a class and not being prepared. When I played baseball, I was always the kid who got picked last. "Ha, ha, you got King," the others would say.

Home was always rented. Our outhouse was painted blue, and that's where we contemplated the sins of our life. My mother worked the midnight shift at a bakery. I'd come home from school and have to tiptoe around so as not to wake her. Our desserts would be broken cookies from the bakery. She was a woman who once went to music school in New York and was a very good pianist. She played the organ on a radio show in New York that was on the NBC network. My feeling is she took herself and her talent to New York to see what she could find.

She was a very hardheaded person when it came to success. She knew what it was like to be ón her own without an education, and she was determined that David and I would go to college. "You're not going to punch a time clock all your life," she told us. She always told us that dreams and ambitions can cause bitterness if they're not realized, and she encouraged me to submit my writings.

We both got scholarships to the University of Maine. When we were there, she'd send us $5 nearly every week for spending money. After she died, I found she had frequently gone without meals to send that money we'd so casually accepted. It was very unsettling.

I had some running battles with those teachers in college who sneered at the popular fiction I carried around all the time. They'd go around all day with essentially unreadable books like *Waiting for Godot*. I was their court jester. "Oh, King, he's got some *peculiar* notions about writing," they'd say.

When I started *Carrie* I had finished my first year of teaching. I was working in the summer at the laundry to try to make ends meet. Our phone was taken out because we couldn't afford it. Our car was a real clunker. When the telegram came saying it was accepted with a $2,500 advance Tabby had to call me at school from across the street. I was in the middle of a teachers' meeting and was on pins and needles waiting to get home and hug her.

My mother was dying then. But she knew everything was going to be all right. She was old-fashioned about *Carrie*. She didn't like the sex parts. But she recognized that a lot of *Carrie* had to do with bullying. If there's a moral in the book it is "Don't mess around with people. You never know whom you may be tangling with." Ah, if my mother had lived, she'd have been the Queen of Durham by now.

Later, after *'Salem's Lot* was finished, we went to Colorado because I wanted a book with a different setting. And nothing was coming. Somebody said we should go to Estes Park, which was about thirty miles away, and stay at the Stanley Hotel, a famous hotel that supposedly was where Johnny Ringo, the legendary badman, was shot down.

We went up there the day before Halloween. It was the last day of the season and everybody had checked out. They said we could stay if we paid cash because their charge-card blanks had been shipped off. Well, we did have cash and we did stay. We were the only guests in the hotel, and we could hear the wind screaming outside.

When we went down to supper we went through these big bat-wing doors into a huge dining room. There were big plastic sheets over all the tables and the chairs were up on the tables. But there was a band, and they were playing. Everybody was duded up in tuxedos, but the place was empty.

I stayed at the bar afterward and had a few beers, and Tabby went upstairs to read. When I went up later, I got lost. It was just a warren of corridors and doorways, with everything shut tight and dark and the wind howling outside. The carpet was ominous, with jungly things woven into a black-and-gold background. There were these old-fashioned fire extinguishers along the walls that were thick and serpentine. I thought, "There's got to be a story in here somewhere."

That night I almost drowned in the bathtub. They were great deep tubs that ought to have had hash marks on the side. I thought, if I could get just a few people in there and shut them up...

I write my nightmares out. Occasionally, somebody will say to me, "I got a nightmare from reading your book," and my immediate reaction is "Serves you right for reading it." Because when you get to the bottom of everything, what I'm involved in is trying to scare the bejeesus out of people. You aren't there for tea and cookies, but to serve people's darker tastes.

My favorite scene in *The Stand* is when Larry Underwood, a rock singer, and his girlfriend are trying to escape New York City. You have to remember nearly everybody in the country is dead. He gets into an argument with her by the Lincoln Tunnel. The tunnel is jammed both ways with cars whose drivers died before they could get out. The only way out is to walk the two miles through the tunnel, around all the cars, and all the bodies inside. And there are no lights.

He starts through the tunnel, alone, and gets about halfway. And he is thinking about all the dead people in their cars and he starts to hear footsteps and car doors opening and closing. I think that's a really wonderful scene. I mean can you *imagine* that poor guy?

Q: As your fame and fortune grow, how do you keep your perspective?

KING: I'm very leery of thinking that I'm somebody. Because nobody really is. Everybody is able to do something well, but in this country there's a premium put on stardom. An actor gets it, and a writer gets it. I read *Publishers Weekly*, and more and more I see people compared to me. In the review of a horror novel they'll write, "In the tradition of Stephen King..." And I can't believe that's me they're talking about. It's very dangerous to look at that too closely, because it may change me from what I want to be, which is just another pilgrim trying to get along. That's all any of us is.

You know, my editor calls New York GWOP, the "glamour world of publishing." Everybody is really a little kid inside, and it's like playtime in New York. It's where we take off our Clark Kent outfit and turn into superwriter.

We had lunch at the Waldorf with people who bought the movie rights to *The Shining*. We sat in leather chairs. Mine was dedicated to George M. Cohan because it was where he used to sit and compose. The waiters are all French. They glide over to you.

And we sat around the table talking seriously about people to play roles in the movie. "What do you think about Robert De Niro for the father?" someone says. Somebody else says, "I think Jack Nicholson would be terrific." And I say, "Don't you think Nicholson is too old for the part?" And so it goes. We're tossing around these names from the fan magazines—except it's for real. Then the check comes and it's $140 *without* drinks, and somebody picks it up without batting an eye.

Then I come back to Maine and pick up the toys and see if the kids are brushing in the back of their mouths, and I'm smoking too many cigarettes and chewing aspirins alone in this office, and the glamour people aren't here. There is a curious loneliness. You have to produce day after day and you have to deal with doubts—that what you're producing is trivial and besides, not even good. So in a way, when I go there, to New York City, I feel like I've earned it. I'm getting my due.

With Joyce Lynch Dewes Moore

Q: Did you shave off your beard again?

KING: Right on schedule. I shave it off when the baseball season starts every year. And when the last game of the World Series is over, I symbolically go into the bathroom, throw out all the razor blades, whatever else there is—the electric razor goes into the drawer—and it doesn't come out again until next year.

Q: That's a wonderful answer to an interview question. Is it true?

KING: It's true, absolutely. To me, the beginning and the end of the baseball season mark, or symbolically bookend, summer. In the summertime I don't want a beard. It's like a blanket; it's hot. But in the wintertime when it's cold, it covers your face, and where I am, in Maine, it's really cold.

Q: You said, "I'm not a great artist but I've always felt impelled to write." What elements do you feel go into making a great artist?

KING: (*taking a deep breath*) More talent than I have, I think... that's just sort of a gut reaction to the question. When you read somebody like Joseph Conrad or Raymond Chandler, you sense that a lot of stuff is going on there. I've always felt that my work has been more humdrum or more mundane than the sort of thing the really great writers do. So you take what talent you have, and you just try to do what you can with it. That's all you can do.

Q: But a lot of people think you are great.

KING: I know, from the letters I get, that there are people who believe that. But the other thing that goes along with that is that you have to evaluate the critical reaction to your work and decide from that what you're doing. You see, I don't think writers are very good judges of their own work. Maybe they're not bad judges, but they're no better judges than anyone else. Everybody has an opinion, but nobody's opinion is better than anybody else's.

I don't think greatness is anything even a great writer can take credit for. The only thing you can take credit for is how much you work at your craft, how much you want to refine what you do, and how much better you can get through work. I mean God gives you so much talent. It's the same way that the butcher gives you so much meat. If you've got a lot of meat, you can have steak. If you don't, you have to make stew. But just because you've got to make stew doesn't mean you can't make a good one. So I work with what I've got.

Q: John D. MacDonald, in his introduction to *Night Shift*, said, "... at the risk of being an iconoclast, I will say I do not give a diddly-whoop what Stephen King chooses as an area in which to write." Then he continues, "*One is led to care.*" Isn't that what great writing is all about?

KING: I shy away from the word "great," but I think if you talk about good writing, one thing about it is that it's antigenre. Good writing is not mystery writing, it's not western writing, horror writing, science fiction writing. Good writing is good writing. It can be appreciated by anyone who picks up the book. In that sense, I think MacDonald is right. It doesn't matter what you write about, there really is not enough of that good stuff to go around.

Q: Most of your books have a psychic theme. Have you or someone you know had psychic experiences?

KING: Not in my immediate family. You hear stories. Because I'm in the business that I am, people bring their ghost stories to me. But I've never had what I would call a genuine psychic experience. The only thing that even comes close to this is that in the last three houses my wife and I have lived in—we've since found out—people have committed suicide. In fact I'm sleeping in a dead man's bed now. This is really strange. My wife bought this beautiful bedroom set. I can't even take credit for it and say I bought it. She could tell you the style and everything, I don't know. But she bought it from a fellow at a used-furniture store in Maine, and he said, "You know, that's funny, but you're the third lady I've sold this to." And she said, "How's that?" It turned out there had been a retired couple on Sebago Lake and he died in the bed. His wife broke up house-keeping and sold the bedroom set to this guy we call the old pagan, because he's open 365 days a year—he doesn't care, he doesn't give a shit; it's all right with him—and he sold it to another couple in another little town. They were also older, and he popped off in the bed. Then he sold it to my wife, and she and I sleep in it.

Q: If the stories you write aren't from personal experience they are, at least, well-researched.

KING: I do research. I get different ideas from one source or another. You know, a lot of the phenomena, the case histories you read of psychic phenomena, things like telekinesis or telepathy or pyrokinesis, those things fascinate me. If you read a few case histories you get a kind of feel for it. Then I'll sit down and write the book. Afterward I do the research. Because when I'm writing a book, my attitude is: don't confuse me with facts. You know, let me go ahead and get on with the work. Afterward, I develop the soul of a true debater or a true carpetbagger, same thing, and find out the things that support my side.

Q: How often are you wrong?

KING: It's a relative term in this field because there are a lot of people who don't believe any of it. I don't believe or disbelieve. It's so subjective there is no right or wrong. It's like arguing the existence of God.

Q: How often is what you've written easily corroborated, verified?

KING: Oh! There's a lot of verification for this stuff. I'm no student of the paranormal or the psychic, but I have a really keen nose for people who are obvious fakes, people I won't believe. In some cases there are people who might be telling the truth, but either their stuff isn't corroborated from another angle or I simply don't believe them.

Q: Some people who saw *The Exorcist* passed it off as a great horror film and just enjoyed being scared. Others were flipped out by the film. Has anybody ever written to you or talked to you about a certain scene in one of your books that has really caused great upset in their lives?

KING: Never. I've gotten a lot of letters from people who have been very excited by the books. Of course, I had an experience when I went to see *The Amityville Horror*. There was a big crowd, and I was surprised when the lights went on because a lot of them were older people. There's a kind of median age for horror movies, maybe seventeen or eighteen; they're fairly young. And this was a fairly old crowd, and they were very, very excited leaving. These people were discussing the film in very animated tones, talking in the way people talk when they feel their lives have touched the unknown in some way, which for most people, in books, is always described as a horrifying experience where people shy away from the unknown. Most people get very excited when they feel they've touched some otherworldly experience. And my response to the people who flipped out at *The Exorcist* is that they're people who would flip out anyway. It was a great horror movie, but to flip out. . . . It scared me when I saw it, and I was very excited by the film. When I came out of the theater I felt as if I'd been given a shot of the real stuff. Which is what I try to do with my books.

Q: You succeed. You're a person who gives people a shot of the real stuff, yet you profess to never having had any contact with. . .

KING: With the real stuff myself. No, but I get as excited as those people coming out of *The Amityville Horror* by the possibility. There was a guy who wrote a lot of flying-saucer books in the 1950s by the name of Donald Kehoe. He collected a number of documented cases which to him seemed to either be supported or were from responsible people. Mike Wallace on the old *Nightbeat* program asked him if he'd ever seen a flying saucer.

Kehoe said no, but that didn't mean they didn't exist. He said nobody had ever seen Pluto either, but they knew it was there by the distortion in the orbit of Uranus and Neptune. And that's the way I feel about a lot of this stuff. There's a scene in *The Dead Zone* where Johnny Smith gives a press conference after he's come out of a coma. News has leaked out that he might be psychic. This reporter who doesn't believe it comes forward with a gold chain from his sister, and he says, "If you're psychic, tell me something about this." And he gives it to Johnny Smith. The scene that follows is kind of the archetype of the psychic experience as I've read about it and understood it, and it's my own feeling about what would really happen if a person were *really* psychic. Johnny just blows the guy away. The guy faints with horror because Johnny Smith is actually able to do it.

Q: Don't you think "psychic" means more than ghosts or moving tables? Isn't it also just plain intuition?

KING: That's right, and we don't argue that intuition exists.

Q: To be intuitive is good, to see spirits is warped, to move things is really whacko, but isn't it all a matter of degree?

KING: Yes, I think it is. I think that most people feel the lack of those things, particularly in an age like the one we now have where there's so much technology and so much emphasis on logic, deductive reasoning, inductive reasoning. This is an age where you go into the 7-Eleven store and find a computer rather than a cash register.

Q: What kind of kid were you?

KING: I was a quiet kid. I've read stuff about Ray Bradbury, and I think I was a lot like Ray as a kid. I went to a lot of movies and read a lot of books and I didn't talk much. You know, a day of interviews like this is very hard for me because, generally speaking, I'm not a very good talker. I'm not used to externalizing my thoughts other than on paper, which is typical of writers.

Q: What about school?

KING: I was about a B average. I think. Not so good that I would call attention to myself and not so bad that cards got sent home to my mother about my performance as a student. If that had happened, she would have gone to work on me.

Q: What kept you going as a young writer after sixty short stories and four novels were rejected?

KING: The traditional answer to give to a question like that is to say, well, I knew in my heart that I was right, or that I would get there eventually. Actually, you get a lot of encouragement along the way. When the first novel was rejected, I just wasn't ready. I think I wrote it between sixteen and seventeen and I was just too young. But I started to sell some short fiction when I was eighteen, and when you're selling stuff you say, well, there must be something, some spark there, because something is happening. I think I was just protected from, say, the age of twelve to about eighteen by the idea "They're rejecting you, what do you expect? You're just a kid."

By the time *Carrie* sold, I was twenty-four. I remember working on that book and having times when I felt depressed and really down. I would say to myself, well, maybe you're after a fool's dream and you're never really going to succeed at this, and what makes you think you can do it when billions of people all over the world are trying to write books. There were times in my life when it seemed that anybody I talked to would say, "Well, yeah, I'm writing a book." It was like being in the Boston Marathon: there were all these other people running, what makes you think you can win?

I would also think, when I was depressed, "Well, you used to say you were just a kid, too young to succeed, but what the hell? You're twenty-four now, and Ira Levin published a book when he was twenty-two, and a lot of people have done that, and pretty soon you're not going to have that excuse anymore. Then how are you going to face it?" But most of the time when I was being my normal self and trying to evaluate things on a real basis, I would say, "Well, I'm selling some short fiction and things take time; you can't have everything at once." And I would simply keep punching away at it.

Writers have big egos. That's the only way you continue in the face of all those rejection slips. You've got a thick skin and you don't bleed maybe as much because of it. When somebody sends back a story and says, "I'm sending this back because the characterization seems wrong to me and it seems like you've gone off the rails at Points A and B," you file the rejection slip. Except I used to have a dart board that I kept mine on, and when I was really feeling down I used to throw darts at them and I would say, "There, that's it for you, *Cosmopolitan*. There, that's it for you *McCalls*. Take that, *Alfred Hitchcock!*"

You read the rejections, the personal letters that explain why they didn't take the story, although they might say something good about it and part of you inside says, "Well, they were wrong." Also, if you read a lot of stuff and you know in your heart that you write better than some of the crap that comes out you say, "Well, if I'm doing better than this and this is published, then it's just a question of continuing to flog the things around until they find a home."

Q: What do you have more problems with: characterization, dialogue, mood, narrative, plotting?

KING: I would say plotting is the most difficult thing. Characterization is only hard because sometimes I feel I get so interested in it that I want to talk too much about the characters and that slows the story down. So I say, "Hey, people want to find out what's going to happen next, they don't want to listen to you spout off about this or that person." But I think even the bad guy deserves to tell his side of the story.

Q: Do you begin your books with an idea or message? Do you know where you're going when you start?

KING: I start with ideas and I know where I'm going but I don't outline. I usually have an idea of what's going to happen, maybe ten pages ahead, but I never write any of it down because that sort of closes you off from an interesting sidetrip that might come along. Theodore Sturgeon told me once that he thinks the only time the reader doesn't know what's going to happen next is when the writer didn't know what was going to happen. That's the situation I've always written in. I'm never sure where the story's going or what's going to happen with it. It's a discovery.

Q: Regarding *The Shining*, is it true you wrote it in a burst, something like four weeks?

KING: The book ran itself off in, I would say, four to six weeks, for the major part of the work. There was never any hold on it, never any delay or any interruptions, because I was working in a rented room at the time I did it. We were living in a small house in Boulder, Colorado. I could not work at home; there just wasn't any place for me. So I rented a room from this woman and never saw her after that. Once a week, I left a check for $17.50 by her coffeepot, and I never saw her again! I went up there, and I knew what I was going to write or at least I thought I knew. I didn't find out until I was into the thing that I had no idea what I was going to write.

Originally I set the book in the form of a Shakespearean tragedy, and that was really all I knew. It was going to be in five acts, which finally translated themselves into parts: Job Interview and Preparatory Matters, Closing Day, Wasp's Nest, Snowbound, and Matters of Life and Death. But I knew what the framework of the book was going to be, the frame that it was going to fit itself into, and there was just never a hitch or snag in the whole writing of the book.

Q: Have you ever had a character take over?

KING: In *Carrie*, the old drunk that tells about the explosion in town had to be pruned back. I got carried away with that guy. He just wanted to go on and on. And Watson, the night watchman in *The Shining*, was supposed to be a minor character. He had a lot more to say than I ever expected he would, but I never pruned him back. I'm glad now I didn't.

Q: What kind of writing schedule do you have?

KING: I work about two hours a day, but I work seven days a week. I write six pages a day, and that's like engraved in stone. With my work, you can take the page number and divide it by six and come out with the number of days I've been working on the book. Unless something catastrophic happens, like the house explodes, in which case I would stop. My wife might say Owen fell down the stairs and broke his neck, and I'd say, "Fine, go take him to the emergency room, and let me finish this page."

Q: Do you rewrite?

KING: Yes, three or four times. I think when you write a book, most of what you want should be there or there's something very wrong, and it means the book is very broken. It's really dangerous to finish the first draft of the book and as you're going along you say, "Well, I sense things are going wrong and getting out of hand, but I'll fix it on the rewrite." You shouldn't have to do that. You should have a lot of it there, and on the second draft go back and fix everything that was a little bit wrong— like taking a deck of cards and squaring them up so they're all even.

On the third draft I concentrate on language and make the sentences feel balanced. I think good writing should be accessible. The reader should be able to get through the barrier of print and into the story without too much effort. It should be like a good car. You have a good car and when the engine is in tune and running right, you can't hear the motor, but that doesn't mean it isn't doing its work. It means that everything is OK. And I think in a good novel the writer's voice should be low enough that you can engage your mind and do what you need to do with the book and make it do what you need it to do.

Q: How do people react to you personally?

KING: They're usually disappointed. They say, "You're not a monster!" Lots of times photographers will look at me with this kind of depressed, sad look and say, "Can you do something spooky?"

With Paul Janeczko

Q: Can creative writing be taught?

KING: I'm of the opinion that it probably can't. I think that you can teach writers who have come a certain distance to do things that make their writing better. You can teach things about point of view, for example. You can teach things about pace. But you cannot teach a writer to find the good story, the story that hasn't been told. With writers who are very good—the naturals—you can't really do anything except give them an environment of friendly criticism, and let them read the story to the class. Hopefully, the teacher's input and the class's input will mean something to the writer in terms of rewriting or grasping that story or the next story more firmly.

To my mind, the most important thing that a creative writing class does is give the writer a friendly atmosphere where you take it seriously and nobody's saying, "Oh, that's a bunch of bullshit. Why do you want to do that? Why don't you get out and learn to fix cars or become a plumber or something?" People must take it seriously, and I think that's an important function in creative writing classes.

Q: Do you think that can be done on a high school level?

KING: Sure. In fact, I think you can do more with creative writing in high school than you can in college. I taught creative writing in high school, and the reaction of the kids who took the creative writing courses as electives was, "Let's have some fun. This is just for fun anyway." The thing about high school is that the students look at school in a different way. They're forced to go there, and a lot of times their attitude is, "Well, we might as well enjoy this and get what we can out of it." Whereas in college, I had the feeling with a lot of my creative writing students that, at least for this month, they really wanted to be writers. Their egos were mortally involved in this. After a while I did the worst thing a creative writing teacher can do, especially with a poetry class. I started to get very timid with all of my criticism because I was afraid that some student would go home and perform the equivalent of hara-kiri. Well, I didn't want to be responsible for destroying anybody's ego completely.

But on the high school level I could say, "This story is crap. Look, this is all wrong. Rip this out and put it here. Take this out entirely." And they'd say, "Okay, okay." And they did it. They took a lot more chances, and they weren't so influenced by what they'd read. They didn't want to be Baudelaire. They didn't want to be Hemingway. They didn't know about these guys. They just wanted to be themselves, and that was that. Unfortunately, with a lot of poetry students you're laboring under a lot of terrible burdens like Rod McKuen and Leonard Nimoy and Hallmark greeting cards. You've got to work against that.

Q: Is there anything else that the writing teacher can do?

KING: I think so. For the people who are writing at a level where you think their work can be published, you can try to help them in that direction. Above that, it would be nice for them if they could see it published for money, just simply because most students don't have any. You may know the names of contacts, for example. You could suggest markets. But, of course, there are various levels for publishing their work, and the teacher should take advantage of them all. It means a lot to a kid to see his stuff in print.

Q: What things should students read?

KING: Well, I had my college students read *Double Indemnity* by James M. Cain, which is only about 125 pages long. And I had them read a novel by David Morrell called *First Blood*. Morrell is a college teacher, and he constructed this very careful novel of predestination. I lean toward all these naturalistic books anyway, where everything just goes to hell. Those are two books that I can think of right now. I had them read primarily novels because it seemed that a short story constantly turned the class into a lit. class, and I wanted them to read, to think, and to write about what they had read. But I never tried to lecture on those books. My own feeling is that it's almost an exercise in futility to assign outside reading in a writing class because if the writer isn't reading, he or she is in bad trouble anyway.

Q: So reading should be a given for a writer?

KING: *I* think so.

Q: Why is reading important to a writer?

KING: The most important thing is it teaches you what *not* to do. I think young writers have reached a real watershed moment in their own lives as writers when they can say very honestly to themselves—maybe not even say it aloud—"I do better stuff than that." They read a book that's been printed and presumably somebody got paid money for it. Or if they didn't get paid money for it, they got copies to give to their relatives and friends. But when they read it, they make that vital critical judgment and say, "I'm better."

When I went to school my important creative writing work was done through paperbacks that I read as a kid. I went to school with John D. MacDonald and learned about character from Ed McBain. From others I learned about pace and plot. And from others I learned about cardboard characters, people who were moving without motivation. Maybe that's the most important thing a writer learns by reading: how important motivation is to the story.

That's one of the reasons, by the way, that I have never had a strong relationship with the people who make films. I don't feel that they understand motivation. They want pretty pictures; they don't want a story. When Stanley Kubrick made *Barry Lyndon*, he gave people a movie that was actually a novel. It did poorly at the box office and it did poorly with the critics because people don't want novels. They want movies.

Q: As a writer of fiction, what do you feel you owe your readers?

KING: A good ride on the roller coaster, and that's all. Anything that they take beyond that is up to them. My idea has always been to tell a story, and the story is boss. Anything else that may come along has got to be put in its place, which is secondary.

I don't like the stories by the Jacqueline Susann, Harold Robbins–type of writers where people seem cardboard and you can almost see the hand of the writer moving them from place to place. I think the characters should be real, and they shouldn't do anything in the course of the story that is false. I don't like that chessboard feeling. Characters should be able to move on their own. I guess I like *The Shining* because the characters seem to do that.

Q: What makes a good horror story?

KING: Character, I think. You care about the people, particularly in *'Salem's Lot* and *The Shining*, which were real screamers. People have said to me that both novels have slow builds. And they do. But the thing is, I want you to feel that the characters are people that you care about, that they are real, and that they are doing real things. That you don't have to dismiss them on the grounds of, "Well, they're just doing this because the writer wants them to do it."

You must feel that the characters are deep. And I don't mean deep in the sense that they have a lot of deep thoughts. They must have thickness. Do they stand off the page? Then the writer puts them into a position where they can't get out. You don't get scared of monsters; you get scared for people.

I think it's important that the reader knows that the writer is not playing. This isn't going to be a Hardy Boys story, where everybody survives at the end and there never was any real danger. I think that you know you've grown up when you say to yourself, "I don't want to read any more Supermans because he is the man of steel and he's always going to get out of this jam, whatever it is and nothing serious is really going to happen to him."

Q: How does Stephen King see the world?

KING: I'm not very optimistic about the world. I think that shows in the books. The books that influenced me the most when I was growing up were by people like Thomas Hardy, Frank Norris, and Theodore Dreiser. All those people of the naturalistic school believed once you pull out one rock, it's sort of a relentless slide into the pit. I don't think that any thinking person can look at the world in our society and see anything very secure. The whole situation is bad. I try to do as well by my family as I can. I try to raise my kids to be good people. You know, the good guys. That sort of thing. But I don't think the future looks very bright.

With Charles L. Grant

Q: There's a story going around that it took a lot of expensive permissions to use the fifties song lyrics for *Christine*. How did you manage to turn up the sources?

KING: We got most of the quotes from a music publishers. A guy named Dave Marsh helped us out. He used to write for *Rolling Stone*. I think he finally got tired of the articles about Farrah Fawcett's clothes in what's supposed to be a rock and roll magazine. No, it wasn't Farrah Fawcett's clothes, it was Linda Ronstadt's clothes, which is even worse. But there are two music organizations, ASCAP and BMI, and in most cases we were able to get information from them. But nobody ever came forward to take credit for "Teen Angel."

Song permissions are really expensive. I think that it turned out to be about $15,000 in royalties for the lyrics used in *Christine*, and the publisher doesn't pay for that, I pay for that. It looks very deceptive when a contract comes back, and it says they only want $50 to allow use of the song for a thousand copies printed. Then you start to think for a minute and you say, now wait a minute. The publisher says, okay, no problem—you know what I mean? But you say to yourself, 300,000 hardcovers and then more paperbacks.... It's a long answer for a simple question.

Q: Which of your stories is your favorite?

KING: As far as short stories are concerned, I like the grizzly ones best. However, the story "Survivor Type" goes a little bit too far, even for me. After four years of fruitless efforts to get the thing published, Charlie Grant bought the story.

Q: Do you really think that story is funny?

KING: I think it's hilarious! A guy cuts himself up and eats himself, piece by piece. It's the grossest thing you've read!

Q: What's it like being married to a novelist?

KING: It's all right. We work on entirely separate tracks, so it isn't much of a problem. Every now and then she'll accuse me of stealing one of her ideas. Now, would I do that? She's got a new book out called *Caretakers*, now available in softcover at a bookstore near you.

Q: In *Danse Macabre* you hypothesized that one of the reasons people are so fascinated with horror stories is that they are rehearsing for the bad or violent death.

KING: In a lot of ways I think that's bull. That's not to put down what I wrote or what you asked, but I just don't think anybody knows. I associate it with mortality because I think that we're the only sentient creatures on the earth, with the possible exception of chimps, whales, and dolphins, that can contemplate their own end. I'm not real sure about chimps because they don't seem to have much of a conception of time.

Time is very important to the idea of mortality. In 200 years, none of us is going to be here. Which reminds me of something else one of my kids said. Out of the mouths of babes.... My six-year-old wanted to know how old Tabby and I would be when he was ninety-nine, and Joe, who was ten, said, "They'll be dead, they'll be in the ground; they'll be all black and things will be falling off of them." That was a real conversation stopper!

The point is, we are observant creatures, and we see that most of the endings are bad ones. I think I said in *Danse Macabre*, in fact I know I did, that I'd like to die in bed of a heart attack. Then it would be like (*snaps fingers*) that. A lot of times it doesn't happen that way and I think we have to prepare for that.

Q: Did your son Jody have a good time making *Creepshow*?

KING: Yeah, Jody had a good time, but he did get freaked out for a while. He was eight or nine at the time, and to be in your pajamas with a whole bunch of people around your bed in a strange house can be very unsettling. All the lights and everything. He just came to the point where it was either freak out or go to work. He went to work.

One of the first things you hear in the movie is an argument between him and his father. He says something to his father, and you hear a smack. They put this very realistic makeup bruise on his face. The night that scene was shot Jody worked late, according to the Screen Actors Guild rules or whatever it was, but we got everything on film, and I enthusiastically assisted in the exploitation of my son. We'd gone over budget by then. When we finished working at around eleven p.m., he wanted to stop at McDonald's on the way back to the place where we were staying. So we went to the drive-up window, and this cat takes one look and his mouth drops open. By the time we left, about fifteen minutes later, everyone in that McDonald's had been outside to see the kid in his pajamas with this great big bruise on the side of his face.

Q: Is there a particular director that you'd like to work with that you haven't worked with before?

KING: I'd like to work with Spielberg. I think that would be fun. I came very, very close to writing *Poltergeist*. I would have liked to work with Don Siegel, the guy who did the original *Invasion of the Body Snatchers*. Another is Sam Peckinpaw. There are a lot of directors I really like, but in most cases the last thing filmmakers want is to work with an author. I'd like to do originals, and I'd like to do some more with George Romero. It was a great experience. I'd like to work with long form on cable sometime. George really wants that mood to spread, y'know. Give that guy nine hours and he'll give everyone in America a heart attack!

Q: When one of your stories is being filmed, do you work closely with the director, as you did with George Romero?

KING: I did work closely with George, but those other guys—no.

Q: Were you pleased with *The Shining?* Many people were disappointed.

KING: *The Shining* is a strange case—perverse. Sometimes I wonder how Bob Bloch, who is a real gentleman, has been able to cope with people asking, "How did you like *Psycho?*"—for twenty-some years. He must be a little bit tired of that question. I'm getting tired of *The Shining* question, and it hasn't been that long, although sometimes it seems like twenty years. I hope people aren't asking me that question in twenty years because I'll just say, "I don't know, leave me alone." Because I really don't know. I don't have a capsule answer.

Q: When, not if, you write another film, would you rather adapt one of your own things, like *The Stand?*

KING: No. I'd like to do another feature: something long. God help me, I'd even like to do a novel for television. Everyone has their own sword planted in the sand, and they go by it twice a day and say, "Sooner or later I must rush on that sword—disembowel myself." I think that's mine: I'm convinced that network TV is still viable. If you give somebody enough time and get the audience involved in the characters, you can scare people. You could even scare people over programs like *The Dukes of Hazzard* if you could kill off one of those creepy kids.

Can you imagine the reaction of all those nerdy eleven- or twelve-year-olds sitting in front of their TVs watching *The Dukes of Hazzard* and some ten-wheeler comes and just runs those Duke boys right down! (*High-pitched voice*) "I see his eyeballs on the highway—Oh, God!" That would be great.

I'd also like to get a bunch of California actors, the ones that look all bubbly inside, like pod people, and run six or seven hours of them and get people, just by force of incremental repetition, to take them seriously as people, the way everybody takes the soap opera people seriously. After you watch *Edge of Night* for about three months, your critical judgment fades. They become real people to you. You have no more perspective. I don't follow *Edge of Night* anymore, and *General Hospital* is too trendy for me, thank you. But imagine some of those people, and then introduce the monster, the slime in the cellar, and have a few of them get eaten. Then you know that no one is safe, anything can happen, and the Neilsen ratings would go through the roof! I'd like to try that sometime.

Q: What do you think of the film version of *Cujo?*

KING: It's one of the scariest things you'll ever see. It's terrifying! *Cujo* was an independent production, with Dee Wallace playing the part of Donna Trent. She played the mommy in *E.T.* It was directed by Lewis Teague. I think this guy is the most unsung film director in America. You never hear his name brought up at parties. Teague did *The Lady in Red* and *Alligator*. He also did a picture called *Fighting Back*. He has absolutely no shame and no moral sense. He just wants to go get ya, and I relate to that!

Q: What kind of literature do you read?

KING: I read a little bit of everything. I read some mysteries when I get a chance, although I'm more apt to buy mysteries, put them on the shelf, and say, "I ought to read that." I read a fair amount of horror, and I like straight novels. I read very little nonfiction because it's all too frightening.

Q: Do you read every day, like you write?

KING: Yes. A day without a book is like a day without sunshine!

Q: How hard are you trying to convince your readers that the situations in your books are real?

KING: I'm very aware that when you work in this field, eventually you cross a line where everything becomes unbelievable. That is to say, the rational audience knows that there aren't any traditional vampires—creatures who live thousands of years and rise at night. So I think in terms of untraditional vampires: literal vampires who may not be immortal. At least we hope they are not immortal. They may have a brain hemorrhage. I'm aware that between reality and unreality you have to stitch a seam, and I try to make that seam as fine as possible so the reader steps over it. I like the whole illusion of reality. When you play with fantasy, and if you do it in a certain way, it highlights it even more.

I'll give you an example. In *The Tommyknockers*, I wrote a scene that I like as well as anything I've ever done. There's a Coca-Cola dispensing machine in the book. It's sort of a thinking Coke machine because this kid has put all kinds of circuits and memory chips in it, and the thing runs on a great big Delco tractor battery. It levitates and cruises around the county roads, very slowly in this ghastly silence—this red-and-white Coke machine with the sun glimmering off the glass panel from which the bottles come out. Every now and then it will find a pedestrian and run him down.

One of the main characters is a real wimp. I was glad to see him go.

He's a reporter and his car stalls. He's walking along and here comes this Coke machine. It's early morning and it is cruising about 6 inches above the ground with its shadow behind it. The machine somehow senses the man and begins to speed up until it's going really fast—like zero to sixty in five seconds.

Coke machines are actually big refrigerators. They weigh about 500 pounds; more if somebody has been putting money into them. So it hits the guy, and he's like a bug on a windshield. He's just smashed on the front of this Coke machine and the glass panel is broken, and all of the money is coming out of the coin return.

That was it for me. I could see it. It was just there and it was absurd, but at the same time it had weight and reality for me. I like that. That's all I know. I like the way unreality smells and feels as well as the way it looks.

Q: Who do you go to for criticism or help on your writing? Say you have a rough draft you're not sure of. Who helps?

KING: I go to my wife because she's there in the house and because I trust her. There are two kinds of critics. There is the kind who tells you he doesn't like something but can't tell you why. Then there are critics who point out what is wrong and then show you how to fix it. That's what a good editor is supposed to do.

Q: Have you ever been rewritten without your knowledge?

KING: I don't think so, but I've had things dropped. You never see the continuity lapses, of course, until after the book has been published. Then you go Ouch! There's a scene in *Christine*, by the way, when the bad guy, Buddy Repperton, drives into a garage with his cuckoo friends and trashes this other fellow's car. He drives into the garage in a Camaro, I think, and comes out in a Duster. Oh...

Q: How are you coming along on the screenplay for *The Stand?*

KING: Let me run this down as well as I can. When I met George Romero, I really liked him. We came to an agreement that we would try to do this thing, so I wrote a draft. The original draft was half as long as the book, which means that instead of 800 or 900 pages of novel, I had 400 pages of screenplay. The rule of thumb for screenplays is that one page equals one minute of running time. A 400-page screenplay comes out to be something like six hours and forty minutes on the screen.

Can't be done. Another problem is what one Warner Bros. executive referred to as "spill and fill," which is one of the ugliest phrases I've ever heard. What it means is that a picture cannot make money unless it can be turned over enough times in one day, and particularly during that time period when there's someone other than people using Golden Age passes, JDs skipping school, and people who have come from their bowling league in the afternoon to see the picture. You've got to be able to get in two evening shows, and sometimes three in the big cities. I heard from one Warner Bros. guy that the reason *The Shining* didn't get into the black until release abroad was that it was two hours and fifteen minutes long, so in a lot of cities the last show was cut. After eleven p.m. the babysitter goes on double time, and it becomes a problem.

So I did a second draft of the screenplay, and it came out about 300 pages long. This was better. We also talked a little about the way to go with it, the novel-for-television idea. But the networks don't want to see the end of the world, particularly in prime time. Advertisers don't want to sponsor the end of the world. Cable didn't have enough money. For a long time I pushed for doing it in two sections—*Stand I* and *Stand II.* I thought it would be possible to build a big artificial climax in the middle that would satisfy audiences for the time being. If it was all shot at once, the films could be released maybe three months or a season apart. The final decision was to go for a very long feature film. I have to try to cut my 300 pages of screenplay in half. I think I know how to do it now, but I don't relish the idea because I know that some of the characters will get squeezed. The film *is* going to happen.

Q: Is it true that your wife retrieved *Carrie* from the garbage?

KING: Yes. Tabby took *Carrie* out of the trashcan, she really did. There are critics who would argue that perhaps she should have left it there. Anyway, I was working in a laundry when that happened, and I had written a lot of horror stories for men's magazines. We got married young, had a kid right away and a second kid almost right after that. I was making the princely sum of $60 or $70 a week and getting all the overtime I could. The only thing that was really keeping our heads above water were these stories for men's magazines. I've autographed a few of those, and it always gives me a cold shudder to think about where I was when I wrote those stories. My underwear had holes in it in those days.

Anyway, one of my college friends, who was still in college and could therefore still afford literary scruples, came to me and said, "Why are you writing all of this macho crap?" I explained that they were for macho magazines and the stories didn't sell too well to *Cosmopolitan*. "You don't have any feminine sensibility at all, he said." I told him I could if I wanted to, but he didn't think so. I said that if you're a writer and a realist about what you're doing, you can do nearly anything you want. In fact, the more of a pragmatist and the more of a carpetbagger you are, the better you can do it.

Here's an example that I think proves my case. There was a pulp writer named Frank Gruber who once accepted a challenge and wrote a story that was accepted in one of these trendy literature magazines. He was hailed as the new Faulkner, but he just did it on a dare. He wrote just this one story and then went back to writing his regular crap.

I had said I could do it, so I sat down and started writing a short story, and that short story was *Carrie*. It had a kind of fairytale structure, and it was going to be a story about a girl who did a terrible thing but who was justified because she had been driven mad by all the teasing. I kept having this image of a bear being baited by a bunch of dogs that were snarling and biting at him—at her. I saw immediately that it was going to be too long for the market, but at the same time I didn't have time to write a novel. I couldn't invest that much time in a project that might not make money. I was getting $200 for the short stories, and that kept the phone in the house and bought medicine for the kids. So I wrote two or three pages, but kept running into mundane problems. For instance, at the beginning someone helped Carrie use sanitary napkins and I didn't even know they came in coin dispensers.

I realized I was making my entry into a woman's world where I would have to deal with many things that I had never considered before. The guy was probably right—"I can't do it." So I tossed it, and Tabby picked it out of the wastebasket and read it. She was amused. I think she liked it but I think she was more amused.

Samuel Johnson once made a comment about women preachers, that they were like dancing dogs. It wasn't that you wanted to see it done well, you were just amused to see it done at all. She asked me to go with it, which I did. Several times during the course of that book Tabby was able to supply doorways at crucial moments. One of those moments was the thing at the prom where I really wanted to reap destruction on these people. I couldn't think of how it was going to happen. Tabby was the one who suggested using the amplifiers and electrical equipment from the rock band.

Q: When you've finished a project or are midway through one, have you ever seen someone else come out with the same idea?

KING: Yes. It happened with *The Stand*. There was a guy named Terry Nation who published a book called *Survivors*. It was exactly the same thing. Isn't that the worst?

Q: How close are you to finishing the sequel to *'Salem's Lot*?

KING: I know what it should be. I know the whole story, but I'm not going to tell it here. It's a pretty good story, too. I don't think it will be as long, and everybody will probably say this is nothing but a sleazy rip-off. Probably that's what it will be, but boy, am I going to have fun doing it! I want to go back there. I love that town.

Q: Can you talk about *It?*

KING: I think the most devastating criticism that I ever read was the criticism of a James Michener novel. The critic said, "I have two pieces of advice about this novel. The first piece of advice is, 'Don't buy this book.' The second piece of advice is, 'If you buy it, don't drop it on your foot.'" *It* is 1,300 pages long, and it started when I was going to pick up a car which had dropped its transmission in Boulder, Colorado.

People ask me, "Where do you get your ideas, man?" . . . They come. That's the huge part of it. You get an idea. Inspiration! Maybe it's a good idea, and maybe it isn't. File it away. Maybe you'll use it, and maybe not. Anyway, this particular day I was walking across a bridge at dusk. This was an industrial park community—way out—but you could see the town through this marshy area. It was real spook stuff. I could hear my boots on the bridge. They made a very echoey sound, and then I got this "telephone call" from my childhood. I thought any second I'm going to hear a voice say, "Who's that walking on my bridge?" Then the troll would just jump out, grab me, and eat me up. It's amusing, but I hurried to get off that bridge. All those things seem much more real when you're by yourself.

For a long time I thought about that troll and it began to cross-pollinate into a lot of other ideas. One of them was the idea of how children become adults, what makes children into adults, how we change, and even the fact that our faces change. When your face changes, what is inside your head changes too, but it doesn't all happen at once. Here was a chance to go back and explore those feelings we had as children: the fears that keep popping up through adulthood. I thought of a way to bring every one of them in. That's what *It* is. Frankenstein is in this book; Wolfman is in this book; Jaws is in the city canal. This kid has been beaten up by his father and he's sitting by the canal dangling his feet over the side into the water. He sees this white fin—Dum Dum, Dum, Dum. . . . It gets him and eats him up. The Mummy is in it, too. It's wonderful. Everything is in it, so it's sort of an epic horror movie in book form.

Q: Have you ever come up with a plot that is too outrageous?

KING: No. I've had ideas which I just don't think will work, and I've had ideas that seem too hard, things I couldn't handle. I've done a lot of hack stuff, and some of it has turned out OK. I think it is possible to go back into the junkyard. Many of those ideas are very good. I won't say *'Salem's Lot* is a rip-off of *Dracula*, but it definitely is a *bounce* off of *Dracula*. It's just a case of going into the junk pile and saying, "Hey, this thing still works. Let's take this home!"

Q: *The Stand* is very antigovernment. Are those your personal feelings?

KING: Oh, I think the government stinks! I pay my taxes. In fact, I must own a missile silo somewhere in Kansas by now. Probably has my name on it. The Stephen King Memorial Missile Silo. I pay my taxes, partially because I don't want to go to jail, but also because this country's been good to me. It has provided an umbrella of relative sanity for myself and my kids. But I believe what I wrote in *The Stand*. It always ends in one way. It's like taking dope or booze. You take enough government, and it's going to kill you. That's the end. Sooner or later it always goes down.

Q: You've got young children. What do you think about the effects of kids reading horror stories?

KING: I don't know. I did, and it warped me really good!

With Keith Bellows

Q: You're incredibly prolific. Where do you get your ideas?

KING: Well, there's a great little bookstore on 42nd Street in New York called Used Ideas. I go down there when I run dry.

Q: What scares people?

KING: There are big things that scare people, like dying, which is the really big casino. Most people get scared anytime you venture into taboo territory. While we've become more explicit about things like sex, we've really tightened up on death and disfigurement. Those things scare people a lot because we put such a premium on being pretty and handsome and young.

Q: Were you a little horror in high school?

KING: I used to crack jokes a lot. From time to time I was in trouble. Not bad trouble, but the kind of thing where you suddenly find yourself with a week's worth of detention slips, and you say, "How did I get these?"

Q: With all the horror of today's society, is it harder to scare people now?

KING: No. In *Creepshow* there's a segment in which this guy is overwhelmed by cockroaches. The guys who handled the bugs, the "roach wranglers," work for the Museum of Natural History in New York, and they're used to handling bugs. We had about 3,000 cockroaches, and at first the roach wranglers were pretty cool. But each day they got a little more freaked out. During filming, these bugs were living in big garbage cans and eating dog chow and bananas—a mixture that just reeked. By the end of the film, the wranglers were so scared that if you'd slapped one on the back, he'd have gone straight to heaven.

The more frightened people become about the real world, the easier they are to scare. Sociologists report that people in cities are hardened to violence. It's possible to get casual about it—to say, "Oh dear, a woman is getting beaten up. What's for dinner?" But the quantum fear grows, and that's why horror films are so popular. People have more fears to get rid of.

Q: You've said that high school students are more sophisticated today than when you were teaching. Do you think they approach the world any differently now?

KING: They approach the world the same way we did. You have a garbage cutter in your mind that chops through all the baloney and lets you focus on things that are important. When you're a teen, you're very conscious of the world around you. You don't want to be like everybody else, but you don't want people to think you're weird, either. So you adopt a lifestyle that encompasses everything from disco to Jordache jeans to video games or whatever. But that's the icing on the cake. The same things go on beneath the surface that went on when *we* were trying to find out what the heck we were up to in the world.

Q: What's the greatest horror that you think high school kids face today?

KING: Not being able to interact, to get along and establish lines of communication. It's the fear I had, the fear of not being able to make friends, the fear of being afraid and not being able to tell anyone you're afraid. The feelings of inadequacy and of not having anybody to turn to—a teacher, a counselor, a girlfriend, a boyfriend, the guy at the next locker—and say, "I'm afraid I can't make it on this level," whether you mean getting a date for the prom or passing Algebra II. There's a constant fear that *I am alone.* Mentally, you feel you're running a fever. That's when people need a close relationship, especially outside the family. Inside the family things are often very tense: people say little more than "Please pass the butter" or "Give me the rolls." And all the time kids are deathly afraid that they won't be able to get along.

With Christopher Evans

KING: I don't really prepare for my novels in any kind of a conscious way. Some of the books have germinated for a long time. That is to say, they are ideas that won't sink. Your mind is like this very deep pool. Some things just sink, and other things keep bobbing up, and you see them, you glimpse them over time and begin to see them in a different way. I don't even know what the right word would be. You go through all your old memories, things you've forgotten, because sooner or later everything comes up; you use everything.

Like the beginning of *The Dead Zone*, where Johnny Smith falls down and cracks his head on the ice. That happened to me. It's one of the earliest things I can remember: being hit by a hockey player, knocked out, and coming to about five minutes later. I was probably no more than four years old. It's one of those things you grab hold of and put in a book because it fits.

Well, I think it's a horror story. If there can be people like this Greg Stillson around, it's horrible. The way I look at it, things in this country have gotten flakier and flakier, and power in some ways has become more concentrated and, in some ways, it's become more diffuse. We haven't really had a strong president in this country since Nixon, and Nixon's strength was vitiated in his last two years by Watergate. People in this country would like to have a strong president. They'd like to have Greg Stillson.

I think most writers write what interests them, what they feel will entertain and divert them. I'm sort of mistrustful of writers who moan about how hard it is to write. I wonder how they live because my feeling is you're going to be with a book for a year and a half, sometimes longer, and you better damn well like the story, or you're going to go crazy.

The Dead Zone is a suspenseful novel. All of my books are related in that way. A suspense novel is basically a scare novel. That's the difference between suspense stories and mystery stories. I see the horror novel as only one room in a very large house, which is the suspense novel. That particular house encloses such classics as Hemingway's *The Old Man and the Sea* and Hawthorne's *The Scarlet Letter*.

One thing I don't want to do is write the same book over and over again. I'm very leery of that. My feeling is that Harold Robbins has written the same book now for about ten years. I think Robbins and originality parted company directly after *The Carpetbaggers*.

I see a correlation between the religious idea and the psychic idea because they are both a sort of struggle for power by people who are powerless. A lot of times, the people who are real fanatical believers in psychic phenomena are people like Vera Smith (the fundamentalist mother of Johnny Smith in *The Dead Zone*). Sometimes fundamentalism and the belief in the psychic cross. Vera Smith is a middle-class or lower-middle-class woman, and I think the lower you go on the financial scale in America, the more people you find reaching outside what we think of as the ordinary channels of power.

A guy who lives in New York on Park Avenue and makes $70,000 a year knows that a maitre d' in a restaurant is going to come immediately when he walks in, and that's a form of power people like Vera Smith and people who are living on welfare don't know about. So they read *Fate* magazine and things like that.

I'm not a churchgoing person but I'm sort of personally religious in that I've been careful about codifying anything I believed in. Belief in itself is a kind of power, and if there's a power deeper than that, for instance, if you take your grandmother to Lourdes and she really does get up and walk, then the belief is sort of a line into The Other Thing. I don't advertise The Other Thing because that's the province of novelists who are more self-confessedly literary than I am.

It's like the Ouija board except I don't think, in very many cases, writers have any kind of a line to a supernatural, outside force that is feeding them the words. Although God knows, enough people have believed that. The Greeks believed in their muse, which was like a little angel.

My favorite cartoon of all times is one in *The New Yorker* of a writer who looks really bummed out. He's sitting at his typewriter and a little angel is flying around his head saying, "I want to go down and get a pizza, and then I want a few beers and see if we can pick up some girls at the Paradise. Hey you, I'm talking to you!"

But really, I think a writer, if he's lucky, has got a pipeline that goes down into his subconscious where there's a little lexicographer setting type all the time. You kind of pull it up, along with a lot of old stuff that ordinarily you wouldn't think of or remember.

CHAPTER THREE

TERROR INK

The horror story makes us children. That's the primary function of the horror story—to knock away all of this stuff, all of the bullshit we cover ourselves up with, to take us over taboo lines, to places we aren't supposed to be. For a long time people have thought that horror is radical—a dangerous thing to deal with. But, actually, people who deal in horror are like Republicans in three-button suits.

With Abe Peck (*Rolling Stone*)

Q: Why do you want to scare people?

KING: Because people want to be scared. I love it when somebody tells me he read *'Salem's Lot* and then slept with a crucifix for three days.

Q: Do you believe in supernatural powers?

KING: I am a Yankee, a New Englander, so when somebody asks me, "What's your sign?" my immediate reaction is to say, "How many centimeters is your asshole?" But I don't disbelieve in the powers, either. They're fascinating if you say to yourself, "For a while, let me take for granted that this exists. Let's say Abe Peck can levitate. What does Abe Peck's wife do when she sees this guy floating around the ceiling? Does she run? Does she laugh?" It opens up a whole can of worms.

Q: Why do you use ordinary situations when so much of traditional horror is set in cemeteries in Transylvania?

KING: Well, all that had changed when I started to read in the fifties. *Weird Tales* was gone, except at rummage sales. Then Richard Matheson and Jack Finney came along; *The Body Snatchers* is at the root of everything that's gone on now, from Tom Tryon (*The Other*) to William Peter Blatty (*The Exorcist*). *The Twilight Zone* also took horror out of the graveyard. Those things formed my idea of what a horror story should do: the monster shouldn't be in a graveyard in decadent old Europe, but in the house down the street.

Q: And why does your style stress accessibility?

KING: Style is like the hood ornament of a car or having your engine chrome-plated. Style is expendable. You don't need it to tell a story. What has to come first is total accessibility to the reader.

Q: You've said in the past that horror is conservative. Why?

KING: By that I meant the attitude almost all horror stories espouse: "I'm okay, you're okay, but *bleh*, look at that." It's a way of confirming the norm.

Q: You once mentioned that you write about people caught in a crunch.

KING: I'm interested in what people do when they can't get out of a situation, particularly when the whole thing seems to slip out of control. I maintain that my novels, taken together, form an allegory for a nation that feels it's in a crunch and things are out of control. We're in that situation now, in terms of our world posture and the economy and oil. How do we cope? What do we do?

Q: What did you want to get at with *Carrie*, and how did it come about?

KING: Somebody had said to me, "You've written all these short stories, but they're really macho parables. You couldn't write about women." The thing hit home, because I had read Leslie Fiedler's *Love and Death in the American Novel*, which says that women in American fiction are either bitches or zeroes. There's no in between, no real women.

Basically, I had had an idea kicking around for six or eight months. It was supposed to be a short story, for $200 for *Cavalier* magazine, about this girl who got back at her classmates for this dirty trick they've pulled on her. But a short story is like a stick of dynamite with a tiny fuse; you light it and that's the end. It suddenly occurred to me that I wanted a longer fuse. I wanted the reader to see that this girl was really being put upon, that what she did was not really evil, not even revenge, but just the way you strike out at somebody when you're badly hurt.

I had done four books before *Carrie*. They're all home in a trunk. None of them are horror stories. It never crossed my mind to write a horror novel because there were none being published. As I worked on it I kept saying to myself, "This is all very fine, but nobody is going to want to read a make-believe story about this little girl in a Maine town. It's downbeat, it's depressing, and it's fantasy." But as I finished the first draft, *boom*, along comes *The Exorcist* and *The Other*, and that's how it was pitched.

I've always seen *Carrie* as a parable of women's consciousness. It's a book about women. The women are the only ones exercising brains, any kind of moral courage, or moral act. I think the film unconsciously takes the attitude that all men are cat's-paws. The guy played by John Travolta says (*geekish voice*), "Jeeze, that's good. Pig's blood. Hi-yuh, hi-yuh." *Carrie* expresses a lot of male fears—about menstruation and about dealing with women who eat you up.

People say, "How do you feel about *Carrie* now?" I have no response. Writing *Carrie* was the way you'd feel if you had the measles. All you can remember is that there was a low-grade pain.

Q: How much of *Carrie* was based on your experience as a high school teacher?

KING: A lot. An awful lot.

Q: That's an age when you really see kids being vicious to one another.

KING: Yeah, it's the last gasp of childhood's unlovely, uncivilized side. You know the book by William Golding, *Lord of the Flies?* That's *Carrie* out of control—high school society run riot.

Q: Kids seem to play a major role in most of your books. Why?

KING: I have three kids in the house. I love 'em, and I don't study 'em in the sense that you'd study bugs under a microscope, but they give me a chance to study what childhood is. None of us adults remember childhood. We think we remember it, which is even more dangerous. Colors are brighter. The sky looks bigger. It's impossible to remember exactly how it was. Kids live in a constant state of shock. The input is so fresh and so strong that it's bound to be frightening. When I was in college, I did twenty-five acid trips, used synthetic mescaline, and that sort of thing— and some of it was very, very powerful. Kids are constantly faced with that feeling. They look at an escalator, and they really think that if they don't take a big step, they'll get sucked in. I had a friend who had a kid who wouldn't go to bed at night because he was afraid of this monster. The parents kept talking about it, trying to get to the root, and it turned out to be a monster his father had talked about: a twilight double-header.

In my next book, I'm going to stop screwing around and try to take on directly the problem of what happens between childhood and adulthood, what changes and how the two connect.

Q: *Firestarter* also has a kid as a heroine.

KING: *Firestarter* started because I got fascinated with pyrokinesis. You read cases in the paper where people just burn up spontaneously. I started to read more about it, and the thing that came out was: Here's this man, Andy McGee; he's in college in 1969, and going to go to graduate school the next year. He's really poor, looking for a way to supplement his income, so he takes part in a psychology experiment where people receive either distilled water or a low-grade hallucinogen, which turns out to be a low-grade telepathic drug. The pyrokinesis came first, and then the idea of genetic mutation, which is also in *Carrie*. My concept is, if there are psychic talents, they're handed down the same way that the Wyeth people hand down artistic talent.

Q: In *Firestarter* you pit Charlie McGee, an eight-year-old girl, against a huge guy, Rainbird. There's almost a Lolita-esque plot.

KING: It's a sexual relationship. I only wanted to touch on it lightly, but it makes the whole conflict more monstrous.

Q: You once said you were afraid that *Firestarter* might be received as *Carrie II*.

KING: Yeah. If you're taken seriously as somebody who's practicing literature as art, you're allowed to return to what you've done before: you're amplifying previous themes. But if you write popular literature and you repeat a theme, the idea is that your head is so empty it's produced an echo.

Q: How did you feel about Stanley Kubrick's version of *The Shining*?

KING: I can't answer that question. I'm too ambivalent about it (*deep breath*). I didn't really want to work with Kubrick. He's got this reputation of running authors down. His view of movies is a zealot's view, which makes for interesting movies but also for a tough working relationship, unless you just say, "Stanley, here's your blank check. Do what you want."

My screenplay, which Kubrick chose not to use, was considerably different from the script that came out of his end. For one, my screenplay was pegged even more heavily than the book on something Kubrick never touched on—the past of the hotel. It says in *'Salem's Lot*, "An evil house calls evil men." That was the idea in *The Shining*. The hotel was not evil because those people had been there, but those people went there because the place was evil.

But I liked the movie for a lot of reasons that don't have anything to do with the book. The tone, the way he creates horror by building atmosphere—not by doing anything overt, just by using camera angles and light. Kubrick is a tremendously talented man, and I thought he would hit it dead bang on target.

Q: Is that what you think now?

KING: Well, no. I visualized a situation in which people would be carried out to ambulances with heart attacks.

Q: I like the book better.

KING: To be honest with you, I like the book better too.

Q: Yet the reviews of the movie knock the book.

KING: Whenever I publish a book, I feel like a trapper caught by the Iroquois. They're all lined up with tomahawks, and the idea is to run through with your head down, and everybody gets to take a swing. They hit you in the head, the back, the ass, the balls. Finally, you get out the other side and you're bleeding and bruised, and *then* it gets turned into a movie, and you're there in front of the same line and everybody's got their tomahawks out again.

Q: What's the difference between horror on film and horror in books?

KING: In a movie, you can do things on an emotional level that just don't work in cold type. For instance, at the end of the film version of *Carrie*, the hand comes out of the ground and the audience goes up in the air. You can do that in a book, but not as successfully.

Movies are a communal experience. You go to see *The Shining* with a huge audience and a feeling sets in: "Well, if I scream, everybody's going to say, 'What a wimp.'" But they do scream, and immediately there is a wave of laughter. That's everybody's way of saying, "It didn't really scare me. I'm laughing now. It's all right." In a book, you split one person off from the herd and...

Q: ...run 'em into the ravine.

KING: That's right.

Q: How would you compare the movie versions of *The Shining* and *Carrie* with the TV presentation of *'Salem's Lot?*

KING: In terms of horror, the ability to scare, I think *Carrie* is the best of them all. I thought Brian De Palma did a super job with *Carrie*. The chemistry was perfect. *Carrie* was a hot book—it just about bleeds on the page—and Brian is as cold as ice. He's very stiff, but he's fearsomely intelligent.

Q: What about *'Salem's Lot*—the way TV handles horror?

KING: The problem is that there are only so many things you can do on TV. The network-executive attitude seems to be that melodrama on TV is best appreciated while in a semidoze.

Q: When you were asked which of your books was your favorite, you said you had a "cold spot" for *'Salem's Lot*.

KING: It's a story of country people, not necessarily good country people. Ever since I was a kid, I always said to myself, "Sometime I'll write about the place where I live." The people form the town, and the town forms its own character. I took *Our Town* as an exercise book on how to do it.

Q: *The Stand* seems to be a different species altogether, more an epic.

KING: I never said this to anybody because it sounds so goddamned pretentious, but I wanted to do *The Lord of the Rings* with an American background. It didn't come out that way, but I thought it would be fun to do an epic fantasy with an American backdrop. So many fantasies take place in some make-believe land. You have to learn a new language to even read the book.

You see, I began to see the energy crisis as just one domino in a complex economic structure that was going to go down completely. The more I thought about this particular Gordian knot, the more I thought, "Suppose you cut right through the middle of it. Suppose everybody died except maybe a certain percentage of the world's population—then there'd be enough oil!" I began to embroider on the idea—the empty towns, the sand dunes.

Q: When is *The Stand* going to be done as a movie?

KING: It will probably be two years before it actually goes into production. The screenplay needs work, and George Romero (*Night of the Living Dead*) who is filming it, has at least one other commitment. Also, he and I have another project called *Creepshow* that'll probably go first, because the budget's a lot easier.

Q: How did the two of you get together?

KING: George turned up on my doorstep in Maine one day when I was teaching school. He said, "I'm on my way to New Hampshire to do a speaking engagement, do you have time for dinner?" I said, "Sure," and we drank a bunch of booze and had some chow, and he said, "Do you want to do a movie?" and I said, "Can we do the movie we want to do?" and he said "I always have."

We knocked around a lot of ideas. Finally, he said, "What do you really *want* to do?" and I said, "I would like to have people walk into a movie theater, be immediately riveted, be in a state of extreme terror for an hour and forty-five minutes, then crawl out." His eyes lit up. George and I share the idea that you don't mess around. If you want to do it, you go in and get people and you get 'em hard.

Q: What's *Creepshow* about?

KING: It starts in a tract house in a tract neighborhood on Maple Street, which is a deliberate choice on my part because I remembered a *Twilight Zone* episode, "The Monsters Are Due on Maple Street." We hear a father yelling at his little boy for reading one of those loathsome horror books. The father throws the comic book on top of a trash barrel. A thunderstorm comes, and the wind picks up. There's lightning and all those gothic conventions. The comic book flies out of the trash can into the gutter, the pages begin to turn, and the camera zooms in. The comic pictures come to life.

There are five stories in the movie, which is about two hours long. George wants to do *Creepshow* this fall if we can get financing and total autonomy. The idea is not just to do an anthology, but to zero in on what's horrible, and pare the build to a bare minimum. In the wake of *The Shining*, it would be a chance for me to say, "This is what I think the horror movie is about."

Q: What about *The Dead Zone*?

KING: I wanted to talk about the seventies with *The Dead Zone*. But I didn't want to hit anybody over the head with it. So I thought, "I'll do a Rip Van Winkle thing," and we can see the seventies pass before us like a newsreel. Also, I wanted to explore the problems of this guy who is an outcast through no fault of his own and to talk about coincidence and luck. The central symbol in *The Dead Zone* is a wheel of fortune that goes around and around. To me, it indicates that things occurring in *The Dead Zone* are questions of luck.

Q: You're angry with the government in *The Dead Zone* and in *Firestarter*. Did this anger come out of the sixties?

KING: It's my own political pilgrimage: I've always lived in Maine. I come from Anglo-Saxon stock. We're all Republicans. Dinosaurs walked the earth, my people were Republicans. One of the reasons I wanted to write a novel about Patty Hearst and the Symbionese Liberation Army was because I understood this upheaval they'd gone through. One of those little girls who was killed in the L.A. shoot-out worked for Goldwater in 1964. I worked for Goldwater in '64. I voted for Nixon in '68. I was convinced that people who burned their draft cards were yellow-bellies. My idea was, "Let's bomb 'em into the Stone Age." I went to college from 1966 to 1970, and it was an accretion of the facts—teaching, seminars, and little by little I came around. It's like someone who converts. . . .

Q: You became a zealot.

KING: That's right. And the marches and everything else followed.

Q: Have you ever written anything that was too radical or weird to publish?

KING: Well, I have a couple of stories that were kicked back by various markets as too horrible. One is about a surgeon shipwrecked on a desert island who ends up eating himself a piece at a time. Autocannibalism. I wondered if that was possible, so I asked a surgeon, and he said (*phony Oxford voice*), "Oh yes, it would work, for a while."

He begins with his foot. He's boiling his foot, singing, "McDonald's is your kind of place. It's such a happy place" (*laughs*). He says, "I was very careful, and I washed it before I ate it."

Q: Weren't you doing a novel on burial customs?

KING: It's done, but it's put away. I have no plans to publish it in the near future. It's too horrible. It's worse than *The Shining* or any of the other things. It's terrifying.* I gave it to my wife. She read two-thirds of it, and—she's never done this before—she gave it back and said, "Why don't you go ahead and put it away?" I said, "Didn't you like it?" And she said, "There's no word for how I felt." I think it's effective...too effective.

I got the idea when my daughter's cat died. It got run over, and we buried the cat. There's a story in *Danse Macabre*—it's Bing Crosby's story. When his kids were little, one of them had a pet turtle that died. The kid was just heartbroken. Bing said, "Well, let's have a funeral, and I'll sing a song for the turtle."

The kid didn't seem to be too comforted, but they painted a box black and put in aluminum foil with a little piece of satin over that. They put the turtle in the box in the hole, and Bing sang a song and the kid gave a little talk.

The kid's eyes were just sparkling with excitement, and Bing said, "Before we bury it, would you like to have one last look at your pet turtle?" The kid said yes, so they opened the box and the turtle started to move around.

The kid looked at Bing and said, "Let's kill it."

So anyway, we buried our cat and I started to think about burials. I said to myself, "If anybody else wanted to write about that, people would say, 'Well, he's really morbid.' But I've got a reputation. I'm like a girl of easy virtue: one more won't hurt."

But really, it's too much. The thing about scaring people is, you can really only do it successfully if the reader cares about the people in the story. The people in this book are the best characters I've ever written....Why are we talking about this book I'm not gonna publish?

---

*Editor's note: This book has since appeared as *Pet Sematary*.

Q: Okay, so tell me how you go about writing?

KING: The actual physical act is like autohypnosis, a series of mental passes you go through before you start. If you've been doing it long enough, you immediately fall into a trance.

I just write about what I feel I want to write about. I'm like a kid. I get an idea, and it's like a kid's toy that you push and tug around the room. It's fun, it's bright, it's pretty and maybe it'll go clack-clack or whiz-whiz, whatever it happens to do. I like to make believe.

Q: Is it like Boy Scout camp, sitting around and telling a story?

KING: No, it's a lot more sinister than that. I don't know if we talked about this or not, but at one point somebody said, "What do you think Kubrick wants from *The Shining?*" And I said, "I think he wants to hurt people."

Well, maybe I was just saying what *I* want. My idea is that you should be able to suck somebody in and really hurt them.

With Michael Kilgore

Q: It seems that you're inclined toward the horrifying when you write. Have you thought about writing other things at this point? Maybe break out of the mold a little bit?

KING: I have written some other stuff. I think if you have an idea and it's an idea for, let's say, a straight novel—a romantic novel or a comedy or something like that—and it's a really good idea and you really want to do it, it would be a terrible mistake to turn away and do something else. It's a mistake to think, "If I write this the fans won't like it; therefore, I'll write a horror novel that I don't really care about," because generally what will happen is that your fans will sense there's something missing, something's not there.

Q: It was hard to know whether the lodge in *The Shining* was haunted or whether the man was insane. You didn't really know until the first physical evidence. I think they found some streamers in the elevator—that was the first time you could be sure that something else was going on.

KING: But consider this: is it possible for a hallucination to pass from one person to another? If so, maybe those streamers weren't there at all.

Q: Both *The Shining* and *'Salem's Lot* were very effective because there was ambiguity about the supernatural, up to a certain point.

KING: Well, I was convinced in my own mind that it was vampires from the word go in 'Salem's Lot. My editor suggested that we rewrite the book a little bit in the beginning to try and keep the reader in the dark for a certain period of time. And I said, "Come on, anybody who reads this sort of thing is going to know it's vampires from the first sign." And he kind of slammed me one—on the back—and he said, "You're not writing for a Weird Tales audience. Don't get the idea that you're writing for an audience of 40,000 people. We want to break you out so that you'll appeal to an audience of millions of people, and they don't read Weird Tales, so come on and do it my way." And I did. And he was right.

Q: So you did disguise the supernatural somewhat in the rewriting?

KING: My idea was to make it vampires from the beginning. In fact, I wanted to have a section in the book called "extracta" the way there's a section in the beginning of Moby Dick called "extracta." Except the "extracta" at the beginning of Melville's book was all about whales, and I wanted to have a lot of background stuff about vampires, stuff from the Bible, stuff from books and movies.

Q: 'Salem's Lot is written in such an intelligent style that the reader is caught unaware when the real horror starts.

KING: There is a feeling that anybody who is working intelligently is not going to go in that direction!

Q: What sorts of things scare you in everyday life?

KING: I think one of the reasons my books are successful is that when it comes to fear I'm sort of an Everyman. I have very ordinary fears. I suspect that just the constant using of my imagination in the course of writing has sharpened them, or sharpened the perceptions of them. I think that mankind has what I would call a pool of fears, and that we all can come and see our own faces or wet our hands in it.

Q: It has been said that vampires are terrifying for two separate reasons: a vampire represents the walking dead returning to life, and a vampire is often a loved one coming back for you. Much of the fear comes from a confrontation with a loved one. In 'Salem's Lot, Mrs. Glick...

KING: Yeah, comes back...I loved writing that. You asked the question, "Do you ever scare yourself?" I do from time to time, and I talk in a kind of careful way with some other writers about this: what do they feel when they're writing something that's really gruesome, something that's really scary? I usually get the same answer, and it applies to my own work. I get a kind of sneaking smile on my face, like heh, heh, heh, I got 'em. There's something very cheerful about knowing that you got 'em.

Q: In *The Shining*, there's a scene where Wendy Torrance is fighting and battling the hotel's evil spirit, and finally she wins and she rests for a second and starts to crawl up the stairs, and then she hears a noise behind her...

KING: It's him! What I liked in that was the idea that he'd always be coming. Visualizing it in my own mind, I thought he would always be coming and that nothing would stop him.

Q: *Sneak Previews* had a program on horror films that talked about changing trends, and how the rules are gone. In *Halloween* the babysitter actually kills this guy five times, and he keeps coming back to life.

KING: Yes. Well, I find myself almost writing against that particular trend in spite of myself, though in a kind of intuitive way I understand that and respond to it. I responded to it in *Halloween*. There's the real feeling as you're sitting in the movie theater that you don't know what's going to happen because this guy, John Carpenter, isn't going to stop. He's going to keep coming at you and coming at you. The first couple of times that it happens you tell yourself, "Well, this is kind of a rip-off of a movie called *Wait Until Dark*, where she does it once and the guy keeps coming back." And that's very distressing.

Q: Do you remember movies from your childhood?

KING: I remember the *Creature from the Black Lagoon*, and I remember one called *Invaders from Mars*, which was sort of an *Invasion of the Body Snatchers* rip-off, where this little boy had seen the saucers and he knew about them. Then all these people started to turn up with little red eyes on various parts of their bodies, and he knew the Martians were taking them over. You'd see people falling down into the ground and coming back with these red marks on their bodies. Finally, he gets away and tells his mother the whole story, and she says it's just a dream. Then she goes to wash the dishes and her hair moves aside, and he sees these red marks on her neck. It's really C-R-E-E-P-Y.

I saw all those teenage horror movies. A lot of times I had to tell my mother I was going to see something like *Bambi* or *Davy Crockett*.

Q: She probably thought it was going to warp your mind.

KING: It did.

Q: You have very strong child characters.

KING: Yeah, I like kids.

Q: The kid in *'Salem's Lot* is stronger than the adults.

KING: Well, the kid in *'Salem's Lot* is kind of a dream kid. He is the boy that any boy would like to be, the kind of boy any boy fantasizes himself to be: he can get out of knots. He's very brave. He's intent on revenging his parents, death, this and that. So for me, he was just sort of a dream figure. He pleased me very much, that boy; I like the way he turned out. He's a bigger-than-life archetypal eleven-year-old boy. And a lot of the kid characters in the books are strong and good. But I think kids are strong. They are good, generally speaking. Unless they've been warped in some way, I've never met a kid I thought was genuinely mean—although I'm not saying there aren't any. I just haven't met one.

Q: No Bad Seeds.

KING: No, I never met a Bad Seed.

Q: In 'Salem's Lot the teacher had a heart attack, and the kid went to sleep in ten minutes. It seemed like you were saying something about the qualities of childhood.

KING: One of the things I've always played around with in the books, in my mind, is that you're dealing with the unbelievable in a lot of these cases, like with vampires coming back. I've been trying all through my career not to shy away from the idea that I'm dealing with the unbeliev- able, but instead to play into it and observe people's reactions.

It's a little bit like, if you looked at your typewriter right now and there was a flower growing out of it. Well, if you saw it and you could feel it and smell it, and other people saw it too, then you'd have to agree it was really a flower. But your reaction would interest me a lot more than the flower itself. It would just be something that had happened. I don't know how else to put it. I think kids deal with that sort of thing better than adults. I think a kid'd come around and say, "There's a flower growing out of your typewriter."

Q: Most of the characters are pretty ordinary people who have managed to persevere.

KING: The overall thing, too, is the concept of reality. We understand what we understand by comparison and contrast. If we say Mark Petrie goes to sleep ten minutes after repulsing a vampire, while the teacher, Matt Burke, has a heart attack, then we're saying something about the ability to assimilate reality. It suggests something about the tunnel of per- ception that we see things in. If kids have wider tunnels of perception, well, then, why is that, and what happens to narrow it as we grow up, to make the strange and unusual so hard to take?

What is it about kids that they can look at the most outrageous thing and just see it and, unless there's a reaction they can play off, just deal with it? If a kid sees a guy that's dead in the street, who's been hit by a car, if he's by himself he'll just look at the dead guy and then maybe run off to find somebody—after he's had a good look to see what it was like. But if a lot of people are standing around crying, then the kid will cry too, because he's got a mirror reaction. Kids by themselves sort of interest me that way; they seem to me to be the place where you should start to explore wherever people come from.

Q: Was there a time when you started writing and said, "I'm not going to write this just so I can scare somebody. I'm going to make 'em think a little bit, too?"

KING: Yes, but I think that if you're doing your job right, it follows almost automatically. You have to begin with the idea in your own mind that you're going to play fair, if you're going to give them the story, then you're going to explore all the ramifications of what you're talking about. That's why in a lot of cases I begin writing novels, stories if you will, and discovered maybe halfway through, or three-quarters of the way through, that I had something to say, that I could use the novel as a vehicle for something.

It's a little bit like saying, "This is a great car, and we can go places in it and have a great time, but we can also put watermelons in the back." Except in this case "watermelons" would be theme and symbol and psychological insight, if you want, or insight into character. Those are not things I feel comfortable talking about. If people take them from my books, that's all very well and good. For instance, in *The Shining*, I think I discovered about halfway through that I wasn't writing a haunted-house story, that I was writing about a family coming apart. It was like a revelation.

One of the things that nobody has ever mentioned to me—and it isn't something I generally bring up—is about Jack Torrance. People ask, "Is it a ghost story or is it just in this guy's mind?" Of course it is a ghost story, because Jack Torrance himself is a haunted house. He's haunted by his father. It pops up again and again and again. He's haunted by that. It's just a case of however you want to define "haunted," OK? Because one way or another, there's haunting going on in that book. It's just a question of what label you want to put on it, whether you want to call it psychological or something else.

Q: You often deal with religious beliefs, most noticeably in *The Stand*. The evil in that book was truly bad. It was about as far as you can go without having the devil himself come down.

KING: I didn't really want the devil! This guy's minor league compared to what I assume the devil to be in a Christian theology, assuming that he really existed. But I wanted to play very consciously off that Revelations idea, where you have a kind of testing, almost like an Old Testament deal.

How it really came about was by saying, "Well, let's do this. We'll do the superflu, but we'll do stuff afterward, too. We'll play out this vision of good and evil, this large-scale concept of good and evil."

A lot of people tell me they like that book, which pleases me very much. It's not on any critic's list of favorites, but in a way it seems to sum up everything I had to say up to that point. The books that have come after *The Stand* have been different. *The Dead Zone* and *Firestarter* are both different books than what went before because with *The Stand* I was saying, "Now let's sum it all up and do it once and get it right—or at least get everything in there, even if we don't get it completely right—then go on and do something else."

Q: The biological-warfare aspect in *The Stand* is very believable.

KING: Originally, I had been trying to write a serious book about the Patty Hearst kidnapping or brainwashing in reverse or whatever you want to call it. I wanted to take this plague and translate into literal terms, kind of a plague of violence. So it would almost seem like a rising tide of darkness that could even take over a nice little rich girl without too many brains.

Q: Are you still considering going back to the Patty Hearst theme?

KING: No, at the time that I was trying to do that she had not been apprehended... so it was the perfect novelist's situation where you could take a roman à clef and make up your own ending. But in some ways, what's happened to her since she was released has been more interesting. I am interested in the idea that she could get so far back. Thomas Wolfe said you can't go home again, but in many ways Patty has done just that.

Q: When you wrote *The Stand*, was there any significance to setting the dark man's base in Las Vegas?

KING: That's pretty simplistic, you know. I expected to get really killed on that in the reviews. It's been identified in the American mind, hyped in the American mind, as Sin City. So I thought, I'll put it here. It's overblown, but what the fuck, everything in the book is overblown, so I might as well. I was in Las Vegas when I originally got the idea to set that part of the book there, and I went back several times to make sure I had it right. Vegas is a very... using Vegas at the end of the book reinforces the idea that evil is banal and ultimately anticreative. Evil has no power of its own, you know, except for the power people give it.

Vegas is an extremely banal place. It's a place where you go and you see a show at the MGM Grand—they have so many bare tits on the stage at one time that your circuits overload. There's no sexual rise because, my God, you just wonder how they keep 'em all up; it's like antigravity. You just watch all this, and these guys who are sixty and seventy sit around and don't look like they're having a good time. They're just sitting there with their watery drinks watching these gigantic, huge production numbers, and then some guy comes on with dogs, a dog act, and they wet their pants applauding. They're in their red pants with the white belts and the white shoes and the checked jackets. And you say to yourself, "If this is Sin City..."

The image that I had of Flagg was of a gigantic evil who will begin to deflate by the end of the book, which is not such an exciting concept. I just hoped that the good characters would carry readers over that. Really, I think that if in the end I could have made him into a sort of cringing salesman, a guy who's going bald and wearing red pants and white shoes, I would have done it. But I didn't quite have the balls to do it.

Q: You did manage to deflate him and yet leave some questions, because Flagg left clothes behind when he disappeared. The good characters in the book are still going to be on guard against him—they say.

KING: He turned up on Hawaii after that. That was one of the parts that was snipped from the book. He just simply came to, naked. There were a few survivors nearby, and he simply stands up and says, "My name is Flagg, and I can't remember where I came from, but I'm happy to be here, and you'll be happy to have me here." And they're all groveling on the sand on this bone-white beach on Waikiki and worshipping him, and he's preparing to start all over again. I think it was snipped because a lot of the people at Doubleday thought that was a rather pessimistic ending, after all those pages.

Q: I think that's implied even as the book ends now.

KING: Well, Flagg is always there, in the human capacity to do evil.

Q: How about modern writers?

KING: Great writers? Well, I think Updike had a chance, but I don't think he's doing very good work anymore. Probably Isaac Singer—oh God, who else?—Thomas Williams, who won the National Book Award, is a really great artist. He's got it all together. I'm going to let myself off the hook here. I just think God hits some people with the talent stick harder than He hits others. And it kills a lot of people. It's like dynamite: they blow up. Like Dylan Thomas or Thomas Wolfe. I guess I'd put Bernard Malamud in that great-artist category; there are some around, I think.

Q: Why do you think that your books are so popular as film vehicles?

KING: The books are visual, I see them almost as movies in my head. When I sign a copy of *Night Shift*, if I'm not pressed for time, what I usually sign is, "I hope you've enjoyed these one-reel horror movies,"— which is essentially what they are. I think that's why so many are being turned into movies. I think it's very tough for a Hollywood person to see a movie in a book that's not very visual—say, a novel of ideas like *Siddhartha* or *Steppenwolf*. I'm not saying that those aren't made into movies sometimes, but it's tougher to see the potential. Movie people have a tendency to just dismiss them as talking heads. Most movie people are pinheads; they don't have any brains at all. What they have, mostly, is a great big eye that has a tendency to see pictures without any sense of motivation or anything else.

Larry McMurtry wrote a piece for *Film Comment*—it was pretty perceptive—about movie people and motivation, just the idea of motivation, which is story. One thing starts and it's like a row of dominoes; it leads to something else and something else and something else. A story is believable because you see each link in the chain as far as motivation goes.

Movie people don't think that way. They say to themselves, "Well, I want to have a race. I want to have a car chase under the El in Manhattan," so William Friedkin goes ahead and does that in *The French Connection* with Gene Hackman. When the thing is over, Hackman walks away. We never see him hauled up on charges; we never see him dropped out of the New York police department for what he's done, which would certainly happen. We get an insight into the motivation of Popeye's character, which is mostly suicidal, but Friedkin never follows up on it. There are intriguing, tantalizing hints all through that movie: Popeye likes women who wear big, tall boots, and stuff like that. He seems like a sadistic, suicidal kind of character, but Friedkin's not really interested in that; he just lets Hackman do certain things.

Q: It's just a series of images.

KING: Yeah, like *Grand Theft Auto* with Ron Howard. All these cars are being wrecked. People like to go to movie theaters and see car wrecks. I like that myself. I go and sit in the second row and watch all those car wrecks and I'm like anybody else. "Oh jeez, look at that." But that's it and there should be something more. This is why movie people need good writers: because you can have all those things and you can have motivation, too. Those two things are not exclusive. But a lot of movie people don't see that. They just say, "Who needs a writer? They just junk things up."

Q: Don't horror writers and movie directors and their audiences all strive to create or experience vicariously the ultimate horror?

KING: No, I don't. I just want to scare people. I'm very humble about that. I don't set my sights anywhere near so high. H. P. Lovecraft tried for the ultimate horror, and at times he's almost ludicrous, because in some of those stories he's like a little kid jumping for a bunch of grapes that he just can't have.

Q: How has your success changed your life?

KING: I think that now I've got more peace of mind than I've ever had before. In some ways, I think my life has changed a little bit. It seems as though I went through a period where I had peace of mind because I was doing what I wanted, and I was making money at it and I wasn't bothered much. But in the last year and a half, some sort of peculiar thing has been going on where there are more and more calls, more and more demands on my time—publicity and that sort of thing. There's a growing pressure to go out and do things—to go on talk shows and that sort of thing.

Part of it is that I *can* at least go on a talk show and talk. A lot of writers can't. Writers tend to be an inarticulate bunch, taken as a whole. And of course, talk shows, TV, and radio don't really want writers to discuss anything. They want you to entertain. You've got to get out there and tap dance your balls off. And a lot of writers can't, or if they can, they won't, because they feel it intrudes on their dignity. I guess I felt I didn't have much dignity anyway, so what the hell. So I've done that, and it seemed to work pretty well, but that means that they want you to come back and do it again. I'm not so cool on that.

Q: Is that an occupational hazard of the successful writer?

KING: The occupational hazard of the successful writer in America is that once you begin to be successful, then you have to avoid being gobbled up. America has developed this sort of cannibalistic cult of celebrity, where first you set the guy up, and then you eat him. It happened to John Lennon; it has happened to a lot of rock stars. But I wish to avoid being eaten. I don't want to be anybody's lunch. In other words, I'd love to be on the cover of *Newsweek*; but I don't want to be on the cover of *Newsweek* because I died.

Q: When you wrote the books, the critics lined up with their tomahawks and ran you through, and then when the movie came out you had to do it again.

KING: It's worse when the movies come out. Movie critics labor under an inferiority complex. They understand that they're dealing with a medium that any illiterate with $4 can experience, even an Ingmar Bergman film—pay $4 and go in and take something back out of that movie, even if it's only a series of very powerful images that disturb him. I think most film critics realize that when they go to see Woody Allen's *Manhattan* and write four or five pages, as say, Pauline Kael did, that basically what they're doing is taking a movie that's made, at the basic level, for illiterates, and criticizing this as if it were the work of Immanuel Kant. In that sense, the novel of *The Shining* is certainly better than the film.

I can't think of half a dozen movies that would compare with the books that spawned them, so far as literacy goes. Movie critics will try to get past the onus of that by stating that "the movie is based on a super-market, best-selling, gothic, piece-of-schlock trash, pulp crap by writer Stephen King!" All I'm trying to say is that I think film critics tend to be the nouveau riche establishment of American letters... and, like nouveaux riches people everywhere, they know that secretly they are being laughed at, or they are inferior....

Q: How did you, the author, feel about your protagonist's attempt to commit murder at the end of *The Dead Zone*?

KING: I was very ambivalent about him. A lot of me wanted him to kill that son of a bitch. And another part of me said, "You don't want to do this because if he kills Greg Stillson in the book, and ten years from now somebody knocks off President Anderson or President Carter, and they ask him, "Why did you do it?" the guy says, "I got the idea from Stephen King's novel, *The Dead Zone*," I would have to quietly pack my bags and move to Costa Rica. So I was ambivalent. A lot of me wanted to kill him and felt the ending was something of a cop-out.

Q: You once mentioned that everyone has a fear of emptiness, of being alone.

KING: Yes, alienation, all these things we think of as being evil. Concepts of evil change from time to time and from place to place. For instance, the idea that abortion could be a good thing would have been unheard of some years ago. It seems to me that while the concrete examples change, that underlying concept remains, that evil is when you buy the Brooklyn Bridge.

Or heroin, for instance. Heroin may feel really good, but basically you sense the evil and the repetitiousness of the process of taking it. It's always the same, you know: the spoon, the needle, the fire, drawing it into the needle, socking it into your arm. And then repeat, again and again and again, there's no creativity in the act. There's simply habit; it's like punching a time clock.

Q: What is Halloween like at your house?

KING: Halloween is really nice. That's the best day of the year. Well no, second best. Fourth of July is my favorite holiday because I always get drunk and shoot off fireworks. But I like Halloween because I can dress up and wear something that's really gross, and when the trick-or-treaters come to the door, I whip it open and go "woo-argh."

Q: Do they know in your neighborhood who you are and what you do?

KING: I'm perceived as The Writer before I'm The Horror Writer, I think. And I think in the back of everybody's mind is the question: "How can he write this stuff? He must be morbid or something." Of course, I am. (*Laughs*)

It's that kind of reaction. People are nice, people are polite. I have some real friends and then other people... you can see the question in their eyes: "Is he all right?"

Q: So the kids really come around, and you dress up and try to scare them?

KING: Well, I don't really want to scare any little kids. I love little children. I wouldn't want to make one cry or anything like that. It's like if you put a voice box on the lawn and when they're walking away you say, "Have a good time." That's really funny, because they really jump. I wouldn't want to leap out of the shadows at them, I wouldn't want to do that. But I don't mind goosing them a little.

With Mat Schaffer

Q: Why is Stephen King so popular?

KING: I don't know. I've often wondered that myself. I guess it's because I write scary stuff and these are scary times. But a lot of stuff that I write is more fantasy and less threatening, say, than the idea of a Korean airliner being shot down by a Russian missile, which seems fantastic. Unfortunately, it happened. Whereas the werewolves and vampires, so far as we know, are not there until it gets very dark and you're all alone. Then you start to believe some of that stuff. But I think that's because it's a safe scare.

Q: Someone once described a Shirley Jackson short story as walking into the kitchen and finding horror under the kitchen table.

KING: I think that's great and very accurate. I would like to write a short story or I'd like to give a feeling of somebody walking into a bright sun-washed kitchen and finding a severed head on the counter. The closest I ever got to that in any of my work—it's still one of my favorite scenes—was in *Firestarter*. There's a scene where the husband begins to feel that something terrible has happened at home and when he goes home he finds that everything is fine. When he goes downstairs to the laundry room everything is the way it's supposed to be except that there's...one bloody fingerprint on the glass porthole in the dryer. And to me that one fingerprint in the middle of all that normality sums up everything.

A writer named Dennis Etchison wrote a story I always envied. It was called *The Late Shift* and it was about those convenience stores that stay open twenty-four hours, and it was about the eleven-to-seven shift. These are the people who work the wee hours. His idea was that they are all dead people who have been reanimated. They're walking corpses. They only know about seven words: please, thank you, I can't make change of over $20. And if you've ever been in one of those stores at two in the morning, that's just the way they are.

Q: There's something about the ordinary that you are able to get horror or terror out of, like a 1958 Plymouth Fury.

KING: *Christine*. I think anybody who's ever owned an old car like that knows that there's plenty of horrors involved with it. Actually I picked *Christine* because it was such an ordinary, forgettable car. It was by no means a classic car from the fifties. It was actually pretty humdrum for a period that had those '57 T-birds that everybody remembers and the gull-wing Chevies and that sort of thing. But the upshot was that when they started to make the movie, they could only find about twenty-six of those cars, the '58 Plymouth Furies.

I got a lot of letters from a lot of people about the back jacket on the hardcover. It shows me sitting on a 1958 Plymouth Fury. We thought. Except that it turns out it was a 1957 Plymouth Savoy. If you think people don't know their cars you should have seen the letters I got.

Q: But there is that sense of things that are normal that you are able to bring terror to.

KING: One of the first things they say in writing class is write about what you know. If I actually did that, nobody would read anything I wrote, because what I know is very, very ordinary. I'm a very ordinary man. I can't write about marital infidelity because I don't play around. And I can't write about going crazy because so far I haven't. You understand what I'm saying. I can write about kitchens. I can write about going down to McDonald's. I can't write about ordering fancy French wine at Ma Maison because I don't know any French wines. I can talk about going down to the 7-Eleven and picking up a six-pack of Bud or something like that. I can't write about famous celebrities in Hollywood because I live in Maine.

I think when I go to California someone should ask to see my passport when I get off the plane, because it's just so weird. The only thing I can do, really, is write about those ordinary things and inject them with the fantasy element—which in my case, a lot of time, turns out to be morbid.

Q: Are there any areas that are verboten?

KING: Yeah, there are things that you can't do for various reasons. Some because they might turn out to be unintentionally comic but most because they are simply verboten. It's still impossible in our society to write a story about the thing that came out of the toilet. You can't write about a monster that has anything to do with the excretory functions or anything like that. You can't create a snot monster. That sort of thing is considered not nice, although I'd love to do that. In fact, in *The Stand* at least, there are a lot of people who are dying in this terrible mess. Well, anybody who's ever had the flu or even a heavy cold knows that, but I got rated by the critics for that, in spite of the fact that we all know what goes on when your nose starts to run and your sinuses clog up. I'd love to be able to do some of those things. I think that there are other things that you *can't* do and rightly, and most of them have to do with a sort of sadistic violence.

Q: *The Stand* marked a departure for you at that point, in terms of theme and also style. In *The Stand* you introduced what was for you a new way of writing, in which you made use of a number of characters and multiple story lines. That was something you explored for the next two or three books.

KING: Yeah. That started with a single character in the first draft, a girl named Franny Goldsmith. I thought, "This is going to be a very long book, and it's going to take place in a lot of parts of the country." What if you built this book like a pyramid and you started off with the one character, the girl, and in the next chapter you had Franny plus this other guy, Stu Redman, and in the next chapter you had Franny, Stu, plus Larry Underwood, who's this rock singer and so on and so forth." Finally they do all get together, and I realized that I had something that was becoming very, very cumbersome, and I ended up doing something that was like a diamond instead of a pyramid. That is, it got fat to a certain point and then it began to shrink to a point again, which was the climax. You're right, it was a departure and I did explore that again in other books, but I think I found out about the possibility of using this wide perspective when I wrote my second novel, 'Salem's Lot.

Q: In doing that it seemed you also reached a point where you could interject yourself as the omnipotent author at times, through narrative asides. It's something that you've continued with your recent book, *Pet Sematary.* For example, you'll interrupt a sentence and say something like, "Come on, folks" and then go back and finish the sentence.

KING: I don't want to stay too close to the story. Being a writer is sort of a godlike function in a way, and that's kind of fun. You get to play God. If you're writing a book you point your finger at somebody, just like God, and say, "You, turkey, you're coming with me," and the character drops dead.

I got a lot of letters about the novel *Cujo.* In the novel, but not in the film, the kid died and I got a lot of letters from people who said, "How could you let that happen?" It was like when things like that happen in real life. My response was that sometimes children do die, by crib death, or they get hit by cars. God help us, they even get killed by dogs. I mean the real impetus to write *Cujo* came from reading a story in the paper in Portland, Maine, where this little kid was savaged by a Saint Bernard and killed. Because little kids are in their sight line, and when you're in a dog's sight line, they're more dangerous to you. So these people would write me letters, as though they can't get through to God when those things happen. You can't write a letter to God care of Viking Press. So they write and say, "How can you let that kid die?" And the only thing I could write back is, "I'm not God. I just wrote the damn book. He died. I didn't want him to die."

Q: That gets into the whole question of how you plot your books. Do you storyboard them? Does it reach a point where the characters really do take over, so that if the boy in *Cujo* is going to die it's not your fault? He's just going to die?

KING: He died. The way that books happen for me is, first a situation will occur, then an opening scene will occur, and then I can think of where this thing might be going or how it might end, even if that's not the way it finally ends up, as in the case of *Cujo*. If I can have those things, if I can have a situation, if I can have an opening scene, if I can see a progression to an end, then I can write the book. The characters don't matter. Characters always serve the novel once they're in the story.

Q: Two things that you're close to, that we see in almost all your books, are children and rock and roll music.

KING: I always wanted to be able to explore a little bit of what childhood really was like, because we lie to ourselves about that.

As for rock and roll, I just always rocked. You talk about rock music. My mother brought me for Christmas in 1956 or 1957 an Elvis 78. That was the first record I owned. "Hound Dog" on one side and "Don't Be Cruel" on the other. I played the grooves out of that record. That was like finding something that was very, very powerful, like a drug, like a rush. It made you bigger than you were. It made you tough even if you weren't tough. Then watching *American Bandstand* and seeing some of those people for the first time, I'd go "My God, these people are really ugly. They really look wasted. They really look weird. They look like me!" But the music made them big, too. I just love rock and roll.

I'm a baby boomer. But I know from the mail that I get that I put a lot of stuff in books that brought a shock of recognition to my generation that they hadn't had otherwise. People would say "You mention AC/DC in a book. How did you know about AC/DC?" It's as though they've gotten used to the idea of being below anybody's notice that's literate, of anybody that cares enough to write at all. But it's so ingrained in me that I don't really know what it is.

Q: How many books do you write at the same time? *Pet Sematary* says it was written between 1979 and 1982, and in between you had some other books out.

KING: Well, everything weaves in and out for me. For instance, when it says 1979 to 1982 that doesn't mean constant working time. It was drafted between January and May of 1979. It sat fallow for a long time. You let it sit for a year. You can go back and pick up any manuscript and read it over again and know more about it than you did. It's great medicine for somebody who thinks he's written something bad as well as something good. Because if you think that you've written something that really stinks and you resist that first impulse to just rip it up and get rid of it, you can go back and find out that it's a little bit better. In between I'd finish the first draft and maybe redraft something like *Firestarter*, that had been sitting around.

Q: Do you feel as if you're part of a tradition, and if so, who are other members of that tradition?

KING: I feel that way very much. I mean, I discovered Poe when I was in grammar school, I guess, and from Poe I went on and discovered people like Ambrose Bierce and some of the other classic short-story writers, and H. P. Lovecraft. And then some of the modernist people who actually brought the story out of the foggy moors and the castles and into those 7-Eleven stores and suburbia. People like Richard Matheson and Robert Bloch. And all of those people played a part in teaching me how to write, and they also made it possible for me to make a living. They created the genre.

Q: You're from a tradition of the storyteller. Your books not only read well, but they listen well.

KING: The story is the only thing that's important. Everything else will take care of itself. It's like what bowlers say. You hear writers talk about character or theme or mood or mode or tense or person. But bowlers say, if you make the spares, the strikes will take care of themselves. If you can tell a story, everything else becomes possible. But without story, nothing is possible, because nobody wants to hear about your sensitive characters if there's nothing happening in the story. And the same is true with mood. Story is the only thing that's important.

Q: Are people looking for a good story because it's tough out there?

KING: It's a tough old world. People are looking for something, and I think people have always looked for story because it's like they say, if you don't dream at night, you'll go crazy after a while. You get psychotic. And if you don't dream while you're awake, too. That's why God gave you an imagination. You've got to work it. Put it another way. Salt's supposed to prevent goiter, where your neck swells up and looks like a Goodyear tire. If you don't get salt for that imaginative thing, if you don't feed your imagination, you'll go crazy right away. So we all make dreams, and to me that's great because people pay me for all these fantasies and I love it.

With Stephen Jones

Q: How soon after the publication of *Carrie* did Hollywood become interested in buying the book?

KING: Well, there was interest in *Carrie* right away. It just wasn't strong in terms of money. So they decided to hold it back until publication, gambling that the book would be a hardcover best-seller and the interest in the movie rights would go up again. When they released the book in hardcover, it didn't exactly die, but it didn't do wonders, either. It was published in April of '74, and the movie rights were sold in August of '74. We didn't do wonderfully well, but I got a piece of the action, so the money end of it was all right.

There are so many guys that write books and the movie will come and they get butchered; my favorite example is *The Day of the Dolphin*. There haven't been that many good horror novels in the last fifteen years or so that were turned into good movies. So, I'm pleased with it.

Q: Were you approached at any time to write the screenplay?

KING: Oh no. On *Carrie* they didn't want to know me, and you can understand that. I was given the chance to adapt my own work over in England by Milton Subotsky. He bought six of the stories from *Night Shift* for two movies, and he said, "Would you like to direct? You're welcome to." It was kind of—I think—a carrot, but it was scary to me. The thing is, you write a book, and a book is something you do by yourself—in your office or wherever. When you talk about directing a movie, you're talking about this "team sport" where a lot of money is at stake, particularly in Subotsky's case, where he runs on a shoestring to begin with, and he's very conscious of the dollar and that's how he makes his money. And in a way, I admire him, because there is no self-indulgence there. Granted, he makes a lot of movies that aren't very good, but he also makes movies that make money. The idea to me was frightening! I was afraid I would get into it and I wouldn't have time to do anything else and that I might fail. I don't like the idea of failing.

I did do a screenplay for an NBC TV movie over here based on three of the stories, and how well they are doing with that, I don't know. The screenplay's in: *Daylight Dead*. Twentieth Century–Fox liked it, they bought it. Five years ago I could have said, "It's going to be made and you'll see it in the spring." But now...the atmosphere in American TV when it comes to violence is terrible. You can't show somebody getting punched in the face anymore on American TV—they cut it. So I don't know what'll happen with that screenplay.

Q: Were you surprised that they picked a director of Kubrick's reputation to make *The Shining?*

KING: They didn't pick him, *he* picked the book. Somebody else had it! An outfit called The Production Company, which was bankrolled by Johnson's Band-Aid money. A lady named Mary Lou Johnson, the Band-Aid heiress, formed a group of people, and they bought it and they were going to do it—probably it would have ended up being a Producers' Circle–Lew Grade production, like *The Boys From Brazil* or *Raise the Titanic!* Kubrick read the book and wanted it and he had a three-picture contract with Warner Brothers; *Barry Lyndon* was one of these pictures, and I think maybe A *Clockwork Orange* was the other one, and this would be the third one. So he said he wanted it and Producers' Circle sold it back to Warner Brothers for him. He had nice things to say about the book. Apparently he had read a lot of books and just sort of thrown them away. I heard this from somebody else, from somebody that he's collaborated with in the past: Kubrick came raving in and shaking the book and saying, "This is the one. This is it! Make the deal. Make the deal!"

Q: Returning to your books. . . . How soon after publication have your novels become best-sellers?

KING: *The Shining* was the first hardback best-seller I ever had. It was a best-seller in terms of whatever that means, over here and in England as well. *Carrie* in paperback—nobody knew me from anything, I was nobody—and it did about 1.3 million, and when the movie came out it went right through the roof! It's done, what, 4 million copies in paperback. And *'Salem's Lot* did well. The books apparently appeal to younger people, and they're not socialized to hardcovers—they don't buy hardcovers—they buy paperbacks.

Q: Do you prefer the longer format of the novel in which to develop your ideas?

KING: I'd *love* to write some more short stories. I'm always saying that when winter comes I'm going to put all these novels off and finish up on what I'm working on and just write short stories for four months, and it just never works out that way.

Q: Do you see yourself continuing to write in the horror-fantasy genre, or do you think that you will branch out into mainstream fiction eventually?

KING: I write what comes to me to write. In the time since *Carrie* was published, I've written two mainstream novels and haven't published either one. I put them away because I'm not sure how they'd be taken. I suppose it's more a business decision. I like them. I mean shit, I *wrote* them, so I *must* like them. You know, one of the things that's going to happen is someday I'm going to wake up and just don't want to write about horror anymore or more trips of fantasy, or anything else. Then probably I'll write *The Man in the Grey Flannel Suit*, and I'll go down the tubes and nobody will ever hear of me again!

With Marty Ketchum, Pat Cadigan, and Lewis Shiner

Q: How long did you work on *The Stand?*
KING: I worked on it for about three years. It got to be like Vietnam. I felt like Lyndon Johnson after a while. I was saying to myself, "Well, another hundred pages and I'll see light at the end of the tunnel." So the thing got done and it was 1,400 pages long, and I cut it and cut it and cut it, and then Doubleday got a hold of it, and they said, "You know this is going to be published at an exorbitant price, and it's going to hurt the book." I said, "Jesus Christ, I don't care, if it hurts the book it hurts the book, it's my goddamn book," and we reached some kind of compromise, which is what you do. It's still a pretty long book.
Q: Are good and evil becoming more popularized in your work?
KING: Nobody in this field talks about good. Everybody talks about evil. Evil is a tremendously attractive force—a tremendously potent force. You've got more and more books lately where evil wins, where evil proves to be the stronger. *Rosemary's Baby* is one. And even in *The Exorcist* it's very hard to tell what happens in the end. The priest dies, that much is sure.

I don't see good as a completely Christian force. It's what I think of as white. White. Just tremendously powerful, something that would run you right over if you got in its way.
Q: In *'Salem's Lot*, where the crosses are glowing, they realize the glow is not...
KING: ...a Christian thing. But it's that, too. That's part of it.

People say that Tolkien is never as good with his good guys, like

Gandalf, as he was at things like the spider and Mordor, but Tolkien is pretty goddamn good at producing that other force. I agree that good is not always interesting, but it's there.

Q: Would you say you're trying to present these forces in a realistic way, rather than simply as fantasy?

KING: The side that's opposite the fantasy in this one is... sociology. As I went on with *The Stand* I got more and more interested in the fact that if almost everybody died, think of everything that would be left around. I'm not just talking about canned Dinty Moore Beef Stew. I'm talking about nuclear weapons and things like that. You could have a society in a place like Schenectady and another one in a place like Boston, and they could get into a theological argument and end up literally exchanging nuclear weapons. I mean, those things are not that hard to run. If you had a guy from Ma Bell or a guy from Con Edison or someplace like that and gave him a missile and the board, they could light it up. Might take them a little while, but it wouldn't take them very long. For that matter you could take a nuclear warhead and put it somewhere and pile dynamite around it and it might go off.

Q: Were you connected with the movie *Carrie?*

KING: Well, the Doubleday subsidiary rights department came up with three people who wanted to buy it, and I thought Monash seemed like the best go. They said to me after they bought, "Who would you pick to direct it if you could get anybody?" I said, "There's this guy named Brian De Palma who did a film called *Sisters.* It was a scary monster."

Q: Do you have an urge to direct?

KING: Yeah, but I'm scared. It's so much money, and if you fuck it up, it's fucked up and everybody goes home hungry. When you're by yourself, you're by yourself.

I'm thirty-one now, and I don't know how long I'll be alive. I've got a book that I've wanted to write for two years, and I haven't had time. It's a book about... Jeez. Scary. You know. About this—this *thing* in a kind of a subway system. It's a scary idea, and I just haven't had time to write it.

If you get involved in the film bullshit, it can go on forever. They screw around, and it's destructive.

I'd like to try it. I'd like to know if I was any good at it. But I've never been any good at administrative things. I was the editor of my high school newspaper, and we got out one issue that year. It was a *good* issue!

Q: What was your first reaction to seeing *Carrie* on film?

KING: That's a weird story, because the screening room where I saw *Carrie* for the first time was the screening room I'd been in about five years before when I was in college. United Artists pulled in a bunch of kids from colleges all over the eastern seaboard to see these two turkey movies. They knew they were turkeys, and they thought that if they primed the pump with some money for college writers to come, they'd do good reviews out of gratitude. They just totally underestimated the ability of college writers to bite the hand that feeds them.

So I sat in this theater between two porno shops on Broadway, and I thought, "History is going to repeat itself, this is going to be the third time, this picture is going to be a real dog."

I thought it was really pretty good. I've lost the feeling of that first impression now, because I've seen the film about five times. I never want to see it again. I watched the baseball playoffs when it was on TV.

Q: What about *The Shining?*

KING: *The Shining* was open right until the end. I didn't know what was going to happen until the very end. That shows in the book. The original plan was for them all to die up there and for Danny to become the controlling force of the hotel after he died. And the psychic force of the hotel would go up exponentially.

Q: Did that feel right to you?

KING: No. If it had still felt good to me when I got to the end of the book I would have done it that way. But I got connected with the kid. In the first draft of the book Jack beat his wife to death with the mallet and it was blood and brains and everything. It was really just terrible and I couldn't do it. I couldn't leave it that way.

Q: Did Kubrick have a free hand in *The Shining?*

KING: Completely. He called me up, he asked for my opinion, and I kept telling him, the few times that I talked to him, I said, "Look. This is a movie. You do your movie."

This bullshit about authors having their books changed. If you don'twant to have that done, why'd you sell the goddamn thing in the first place? I love movies.

Jerzy Kosinski doesn't sell movie rights. He doesn't want any movies made out of his books.

Q: Can you imagine *The Painted Bird* as a movie?

KING: He's been offered! But a story changes, and it should. It's right that it should.

I like the movies. But there are things that I won't do. Jon Peters wanted to buy *The Dead Zone*. I couldn't see it, because he makes me nervous. I don't think he's in movies for anything other than as a thing to do. I saw *The Eyes of Laura Mars*, and I didn't care for it, and *A Star Is Born*, and didn't care for that. In other words, you don't sell them just to make money; you try to sell them to somebody who's going to do a good job of it.

Q: So if you didn't like Kubrick, you wouldn't have sold it to him?

KING: I didn't have the choice. I was not in a good position when the film rights were sold.

Q: Did you have any preferences for the casting?

KING: Sure. I wanted a lot of different people that weren't "bankable." They used that word, "bankable." A guy named Michael Moriarty would have been good as Jack Torrance. I also thought Martin Sheen would be very good as Jack Torrance.

Q: Doesn't Warner's also have the rights to *'Salem's Lot?*

KING: Yes. They came to me on this one finally, and I said, "I'm not going to try it. Get Richard Matheson to do it. He says that he knows how it could be done, and he'd like to do it." But they wouldn't do it. It's almost willful. They don't want to go to the person who could do it; they want to go to a Sterling Silliphant.

I said last night that Matheson's the best screenwriter in Hollywood, and somebody said, "What about Paul Schrader?" And I agreed, Paul Schrader's pretty good, though he's weak on motivation. Matheson's great, and he's never done a major motion picture, never. He could do movies, but they won't give him a shot.

Q: How much is planned in advance?

KING: I have an idea what's going to happen. I know there will probably end up being some variance. The same thing happened in *'Salem's Lot*. The book was a homage to *Dracula*, and in *Dracula* what happens is that everybody lives except Quincy, who gives up his life toward the end. Everybody was going to die, except for the writer, who would be driven out of town by all these vampires. And—I fell in love with the little boy that I was writing about, and I couldn't let him go, and he ended up going along.

People say to me since then that what I wrote there was a classical sub rosa homosexual relationship. I say bullshit, it's father-son.

Q: Do you pattern your characters after people you know?

KING: Bits and pieces of various people that I know. There really was a Weasel Craig, he's a real guy. He used to cruise the bars and come back in—he was about sixty-five, a total lush, going to hell except for his white hair, which he kept combed back like Elvis Presley, and this motorcycle jacket, with all the zippers—and he'd come back with these big-bosomed chicks, I mean, gigantic, and you'd hear the bedsprings in the night, crash...crash...crash...it was really funny.

Q: Do you have a particular technique for creating fear?

KING: Not really. I just try to create sympathy for my characters, then turn the monsters loose.

With Waldenbooks

KING: I've been asked if *Different Seasons*, my book of four short novels, means that I've reached the end of my interest in such uplifting and mentally edifying subjects as ghouls, ghosts, vampires, and unspeakable things lurking in the closets of little kids. After all, these questioners point out, three of the four novellas deal with nonhorror themes—prison escape, little boys whose curiosity is perhaps too big for their own good, more little boys on an unlikely—but all too possible—quest. My response is to point out that the *fourth* story in *Different Seasons* (which my youngest son, Owen, persists in calling *Different Sneezes*) is pretty gruesome. It concerns a doctor, a rather peculiar men's club, and an unwed mother who is extremely determined to give birth to her baby.

No, I've always been one of the Halloween people, and I guess I always will be. I've got a vampire bat and a rattlesnake on my desk—both mercifully stuffed—you get the idea. Yet I don't think anyone can write just one sort of fiction *all* the time. Herman Wouk, author of such grim and sweeping epics as *The Winds of War* and *The Caine Mutiny*, has also written a hilarious novel of childhood, *The City Boy*. Gregory Mcdonald, known for those two unlikely detectives Fletch and Flynn, has written an amusing novel about a lonely-hearts columnist on a city newspaper (*Love Among the Mashed Potatoes*). Travis McGee fans might be surprised to learn that John D. MacDonald has written a good deal of science fiction, including two damn fine science fiction novels (*Wine of the Dreamers, Ballroom of the Skies*). And Evan Hunter (aka Ed McBain), who is often associated with the gritty world of urban crime courtesy of the 87th Precinct, has written at least one western (*The Chisolms*) and a science fiction novel (*Find the Feathered Serpent*).

Writers of grue sometimes also go straight. Richard Matheson, who has created vampires aplenty in *I Am Legend* (filmed as *The Omega Man*, with Charlton Heston) and is the author of innumerable classic short stories (*Duel*, for instance, which became the classic Steven Spielberg film of the same name) in the horror field, has published a war novel (*The Beardless Warriors*). Roald Dahl, first known for the grimly ironic stories in *Kiss Kiss* and *Someone Like You*, is now as well-known for his whimsical stories for children.

The point is, when you live in your imagination a lot of the time, it may take you anywhere—anywhere at all. The four stories in *Different Seasons* were written for love, not money, usually in between other writing projects. They have a pleasant, open-air feel, I think—even at the grimmest moments (I haven't been able to get away from horror entirely, even here—there's a scene in one of the stories where a fellow tosses a cat into the oven and bakes it—*you're warned*) there's something about them, I hope, that says the writer was having a good time, hanging loose, worrying not about the storyteller but only the tale.

I had some fun with 'em, and that's usually a pretty good sign that the reader will have some fun too. I hope so, anyway. That's enough for now, I guess, so let me close with just a cordial word of warning: remember that when you turn out the light this evening and climb into your bed, *anything* could be under it—anything at all.

CHAPTER FOUR

━━┼━━

HOLLYWOOD HORRORS

━━┼━━

Brian De Palma did a nice job with *Carrie*. When you think of all the terrible movies made of recent books, I have this basic feeling that mine wasn't screwed up too badly. The character of Carrie was based on a kid I went to school with and on some of the high school students I taught, the ones that were always picked on and eventually walked out because they couldn't take it anymore.

With Bhob Stewart

Q: What is the origin of the phrase "the shining" as a description of psychic power?
KING: The origin of that was a song by John Lennon and the Plastic Ono Band called "Instant Karma." The refrain went "We all shine on." I really liked that, and I used it. The name of *The Shining* originally was *The Shine*, but somebody said, "You can't use that because it's a pejorative word for Black." Since nobody likes to have a joke played on themselves, I said, "Okay, let's change it. What'll we change it to?" They said, "How about *The Shining?*" I said, "It sounds kind of awkward." But they said, "It gets the point across, and we won't have to make any major changes in the book." So we did, and it became *The Shining* instead of *The Shine*.
Q: Who is the writer who worked on *The Shining* screenplay with Kubrick?
KING: Diane Johnson. She did a novel called *The Shadow Knows*. She just published another one this year. She's a good writer. She writes reviews for *The New York Times Book Review* sometimes; she had one not too long ago on a book of letters by or about William Butler Yeats. Quite a smart lady.

Q: What is the title of your haunted radio station screenplay?

KING: It doesn't have a title. I think the perfect title would be something that had four letters, but I can't think of a good word—like W something—that would be creepy. Jesus, it's a wonderful idea!

Q: Oh, you mean a title made out of the call letters of the radio station—like Robert Stone's *WUSA?*

KING: Yeah. Like that! Like that! Only I'd like to be able to do something—

Q: Ah, like *WEIR.*

KING: Yeah, *WEIR.* That would be real good. Yeah. It's based on this automated radio station. They go completely automatic. They have these big long drums of tape that do everything. They punch in the time. They make donuts for the announcer who comes in to give the weather. But mostly, it's just this: "Aren't you glad you tuned in WEIR?... Hi! This is WEIR, you fucking son of a bitch. You're going to *die* tonight." Irony like that in a syrupy voice.

Q: Is someone interested in this right now?

KING: I've got to finish it. I'm not trying to do anything with it except finish it. I take it out every once in a while and tinker with it, but I don't really seem to have the kicker yet. There's no real urge to push it through; there's no excitement there just yet. I've got the idea; I just can't seem to hook it up.

Q: In *Night Shift* the E. C. influence is most apparent, yet you were very young when E. C. Comics were on the newsstands during the early fifties, right?

KING: I used to get some comics; I don't think they were E. C.'s, but I used to buy them with the covers torn off. There was always somebody being chopped off and spitted on barbecue grills and buried alive. My guess is the comics predated 1955. I would have bought them, say, in the period 1958 to 1960. But they might have been sitting in some guy's warehouse.

Q: When did you first become conscious of E. C.?

KING: I think we must have swapped the magazines around when I was younger. I can't really say when I became conscious of it. People would talk about them, and if you saw some of these things, you'd pick them up—even if it cost a buck. At that time you might have been able to get three for a buck; now they cost a lot more than that. When E. C. started to produce supernatural tales, they did it after the worst holocaust that people had ever known—World War II and the death of 6 million Jews and the bombings of Hiroshima and Nagasaki. All at once, Lovecraft, baroque horrors, and the M. R. James ghost that you'd hear about secondhand from some guy in his club began to seem a little bit too tame. People began to talk about more physical horrors—the undead, the thing that comes out of the grave.

Q: When you were a kid, did you read *Castle of Frankenstein?*

KING: Yes, yes. I had about seven or eight issues in sequence, and I don't know what's become of them. For every fan that's an old sad song, but I had them all. It was by far the best of any of the monster magazines. I think, probably like most of us, I came to *Famous Monsters of Filmland* first. I just discovered that poking off a drugstore rack one day, and then I was a freak for it, every issue. I couldn't wait for it to come out. And then when *Castle of Frankenstein* appeared, I saw an entirely different level to this: really responsible film criticism. The thing that really impressed me about it was how small the print was. You know, they were really cramming; there was a *lot* of written material in there. The pictures were really secondary.

Q: I was the editor.

KING: Were you really? Doubly nice to meet you. *Castle of Frankenstein* was so thick, so meaty, that you could read it for a week. I used to read it from cover to cover, and I can't imagine I was alone in that. It had a wonderful book column that would talk about Russell Kirk and other people, and just go on and on. There was a wonderful project where all the horror movies of all time were going to be cataloged.

Q: We never got past the letter R in that alphabetical listing. You credit films as a source for your writing, but how can this apply to syntax and style? What's an example of how you might have translated film grammar into fiction?

KING: The best example of that was probably *The Shining*. Each chapter was a limited scene in one place—and each scene was in a different place, until near the very end, where it really becomes a movie, and you go outside for the part where Hallorann is coming across the country on his snowmobile. Then you can almost see the camera traveling along beside him.

You learn syntax and you learn grammar through your reading, and you don't really study it. It just kind of sets in your mind after a while because you've read enough. Even now, if you gave me a sentence with a subordinate clause, I'm not sure I could diagram it on paper, but I could tell you whether or not it was correct because that's the mindset that I have. But to visualize so strong: as a kid in Connecticut I watched the *Million Dollar Movie* over and over again. You begin to see things as you write—in a frame like a movie screen.

Although I can't always see what the characters look like, I always know my right from my left in any scene, and I know how far it is to the door and to the windows and how far apart the windows are and the depth-of-field. The way that you would see it in a film, in *The Blue Dahlia* or something like that.

Q: If you visualize this with sharp focus and depth-of-field, then why do you say you don't know what they look like?

KING: What they look like isn't terribly important to me. It doesn't have to be John Wayne in *True Grit*. It doesn't have to be Boris Karloff as Frankenstein's monster. It doesn't matter to me. Some actors are better than others: I thought Lugosi was terrible as Dracula; he was all right until he opened his mouth, and then I just dissolved into gales of laughter.

Q: As you write, do you ever slip into the styles of different directors?

KING: No, no. Very rarely do I ever think of anything like that. One of the strange things that happened to me was I got beaten in the Sunday *New York Times* on *The Shining*; I got a really terrible review of *The Shining*, accusing me of cribbing from foreign suspense films. I think one of them was *Knife in the Water*, and one of them was *Diabolique*.

Q: Because of the body in the bathtub?

KING: Yes. What was so funny about the criticism was that, by god, I live in Maine! The only foreign films we get are Swedish sex films. I've never seen *Diabolique*; I've never seen any of those pictures. If I came up with them, it was just that there are only so many things you can do in the horror field. Its movements are as stylized as the movements of a dance. You've got your gothic story somewhere in the gothic castle with a clank of chains in the night. In *The Shining*, instead of a gothic castle, you have a gothic hotel, and instead of chains rattling in the basement, the elevator goes up and down—which is another kind of rattling chain.

When Sissy Spacek was announced as the lead of *Carrie*, a lot of people said to me, "Don't you think that's dreadful miscasting?" Because in the book Carrie is presented as this chunky, solid, beefy girl with a pudding plain face who is transformed at the prom into being pretty. I didn't give a shit *what* she looked like as long as she could look sort of ugly before and then look nice at the prom. She could have had brown hair or red hair or anything, and it didn't really matter who—because I didn't have a very clear picture. But I had a clear picture of her heart, I think. And that's important to me. I want to know what my characters feel and what makes them move.

Q: It's pretty obvious that the jacket on the hardback *Carrie* has nothing to do with the book.

KING: Yes, well, it doesn't. My editor and I had our own concept for that, but Bill Thompson, my editor, was a man with relatively little power at Doubleday, and it kept showing up in funny little ways. When I left Doubleday, they canned him. It was like a tantrum: "We'll kill the messenger that brought the bad news."

Our concept of the jacket was to have a Grandma Moses–type primitive painting of a New England village that would go around in a wrap to the back. But the jacket was done by Alex Gotfryd, who does have a lot of power at Doubleday. What he gave us was a photograph of a New York model who looks like a New York model. She doesn't even look like a teenager.

Q: How do you feel about the montage on *The Shining* hardback?

KING: Don't care for that either. It makes the people look too specific. It's almost a gothic-romance jacket. There are some nice things about that jacket; I object to the faces of Jack, Wendy, and the little boy, but I like the concept of having the hedge animals. The hardback *Night Shift* has a classy jacket using just words, but it looks like a Doubleday-type jacket for a book they didn't expect to sell. There's nothing really exciting about that graphic.

Q: The long-distance view of the town on the *'Salem's Lot* hardback doesn't indicate the book's true nature.

KING: I think that was intentional. The flap copy on *'Salem's Lot* is a real collaboration: my editor wrote part of it, his secretary wrote part of it, I wrote part of it, and my wife wrote part of it. It was just an effort to say something without saying anything. Of all the Doubleday jackets I think that I like *The Stand* the best, but *'Salem's Lot* runs that a close second. I like the idea of the black background with the town inset in the O of *Lot*; you can look into the town, and you see the Marsten house. That's a pretty decent jacket. That was the best-produced book by Doubleday; all the way around, that was a good piece of work. The illustration for the hardback of *The Stand* was taken from a Goya painting, *The Battle of Good and Evil*; it was repainted. I was mad that they didn't give poor old

Goya a credit. There are a lot of people who are rather literal-minded, kind of nerdy about book jackets, who don't like it because they say that it doesn't look like what the book is about. But it looks like what the spirit of the book is about. New American Library's *The Stand* cover is super. I think that it's a good one; I like the dark blues and turquoises in it. The paperback covers have always been better because paperback people seem to understand how to market books, how to go about that. Illustrators and designers don't get credit on paperback jackets the way they do on hardcovers.

Q: Then there's *The Shining* in mylar—

KING: Except that it was discontinued, as was the dead black cover on *'Salem's Lot*. Both of those were expensive covers. The *'Salem's Lot* cover cost 7 cents right off the top of a book that originally sold for $6.95. The mylar was 9 cents, and, in addition, the mylar cover buffs. It doesn't peel, but the lettering and picture gradually buff off the book. Now they just have a plain paper cover with the same picture; it's not as eye-catching, but it lasts longer.

There are people who treasure those original copies; someday maybe those will be worth some money, especially the ones that are in good condition, because on the ones that have been read, the cover wears off very quickly. The mylar was really discontinued not just because it buffed in people's hands, but because it buffed in the boxes when they were shipped. I also like the paperback *Night Shift* cover; it's a deep, dark, rich blue. Some of the editions are perfect, and, on some, the holes are not over the eyes. Again, that was a difficult one to do; there is such a thing as being too clever by half.

Q: What was on the *Carrie* paperback before the movie tie-in?

KING: That cover has gone totally out of print. The original paperback had no title, no author, no printed material of any kind on the front cover. It simply showed a girl's head floating against this blue backdrop— a pretty girl with very dark hair swept back. It was a painting, a rather nice one. Inside, there was a second jacket. Originally, it was to have been die-cut down the side in a two-step effect; the title *Carrie*, reading vertically down the right-hand margin, was supposed to show, and, at the last minute, their printer told them that he couldn't do it. Inside, there's this town going up in flames, and that is an interesting effect. You reach the end of the book, and there's a photograph on what they call the "third cover" of the same town crumpled up into nothing but ash. I don't know if that's ever been done before: having another picture inside the back jacket. These were photographs of flames and a model town that looks as though it was one of these origami things created out of cardboard.

Q: The One + One Studio's design for *The Dead Zone* (from Viking) illustrates the repetitive Wheel of Fortune device used throughout the novel.

KING: I like that jacket pretty well. I think that, in a large measure, it's been responsible for some of the book's success because it's a very high contrast type, something I think Viking might have lifted from the paperback houses. It comes out at the reader because there's so much black. The thing I don't like is the photographic effect; I've never cared for photographed jackets. I can't really even say why, but they seem too realistic to me. I would have liked that jacket better if it had been that same cover design, only painted.

By the time you get up to six books, you have mixed feelings. *'Salem's Lot* was the best-produced of the Doubleday books; *Night Shift* would be second, and probably *The Shining* third. *The Dead Zone* is the best-produced of all the works. But it's more than just cover. The cover is something that, you hope, entices readers who don't know your work to look. But it probably doesn't mean that much to people who have read you before. If they really turn on to what you're doing, they look for the name, and they'll buy the book on the basis of that. Like this new Led Zeppelin album packaged in burlap with "Led Zeppelin" stamped on the front—you buy the name. I like books that are nicely made, and, with the exception of *'Salem's Lot* and *Night Shift*, none of the Doubleday books were especially well made. They have a ragged, machine-produced look to them, as though they were built to fall apart. *The Stand* is worse that way: it looks like a brick. It's this little, tiny squatty thing that looks much bigger than it is. *The Dead Zone* is really nicely put together. It's got a nice cloth binding, and it's just a nice product.

Q: In *Strawberry Spring* you wrote about Springheel Jack. The few mentions of Springheel Jack that I've run across seem to indicate that he was a mythical British character who was luminous and was witnessed leaping twenty-five or thirty feet.

KING: Yeah. That's him! That's him! My Springheel Jack is a cross between Jack the Ripper and a mythical strangler—like Burke and Hare or somebody like that.

Q: But you embellished that history?

KING: Yeah, right, I did. Robert Bloch has also done some of this embellishing, and he mentions Springheel Jack in a third context. He's like *Plastic Man* or *Superman*—a weird folk hero.

Q: I think it was a nonfiction UFO book where I first encountered a description of him suggesting that he was—

KING: —a creature from outer space.

Q: What happened to the *Night Shift* TV anthology pilot (a planned trilogy of *Strawberry Spring*, *I Know What You Need*, and *Battleground*)?

KING: It's not going to be done for TV because NBC nixed it...too gruesome, too violent, too intense. It's the atmosphere of TV today; five years ago it would have been done, but the Standards and Practices people just said no. The production company people have since gone to Martin Poll in New York, and he would like to produce it. So we'll see what happens. I don't think anybody's falling over themselves to do it right now.

Q: *Battleground* seems more like a story that would work in a Milton Subotsky film rather than being grouped with the stories set in a college town.

KING: The way this works out is that I can see a lot of possibilities that just can't be realized, because people take these options in a harum-scarum way and then they're cut out. We discussed this with the trilogy for NBC: There's a rooming house in the town, and the hit man from *Battleground* lives in this rooming house. The premise is that reality is thinner in this town, and things are weird in this one particular place. There are forces which focus on this town and cause things to happen.

Q: In *The Shining* there's a mention of hedge billboards in Vermont. Do these exist, and is this what inspired your topiary?

KING: They're really there. The idea for the hedge maze is Kubrick's and not mine. I had considered it, but then I realized it had been done in the movie *The Maze* with Richard Carlson, and I rejected the maze idea for that reason. I have no knowledge as to whether or not Kubrick has ever seen that movie or if it just happens to be coincidence.

The billboards advertise some kind of ice cream; they're on Route 2 in Vermont. As you come across this open space where there are no trees, you can look across this rolling meadow to the land which, I assume, the ice cream factory owns. The words of the ad have been clipped out of hedges. To hype the contrast, these hedges have been surrounded with white crushed stone so that the letters just leap right out at you. You know the first time you see them that there's something very peculiar about them, and then you realize, as you get closer, that it may be one of the world's few living signs—because they're hedges.

But I got the idea for the topiary from Camden, Maine, where *Peyton Place* was filmed. You come down Route 6, you go through Camden, and there are several houses there that have clipped shrubs. They're not clipped into the shapes of animals, but they're clipped into very definite geometric shapes. There's a hedge that's clipped to look like a diamond. That was my first real experience with the topiary. There is a topiary at Disney World where the hedges are clipped to look like animals, but I saw that long after the book was published.

In some ways, I like Kubrick's idea to use a maze. Because it's been pointed out to me—and I think there's some truth to this—that the hedge animals in my novel are the only outward empiric supernatural event that goes on in the book. Everything else can be taken as the hotel actually working on people's minds. That is to say, nothing is going on outwardly. It's all going on inwardly, and it's spreading from Danny to Jack and, finally, to Wendy who is the least imaginative of the three. But the hedge animals are *real*, apparently, because they cut open Danny's leg at one point in the book. Later on, when Hallorann comes up the mountain, they attack him. They are really, really there. Kubrick told me, and he's told other people as well, that his only basis for taking the hedge animals out was because they would be difficult to do with the special effects—to make it look real. My thinking is that maybe the maze is better because maybe the maze can be used in that same kind of interior way. A person could get into a maze and just be unable to get out and gradually get the idea that the maze was deliberately keeping him in, that it was changing its passages—like the mirror maze in *Something Wicked This Way Comes*.

Q: Why did Kubrick acquire *The Shining*?

KING: I heard a story from a Warner Brothers flack that's kind of amusing. He said that the secretary in Kubrick's office got used to this steady "Thump! Thump! Thump!" from the inner office—which was Kubrick picking up books, reading about forty pages, and then throwing them against the wall. He was really looking for a property. One day, along about ten o'clock, the thumps stopped coming, and she buzzed him. He didn't answer the buzz; she got really worried, thinking he'd had a heart attack or something. She went in, and he was reading *The Shining*. He was about halfway through it. He looked up and said, "This is the book." Shortly after that, Warners in California wanted to know if the book had been bought, and, if so, who owned it and if a purchase deal could be worked out—which was easy, since Warners itself owned the book. I do think that if he wanted to make an all-out horror picture, he picked a perfectly good book to do it with. It's a scary book.

Q: In *The Shining* I noticed a curious bit of synchronicity. Danny's experience in Room 267 takes place on page 267.

KING: It's been pointed out to me before. It's peculiar.

This Judith Wax book here, *Starting in the Middle*, this is *really* creepy. She was one of the people killed on the DC-10 that crashed in Chicago.

Q: She did the annual *Playboy* feature "That Was the Year That Was."

KING: She worked for *Playboy*, and she also wrote humorous books. She talks in that book about her fear of flying and how she's convinced that she's going to die on a plane—which she did. The passage where she discusses that is on page 696 of the book, and the flight number of the plane that crashed was 696.

Q: Did she write that as a humor piece?

KING: She approached it humorously, but, at the same time, people who have read the book say you can see that she really hated to fly.

Q: It seems to me that you often take the most preposterous situation you can dream up, and then you set out to convince the reader it's plausible.

KING: Yes. I do. I've got a short novel in *Skeleton Crew* called "The Mist." I said to myself, "You know all these grade B movies, these drive-in pictures." The real proponent of what I was trying to get at in this story was a guy named Bert I. Gordon. He does big bugs and things like this— or he did. They're always sort of funny; there's nothing really terrifying about even the best of them. They're just sort of fun when they're good. The one of his I like the best, *Empire of the Ants*, is just fun; it's about people inspecting an island where there are going to be condominiums, and the ants are out of control.

I said to myself, "Let's take all those B movie conventions. Let's take the giant bugs and everything, and let's take the most mundane setting I can think of." Which, in this case, was a supermarket. And I said, "I want to set these things loose outside and see if I can do it and really scare people...see if I can make that work." And, by god, I think I did.

You can judge for yourself. The story is about 40,000 words long, and I think it's really good.

Q: Did your *New York Times Book Review* piece on David Madden prompt any increase of interest in his novel *Bijou?*

KING: I don't know if it has or not. Madden has just published a sequel to it called *Pleasure Dome,* and I knew that he was working on that. He and I correspond back and forth at irregular intervals, and I mean really irregular because he's not a very good correspondent and neither am I. He's interested in a lot of the same things I am: the hard-boiled writers of the thirties, the sort of writers who produced the *film noir* in the forties—Cain and Dashiell Hammett and people like that. He's got a critical magazine called *Tough Guys* for which he writes these critical, very literary pieces, and he asked me if I would contribute a piece on Cain. I told him, yeah, I would, but I never have. Mostly because that literary, sort of stuffy style kind of bums me out.

Q: What was the name of the NBC radio program on which your mother played the organ?

KING: Ah, God! It was a church show. It was on at ten o'clock, NBC, on Sunday mornings, and it was something like *The Church Today.* I guess it really was a radio broadcast from the church where they had the remote.

Q: Since you did not want to host the proposed *Night Shift* TV show, and since you also turned down a directing offer from Milton Subotsky, one might assume that you have a desire to avoid the celebrity game.

KING: I don't want to be a celebrity, but neither do I want to avoid it just to avoid being a celebrity. Writers are anonymous. I could walk out here anywhere, and nobody would know who I was. When I'm in Maine sometimes I get recognized. They know your name, and sometimes if you say, "I'm Stephen King," they say, "Are you the person who wrote *'Salem's Lot?*" If Paul Newman walked down the street, he would be recognized immediately. If the right opportunity came along, I wouldn't let the idea of becoming a celebrity stop me, but the idea of being host for a TV program is not a very good idea right now because I want to scare people. Television is so hamstrung; its hands are tied. It's castrated. You can't scare people on TV. It's ridiculous to talk about having a series frightening people on TV when we're locked into the age of *Diff'rent Strokes, Charlie's Angels,* and *Vega$.* If I ever did a horror-type program on TV, I'd want it to be a success. Since *The Outer Limits* and *The Twilight*

Zone went off the air, I don't really think that there have been any successful horror programs on TV, and one of the reasons why is I don't think you can scare people.

I talked with Aaron Spelling about this on the telephone; he was interested in an anthology program. He dangled this particular carrot in front of me: "Wouldn't you like to be Rod Serling or Alfred Hitchcock and introduce the programs?" I said, "Not for six weeks." He was kind of quiet, and he said, "What do you mean?" I said, "Do you remember the old *Thriller?*" He said he did, and I said, "They did an adaptation of the old Robert Howard story *Pigeons from Hell*, and there's one scene where a guy staggers down the stairs with a hatchet in his head. If you can give me an assurance that I can run a program with the equivalent of a hatchet in the head, we got a deal." There was this long pause, and he said, "Well, we could show him with the hatchet in his chest." And I said, "I just don't believe it!" That's where the negotiations on that stand.

As far as the movie goes, I thought Milton Subotsky was a very nice man. In fact, I call him the Hubert Humphrey of horror pictures. He's a constant Pollyanna, and he wants all his pictures to have an upbeat, moralistic ending. It's all right for a guy to get strangled by the snake when it comes out of the basket as long as we see beforehand that he's really a rotten guy and he deserved to go. There has to be this uplifting tone to it. He did hold out this directorial thing. It was interesting to me, but I saw real problems in getting along with him and having a working relationship. I'd rather avoid that at the start than get into it and not be able to get back out of it again.

Q: You foresaw creative conflicts?

KING: Yes, and in the creative conflicts in this business, sooner or later, somebody ends up getting sued, or there are hard feelings. The way I feel about Milton right now is quite well; he feels all right toward me, but there is that creative difference of opinion about what horror is supposed to do. So it's better just to avoid the whole thing.

I don't want to be on view just for the sake of being on view. I don't want to be Charo, and I don't want to be Monte Rock III. If I have to be on view to do my job, okay—that's something different. I've been on tour because it's good for the book to do it. I don't really mind it, but if the situation were different, and I could do it another way, I'd sit at home.

Q: Would such activities be damaging to your output?

KING: No, I think it would just be a question of rearranging the priorities a little bit. There are people who write novels and still manage to do other things. I don't think it's ever easy. Richard Matheson goes on writing books even though he does screenplays. So does William Goldman. It could be arranged.

If PBS came to me and said, "We're going to do a ten-week series of famous horror stories. Would you introduce them?" I would do it because the Neilsen ratings don't affect that sort of thing. If they were very, very good, they might repeat it with a second series, but if they only got 2 percent of the viewing audience, they wouldn't cancel the series—because they're used to that. I just don't want to go on network TV and put my face and my name in front of a bunch of junk.

With Freff

KING: New Hampshire is the center of craziness here. I don't even like to go through there. It's like I hold my breath. That's the state where the governor, three or four years ago, tried to get tactical nuclear weapons for the National Guard. And they put a guy in jail for a while for covering up the "Live Free or Die" on his license plate with adhesive tape. They've also got a place over there—it's a great tourist attraction—called Six Gun City; and it's just like *Westworld,* except that they're actors instead of robots, and you get to draw on them with blanks and pretend you've shot them down.

But even Maine is different. Really different. People keep themselves to themselves, and they take the outsiders' money, and on the surface, at least, they're polite about it. But they keep themselves to themselves. That's the only way I can put it. I'm glad I was born in Maine. I always think of that Shirley Jackson story about the Summer People—you know, where they stay after Labor Day and the townspeople stone them. It's not beyond belief.

Q: What effect has Maine's peculiar rural atmosphere had on your work?
KING: You write about the places you know. I would still write horror stories if I had grown up in New York City. The only difference is that they would be urban horror stories. There are things in New York that

fascinate me, that I'd love to write about. A cab driver told me once that there was an abandoned subway tunnel under Central Park. I thought, "This is fantastic!" In fact I've even had a book that I've wanted to write for about three years where that would work right in. It would be a snap. But I'm never going to try to do it because I don't feel I know it well enough, even though I know it a lot better than any other place I've been to in the last three years.

Q: Why not approach it deliberately as an outsider? That could be very effective.

KING: Yeah, but still, think of all the research I'd have to do. I'd have to go into the city and shuffle up and down 64th Street.

I did *The Shining* after we went to Colorado. I also really like Nebraska. It's made a tremendous impression on me. All those wide open spaces and that big, big sky. Very strange. Very Lovecraftian. Some of the stories in *Night Shift*—"Children of the Corn," "The Last Rung of the Ladder"—are set there.

Q: When was the last time you were terrified?

KING: I think that somebody who writes this sort of thing has a lower threshold of fear. I'm not saying the writer of horror fiction must be a coward. It can be controllable fear; people may not know. I can tell you the last time I was frightened. Yesterday when I was coming home from Portland I saw this cop car coming like hell behind me, with all his lights going, and the flashers, and the siren—and he was obviously not after me or anyone else. I pulled over and he zapped by. As I got going again, I thought, "Jesus, suppose he's going down my road...suppose something happened to one of the kids...suppose I get down the driveway and I see the cop car with the lights going, and they're taking something covered with a rubber sheet from the house, or something like that." That was the last time I was afraid.

The last time I was really *terrified* was probably the time that Joe got hit with a snow shovel. Joe was a little younger than three. It was snowing. We were going to the library. Joe and Naomi were scooting around with a snow shovel and I had a bunch of library books. Then I heard Joe start to cry, and when I turned around he was face down in the snow. I thought: the kid is crying because he got his face washed—that's what we used to call it, falling on your face in the snow—and then he got up on his knees and his face was totally gone. It was covered with blood from top to bottom, and there was blood streaming down the front of his jacket. I ran to him. His eye was gone; it was just a sort of big glob of blood, but we took him in and then we ran around like chickens with our heads cut off, my wife and I. Naomi and Joe had apparently been squabbling over the snow shovel, and somehow it had slipped and the corner severed his tear duct. He was in the hospital for a week. That was the last time I can remember experiencing really acute terror, when he got up on his knees from that face-washing, and there was no face, just blood.

Q: Never ask the native guide for straight directions unless you really want them.

KING: The horror story makes us children, OK? That's the primary function of the horror story—to knock away all of this stuff, all of the bullshit we cover ourselves up with.

Horror is seen as this barren thing that's supposed to take us over taboo lines, to places we aren't supposed to be. For a long time people have thought that horror is some kind of radical—a dangerous thing to deal with. But, actually, people who deal in horror are like Republicans in three-button suits. They're very reactionary. They're agents of the norm. They say, "This is the monster, this is a horrible thing," but at the same time they're saying, "No problem with you. You're cool, because you don't look like this awful thing which has just crawled out of the crater," or whatever.

So horror stories make us children. That's what they do. And children are able to feel things adults can't, because of all the experience we've had.

Q: The roots of appreciating horror are in all of us, and they date back to fairy tales most of us have forgotten we were ever told.

KING: One of the things the fairy tale has always done best is to make children feel bad, to make them cry. My kids have got a videotape of *Frosty the Snowman*—and they watch it over and over again. They love it. But the part I think they love best is when the evil guy in the North takes Frosty's magic hat away and turns him back into just an ordinary snowman. And Frosty's family—somehow he's got a snowman family; sex among snowpeople must be strange, but maybe they do it with carrots—they're all weeping over him, and my kids weep over it, too. But they're enjoying it.

We're afraid of things that deviate from the norm, that break taboo lines. And yet children cry when King Kong falls off the Empire State Building and dies, because they're able to jump over that for a while and feel sympathy for someone who's an outsider.

Q: What were your emotions as you watched 'Salem's Lot?

KING: The major emotion that went through my mind was relief, because TV is this magic medium which seems to turn almost everything it touches into shit, and I felt that 'Salem's Lot mostly survived that. You see, I have no emotional investment in this thing at all. Basically Warner Brothers bought the property and tried to get it off the ground as a theatrical movie, but it didn't work out. If you want to see something that's terrible, you have to look at some of the early scripts. You have to look at Silliphant's, which is worse than what he did for The Swarm. You see those, and you realize what kind of escape I actually had.

I didn't particularly approve of them turning Barlow into a Nosferatu, who says nothing at all and becomes sort of minor by comparison. That's a different concept than mine altogether, and I think it's one that's a little bit empty. "We couldn't think of anything else to do, so we fell back on this." There are all sorts of problems with the timing. When Susan comes back at the end—this is probably something that's less defensible—she's beautiful. Now, all the other vampires are ugly. Totally ugly. Marjorie Glick was only dead a day, and when she rises she looks *dead*, you know? But even though Susan has been dead for two years, she looks like she hasn't aged a day. But even with all this it still isn't like the TV version of Harvest Home, where there's the appearance that everyone involved was asleep. By comparison, this looks really good. I think the people who made it cared about it.

Q: Is religion a major element in your work?

KING: There are a lot of people my age who have got it figured out to their satisfaction. You know, either you go to hell if you're not saved by the blood of Jesus, or there is no hell, or we're reincarnated when we die, or just fill in your own blank. But I haven't figured it out to my satisfaction. I'm pretty convinced there is a God, an Oversoul, some kind of sentient being who's in charge of everything that goes on here.

People blather to me and they say, "How can there be a God if He allows the Holocaust or World War II to happen?" or "How can there be a God who lets Chad Green die of leukemia?" But, hey! We just happen to have this ionospheric screen that keeps out killing radiation. And we just happen never to have been hit by a meteor big enough to destroy this planet, even though space is full of that shit, like dandruff on a guy with psoriasis. So to me the idea of saying, "There can be no God because God allowed 6 million Jews to be killed by the Nazis" is like saying "There can be no God because God let somebody fart in an elevator." The cosmos is just too big.

The question is to try and figure out what we are going to do about this. We fall from a mystery into a mystery, you know. We don't know where we were before we were born. We know that people die, and that at that point of death something happens to the thinking being, to the spirit of the *mentus* or whatever you want to call it, but we don't know what happens. Maybe it clicks out, maybe it goes on, maybe it changes....

So a lot of the religious mania in my books comes out of my concern with this. I'm trying to put it in order in my mind. I was brought up in a fairly fundamentalist family, where you were taught to believe there were fires down there and all that stuff. I went to church two or three times a week. I read a lot of the Bible. Loved the Bible; loved the stuff that's in it. Try not to read it for its prose, try to get the meat of it.

My wife was raised Catholic, though she's now nonpracticing, and I was raised Methodist and am now nonpracticing. I try to keep church in my heart. I don't want to say that I'm a pantheist or that I try to go out and look on Nature as the work of God—because it isn't like that. It's trying to feel what it is that the world has to tell us about something that is more than the world. Now, it bothers me that my children don't have any formal kind of religious training that they can leave. Because if you have religious training, and then leave it, you understand what you are leaving. Moving away from belief is completely in your head, it's something you do mentally.

You start thinking things like: The Bible says Cain slew his brother Abel with a rock, and God said, "Cain, I know you did it, and you're going to go off and live in the land of Nod for the rest of your life." And he did. But the Bible also says that Adam and Eve were the first people on earth, and that they had Cain and then they had Abel—so who the hell did Cain go live with?

I'm not anywhere on the path, you know. The only thing I've pretty much excluded is reincarnation. I realize that in India they believe, and it is very old and time-honored, but what do you expect from a culture that was eating cowdung pies as late as 1850? I just don't believe it, to be honest. But I have times when I say, "All this fundamentalist stuff is right.

You miss your chance and you're going to be down there in the corridors of hell for all eternity, screaming for water every minute of every hour of every day of every year of every century, forever." And there are the times when I say to myself, "You die, hey, you go through a greyness, and then you approach the throne of God—and it's Mickey Rooney." I've always wanted to write a story about that.

With Craig Modderno (*USA Today*)

Q: Do you ever have a difficult time thinking of new ways to kill people for your work?

KING: (*Laughs*) That never even crosses my mind. I never even try to—the old ways work just fine. I have never yet strapped anybody to a power drill or anything like that.

Q: Have you been satisfied with the way Hollywood has adapted your novels into films?

KING: I don't feel good or bad about them. I liked *Cujo* very much. I liked *Carrie* very much. I was very lucky to have Brian De Palma adapt me and I would like him to do it some time again. I liked *Cat's Eye*. It really works, and I'm sort of disappointed that it's not doing any better.

Q: What's hindering it?

KING: It's probably because the gore-hounds are going to it, and they're not getting what they want. A lot of the other ones are just sort of not there. None of them are really bad. None of them are really embarrassing, although "Children of the Corn" is pretty bad. *Firestarter* missed by just an inch being a picture like *Myra Breckenridge* or *Mommy Dearest*. But it didn't happen.

Q: You wrote one of the scariest books ever written, *The Shining*. Some critics said, however, that the film isn't that scary. What went wrong?

KING: Diane Johnson and Stanley Kubrick collaborated on the screenplay, and, of course, Kubrick directed. Neither one of them had any background in the field. I read an interview that Diane Johnson gave to *The New York Times* about three months before the movie was actually released in which she said that she and Stanley had read a lot of literature and that they had tried to figure out why people are always so instinctively frightened of dolls or inanimate objects with faces and features. All of that was very interesting, but nothing in the movie is really scary. You don't necessarily have to be a wiring expert to turn electric lights on and off. They had no real background in the field.

Q: How was the movie flawed?

KING: The movie builds to a point showing Jack Torrance, played by Jack Nicholson, as a caretaker of the Overlook Hotel in 1926 or 1923. This is supposed to be our final shock of the film, when in fact it is something that was done on *The Twilight Zone* twice. So you have that and a basic ignorance of the field causing a lead-up to a big bang that isn't a big bang. It's sort of a dud firecracker. Then you have other things that they don't even do in the *Friday the 13th* films. For instance, there's a wonderful wasted moment where Jack has been working and working on this book and finally his wife screws up her courage to go to the manuscript and look through it, and it says in a thousand different ways, on a thousand different pages, "All work and no play makes Jack a dull boy."

Q: What's wasted about this moment?

KING: We know he's coming. Anybody who has seen a horror film knows that he's going to catch her. That's what happens when you sneak; you get caught. We learn it as kids. Part of us wants him to catch her. Most of us are hoping she'll hurry up and put it down and get away with it. What we want is for her to turn around and he'll be right there, and our hearts will jump up into our throat—that sort of thing. Instead, Kubrick cuts away and shows him walking over to her. That confuses it. It's like a guy who doesn't know how to tell a joke, and I don't mean that to sound vitriolic. *The Shining* is a beautiful film. It's like this great big gorgeous car with no engine in it—that's all.

Q: Have Hollywood producers made too many of your movies lately?

KING: No, they haven't done too many. They just need to do them better. But right now, there's not all that much material. I don't know how to respond anymore to the "Stephen King's movie-of-the-month" sort of thing because there have been so many of them, but that's not my fault. I don't buy my own film rights and inflict these films on the public. People who blame me for that are putting the blame in the wrong place.

Q: How do you feel about not having control over what happens to your book when the moviemakers take over?

KING: My feeling for most of these things is like a guy who sends his daughter off to college. You hope she'll do well. You hope that she won't fall in with the wrong people. You hope she won't be raped at a fraternity party, which is really close to what happened to "Children of the Corn," in a metaphoric sense. So you can't control those sort of things. You hope they'll turn out well. With the exception of "Children of the Corn," every one of the projects looked great on paper.

Q: Do Hollywood producers generally treat you with respect?

KING: Dino De Laurentiis has treated me the way he treats a friend. He's treated me with a lot of dignity and respect. I respect him. That's why I've done more business with him than anybody else.

Q: This summer you're going to direct your first film, *Maximum Overdrive*.

KING: That's right. It's based on a short story called "Trucks." The process by which I got into this was very simple. Dino asked me if I would write a screenplay for it. I said, "No." He said, "OK, think about it." And I went back, and I thought I could have some fun with it and, most importantly, I saw a way it could be expanded to a feature film. So after I agreed, he asked if I would direct. Dino is the sort of a guy who would take a chance on Jack the Ripper if he thought he could get a good picture out of him. I wanted to do it once because I thought I might be able to do a better job than some of the people who have done it. I can't imagine wanting to go back and do it again. It's like being one part on tour and two parts day labor and three parts detention hall monitor. I don't think it's the world's most glamorous job. I'm far enough into it already to tell you that.

Q: What is it about?

KING: It's about machines out of control, and we're going to film down in Wilmington, N.C., where Dino has a studio, and we're going to blow up a lot of trucks, and we're going to have a lot of runaway electric knives and lawn mowers and stuff like that. We start shooting July 6, I think.

Q: What do you think is your best work?

KING: The best I've done so far is *The Dead Zone*, because it's a real novel. It's very complex. There's an actual story. Most of my fictions are simply situations that are allowed to develop themselves. That one has a nice layered texture, a thematic structure that underlies it, and it works on most levels. I never ask a book to do any more than that. If it works, I'm happy.

Q: Is there anything you would like to do over again?

KING: If I had had my way about it, I still would not have published *Pet Sematary*. I don't like it. It's a terrible book—not in terms of the writing, but it just spirals down into darkness. It seems to be saying nothing works and nothing is worth it, and I don't really believe that.

Q: When you are working on a novel, do you write every day?

KING: I sit down and work on it every day. Basically it's as simple as that. I do about six pages a day, which probably figures out to around 1,800 and 2,200 words. I would say I'm pretty disciplined to get that done—get that out every single day.

Q: Have there been subjects that you couldn't attach a story to?

KING: Yes. For a long time I've wanted to write a magic-carpet story. It would be a fantastic story, but so far I can't hook it up. It's like a car with a bad transmission.

Q: You're a big rock-and-roll fan. Have you ever thought of a book on that subject?

KING: That's another one. Actually, I'd like to write an Elvis novel. I'd really like to write a rock-and-roll novel. But it's very, very hard to write about music, so I haven't been able to hook that one up.

Q: Why did you use a pseudonym on the book *Thinner?*

KING: I simply had too much stuff in print, and that book was too good to hold, so I did it that way.

Q: Didn't you think anybody would discover your identity?

KING: In a way I didn't exactly care, and I was prepared to stonewall it as long as I could. I would still be stonewalling it, too, if somebody from New American Library hadn't stuck my name on one of the copyright forms in the early books, where I was writing under the pen name of Richard Bachman. In fact, that happened with the first Bachman book, which goes back to 1977. The other ones were filed in my agent's name. I think if it hadn't been for that, I would still be sitting here saying, "I don't care what you think, I'm not Richard—"

Q: Do you try to get yourself into a scary mood before you start writing?

KING: No.

With Tim Hewitt

Q: Is it true that *Cat's Eye* began as a script for Drew Barrymore?

KING: Yes.

Q: How did that script work its way in with the adaptations of the other two stories, "Quitter's, Inc." and "The Ledge"?

KING: Dino De Laurentiis owned some of the *Night Shift* stories, which he had acquired from, I think, an outfit in California called The Production Company, who had optioned them originally to do a TV movie for NBC. He liked some of these stories, and he was very taken with some of my other stories owned by an Englishman, Milton Subotsky. Dino was able to make an arrangement with Subotsky, which made me very happy because I knew I wanted to see some of those things made, and I thought that if Subotsky made them, it would actually be worse than if they were never made at all. I don't like to root for my things not to be made, except in certain cases, *but...*

So Dino had some stories and he had some ideas about doing a film that would interrelate the stories, and he was very taken with Drew Barrymore, and he asked could I write an original. I was down here and I was looking at *Firestarter* at that time. As a matter of fact, I had had an idea for a short story for some time. It dealt with a little boy who was saved from a monster that lived in his wall by his pet cat, and the cat would have a bad rep because the mother would think that cats can steal your breath and all that stuff. I liked the idea because it was "Kitty Come Home" instead of "Lassie Come Home," but I don't know if I ever would've written it as a short story. But it was easy enough to turn it into a little short screenplay. After the sex of the part was changed from boy to girl, it fit Drew perfectly.

Dino was very taken with the concept of the little girl and the cat, and he thought that the cat would make a wonderful device to bind the three stories together. He said, "Stephen, can you put the cat in all three stories? Do you see a way that that could be done?" And I thought to myself, "C'mon, the guy's got to be crazy. It's impossible." But I went back and I thought about it and I actually saw a way that it could be done. I got very excited about it and I called him up: "Dino! Dino! I know how you can do this!" He says (*imitating De Laurentiis*) "Ees wonderfol. Now, what about de goirl?" and I said, "Dino, do you know what you're asking?" But I saw a way that that could be done as well. Then, I thought the concept was so unusual and so spacy that I wanted to write it myself. I thought that he might offer me the chance to do the whole screenplay, and when he did I jumped at it.

It actually made a film that isn't an anthology film like *Creepshow* at all. It's actually a real movie. And that's how it happened. Dino De Laurentiis led me on.

Q: So the cat is the hero of *Cat's Eye?*

KING: Yes, he and the girl that Drew plays. By that I mean The Girl. She's Amanda in the last story, but she's the same girl all the way through it. Those are the two hero-characters. The cat's the real hero though.

Q: Ostensibly you wrote the screenplay for *Cujo* which was then gone over by some other writers. But to date you've only received screen credit, at least, on the two films that are both anthologies. Any comment on that.

KING: Well, I did a screenplay for *The Dead Zone* which was a Dino De Laurentiis production, and his feeling about that screenplay was that it was too involved, too convoluted. So they went back to Jeff—Jeffrey Boam, who had done a really dreadful first draft—and they all sat down and they hammered out a pretty decent script.

Now, when I did a screenplay for *Cujo* that I thought was pretty good, it was not as faithful to the book as was the final result. That was Taft International, and they badly wanted my name on the film, uh, for screen credit because it would—they felt that it would hype box office. I think that they might've been right. So it was submitted to the Screen Writers Guild of America for screen credit: "Screenplay by Stephen King." At which point, the woman who cowrote the screenplay, Lauren Currier, lodged a protest and I got a letter from the Writers Guild asking if I would like to respond to her protest and allow a split credit or a three-way credit. They sent me a copy of the final screenplay, which I read over, and I saw a lot of my stuff still in there. But at the time that the thing reached me I was in England doing a promotional round for *Christine* and I didn't want to fight about it. So, I let it go and it became a split credit between Lauren Currier and Don Carlos Dunaway.

Now on *Children of the Corn*, once again, the screenplay was submitted to the Writers Guild of America with my name on it and again there was a protest, this time by the fellow who got the screenwriting credit, George Clayton—I think his name is actually George Goldsmith—and they sent me a copy of the screenplay. Now the copy of the screenplay that I saw for *Children of the Corn*, supposedly the final screenplay, had large portions of my screenplay that I had written four or five years ago. I even recognized the typescript from the Olivetti that I used at the time. I thought about it a long, long time, and at that point the question was, "Could I trust New World Pictures? Was that really the final script?"

They were so hot to have *my name* on the screenplay! On the other hand, I didn't need the screen credit, and what happens, number one, if the picture's a dog and your name is on it and it's not supposed to be? That's one thing. You can't petition for a change after the picture's out, you know. In other words, I'll take the credit if the reaction's good, and I won't if everybody says that this is a real piece of shit.

And then, the second, very moral question is, "Do you have any right, just because you're a big shot, to steal the screen credit from somebody who's an unknown? What if it's a great film?" So I thought about that one very very hard for about three days, and then I decided, essentially, I couldn't trust New World Pictures. I sent a telegram to the Writers Guild and said that I didn't want to respond to Clayton's (Goldsmith's) petition to have sole screen credit on the picture, so he was granted sole screen credit. I'm delighted that he was on both counts. Number one, the picture was a dog; it was not a good movie at all, and number two, it was a shuck-and-jive situation. What they had sent me and represented as the final screenplay had nothing in common at all with what finally made it to the screen. It was basically, I think, an effort to fool me into accepting a screen credit that didn't belong to me.

Q: *Creepshow* was funny to a degree. And *Cat's Eye* was promoted as a "humorous thriller." Is this an effort to show that Stephen King can write more than just scary, horrifying stuff?

KING: Well, *Cat's Eye*'s got a lot of teeth in it. I would love to see them promote *Cat's Eye* as *Saturday the 14th*, or "this is a laugh riot"—L-A-F-F—you know, a "laff riot," because then we'd get a lot of people in there, particularly young children, and unprepared older people, and scare them until they wet their pants or had heart attacks, or whatever, because it's a pretty scary picture. Lewis Teague understands that. And in an odd sort of way, Dino understands it too, although he never speaks of it in exactly the same way that I think of it. But Dino has never seen *Creepshow*. I can't really do Dino's accent, but he came up to talk about this and he says (*imitating De Laurentiis*) "Stephen! De ting about dees stories, dey are horrible!" And then he kind of looked like he was going to say something that was a little bit nasty or off-color and he says, "But ees funny. Ees funny!" And I said, "Oh," you know, like, "Gee, I never thought of that."

Well, they're hilarious, they're pretty funny. But I had no problem with that because it's also the kind of picture where if there weren't a ratings system and you were allowed to go as far as you legitimately could go, you would be laughing so hard you wouldn't notice you just puked on your shoes. It's got a lot of really strong moments in it, but it's also got some hilarious stuff. I mean, I saw part of the "Quitter's, Inc." story, and I laughed harder than I've laughed at anything that I've seen in theaters this year, with the exception of *Star Trek III*. I laughed and laughed at that. I couldn't stop.

I have a different reference. My brother went bald at eighteen, got Jesus at twenty-three, and then got Amway at thirty. Now he wears this wig and he looks like a sort of gone-to-seed William Shatner. I made that connection, and I just started to laugh.

But I don't think it's an effort to do any one thing in particular. It's just that Dino was the first one to have consciously latched onto the idea that some of this stuff was funny, and even he said it in a kind of a, "What's Stephen King going to do if I say this out loud" tone. But when we shot *Creepshow*, we thought we were shooting this really scary picture. We were having a helluva time, but that's what we were trying to do. It's true it was a comic book, but then these reactions started to come in: "This is hilarious." "This is one of the funniest things we've ever seen."—from some of the people that were associated with the movie. Obviously not everybody felt that way. A lot of people felt it was neither fish nor fowl, that it fell between the shoes. With *Cat's Eye* there was a conscious effort to look at the absurdity, but there wasn't any effort to play the material itself for laughs.

Q: And you're also writing a script for *Pet Sematary*.

KING: Yeah, but there's no real hurry about that as of right now.

Q: You wrote in *Danse Macabre* that there is humor implicit in horror. There's a lot of black humor in your writing.

KING: Let's put it this way: the ethics of *Cat's Eye* are very muddy to me. It's the same way that I think of the ethics of a movie like *Gremlins*. Kids love that movie *Gremlins*, but I think a lot of adults are made very uneasy by it, because the ethics of it are so murky. It's like a Gahan Wilson Christmas card, isn't it really? I mean, the girl talking about "That's when I found out there was no Santa Claus" when her father's corpse got crisped in the chimney. *Cat's Eye* is like that. The funniest things in *Cat's Eye* proceed from some really awful things that happen. So, that's the best I can answer your question for you.

Q: You really championed *The Evil Dead*.

KING: I did.

Q: That's a pretty grotesque movie. And then there's the famous missing scene from your novel *'Salem's Lot*.

KING: Ah!

Q: With the rats in the mouth.

KING: Yeah! You're trying to ask me why I like all that awful, horrible stuff.

Q: No. Not really why you like it, but why you gave in when they wanted to cut it out of *'Salem's Lot?*

KING: Well, because it was my second book and I was afraid that if I didn't give in, then they would just say, "Okay that's it, we're not going to publish this book." At a certain point that's every writer's fear, and at the same time it can be a writer's salvation because editors can be right as well as wrong. My editor might've been right in that case. I'm not entirely convinced of it, but I do know that if *'Salem's Lot* had been my seventh book instead of my second, and an editor had come along and said that, I could and probably would have said, "No, we're going to keep that in." We would've kept it in.

Q: Moving away from films for a minute. Your best novels seem to be those that are set in Maine.

KING: Uh-huh.

Q: How much of a factor do you think regionalism plays in your writing? Do you think of yourself as a "regional writer"?

KING: Sure. Oh, yeah, because I've lived there all my life, and you have to be. If you're going to live in a place all your life, and if you want to write seriously, you almost have to write about that place. I mean, there are guys that have lived in one place all their lives and who write about other places. There's a guy who's never left England who writes westerns. He's very successful. He researches them, and he does pretty well that way. But if you're going to write about something seriously, and you've always lived in one place, you have to write a certain amount of stuff about "there." But if I wrote about Maine—New England—all the time, I'd go crazy too. So, I get away from there every once in a while. But the novels and other stuff that I've got done are pretty exclusively set in that area. There is nothing wrong with that, because you can find universal factors anywhere.

Q: What about the publication of *Fear Itself*? Do you think that lends a sort of legitimacy to your work in the eyes of people who have, over the years, criticized you?

KING: I don't really think so, because I don't think it's a very good book. I think a lot of the essays in it are kind of sophomoric. They're sort of like essay questions on a junior-level college English exam. Probably the most painful one that actually made print is Alan Ryan's essay on the Marston house which really does read like—Alan's a good writer, but that reads like a bullshit essay for a final exam situation.

Douglas Winter's done a book called *The Art of Darkness*, published in hardcover by New American Library. I sometimes wish it had been a different publisher because I think that would lend it more legitimacy. There are cracks made in the publishing industry—my wife publishes there too—about the "Stephen King Publishing Company." We'd like to get away from that, but Doug's done a good job. He's a wonderful writer. We'll just wait and see whether or not the word gets out and it's taken seriously or not.

Q: Did you work closely with *Cat's Eye* during production?

KING: Without a doubt. I made a conscious decision after I had read my first draft of it and seen the way the material clicked together, that I'd go down the line with it, all the way. Everything else that I've done, even *Silver Bullet*, includes what I call a divorce clause, a no-fault divorce clause. That I could use if Dino comes back to me, or the director comes back to me, and says, "Gee, we like this, but we want to set it in outer space," or "We like this, but what would you think about changing the part of the werewolf so that we can have her played by Meryl Streep," or something like that. . . . Actually, that's not a bad idea.

But I loved what I had, and frankly, I didn't want anyone else to screw around with it. And I thought, well, I can stand up for what I think is right as well as anybody else. So, with *Cat's Eye* I stuck it out and I went down the line with it.

CHAPTER FIVE

+

PARTNERS IN FEAR

+

Look at Joseph Heller. It took him seven years to write *Something Happened*. Now, it doesn't take seven years to write a book. You're jerking off is what you're doing. You're writing a little bit, and then you're jerking off, and then you write a bit more. To me, that's a waste of energy.

With Stanley Wiater and Peter Straub

1979 *World Fantasy Convention, Providence, Rhode Island*

Q: All right, the first thing we want to know about is this terrible rivalry between you two....

STRAUB: We don't have any rivalry. I love Steve's work.

KING: Yeah—I like Peter's work, too. We don't quarrel...nope...no quarrel.

Q: Well, the number of professional horror writers is so small, I would think one can't help but have some kind of camaraderie.

KING: Well, yeah, but you know on that discussion panel we were on, nobody mentioned Ira Levin? He's been in the field a long time! He's done some great work....

STRAUB: You're right—talk about mainstream!

KING: He is Mister Mainstream. I always felt he had his tongue a little bit in his cheek, though.

STRAUB: I guess so. I haven't seen that play of his, *Deathtrap*, though I'd like to see it. I'll bet it's very ingenious.

Q: Why the sudden respect for the genre, which for so long has been relegated to the bottom of the paperback rack but now can be found at the top of the hardcover best-seller lists?

KING: I'll tell you something. People have been asking me why there's been a boom in horror for the seven years I've been publishing books. And there really hasn't been! *Carrie* came in at the very end of the boom; it was not a hardcover best-seller. It did well in paperback *after* the movie came out. It did well before—it sold a million copies—but it really took off afterward. And there's never really been any "boom" in it. There was a short one near the end of the sixties and in the early seventies: *The Exorcist, The Other, Rosemary's Baby*. Those three, and then what've you got in the middle? You've got one book by Frank DeFellita, which I would argue isn't even a horror novel at all—and it even isn't that good a book!

STRAUB: *Audrey Rose*. And that in fact never met the publisher's expectations.

KING: No, I don't think that it did either. And they really thought they were going to have another *Exorcist*-type book. But, you know, the other thing is, a lot of times, when the books do come on the lists, they don't demonstrate tremendous "legs." They don't sell and resell. *The Shining* was on *The New York Times* best-seller list in hardcover for *one* week. But Peter's book *Ghost Story* was on for nineteen weeks. It just rode and rode and rode. But even that's not like *War and Remembrance*, which is week fifty-two this week, so...

STRAUB: Steve and I have a little theory—that is, Steve had the theory first and I believe in it—that the established writers of best-sellers are getting pretty well on in years. And there is a kind of vacuum, you know? There's a shortage at the top, and publishers are trying like crazy to push people into those slots. It's a question of the strength of the book, really; if the book is really strong enough, there's room on the list for it.

KING: One of the reasons *The Dead Zone* got to number one was when the book came on the list there was nothing that was strong on the list at all. It was a very weak list at that time. When your book was on there, *War and Remembrance* was number one, *Fools Die* was still on the list.

STRAUB: And then *Sophie's Choice* came along....

KING: Yeah.... I was convinced from the time I was a teenager trying to sell my first novel that, sooner or later, I'd break through and get published simply because they've got to publish *something*, and these old farts are going to die off! I mean, they're not farts, but they're on the lists forever. Like that woman—Taylor Caldwell.

STRAUB: Boy, hasn't she been around a long time!

Q: Yes, but why do you think horror finally took off as a truly contemporary genre? It's never really disappeared from the scene, except perhaps in the fifties.

KING: Well, they're around. Even if you go back to a period like the fifties when this stuff was very—I mean, *Weird Tales* magazine died from lack of interest as much as anything—but the stuff was there, and it would crop up every now and then. There was *The Search for Bridey Murphy*, which was the fifties' answer to *The Amityville Horror* and just as hoaxy, apparently.

STRAUB: That's right.

KING: And it's just that people have to have this stuff! You need it—like a little salt in your diet.

STRAUB: Yeah, I think that's right: people have always enjoyed it, and always *will* enjoy it. But I have another little theory—which I've just invented—that the whole fiction market, the whole publishing world, changed a couple of years ago when the price of paper went so high. Publishers started turning down books that they normally would have accepted. It got much harder to be a first novelist. It was much harder to be a first novelist in 1977 than it was in 1973, when I was a first novelist. There was a certain handwriting on the wall, and I think one by-product of this is that many younger writers read the writing on the wall and wanted to exercise their talent in some form that would be acceptable to publishers. If you're very, very good—if you're *really* good—there's always a place for you: you're always going to be read, and you're always going to be published.

Q: In other words, some writers embraced the horror genre specifically because they figured they had a slightly better chance of seeing that first novel getting published?

STRAUB: That's right. I think so. I'm pretty sure that's what's been happening. Barry Malzberg said the reason he wrote science fiction was because he wanted to make sure he got into print. I think that once you get into a genre, you discover how rich it is, and how varied it is. And just how much you can do with it! And of course you gravitate toward that genre to which you feel close to anyhow, so it's not an act of "hackery." It's an act of prudence.

KING: I don't know. . . . I've always been sort of working in this field. But I was really surprised when New American Library bought *Carrie* for enough money to put me over the top, to be able to stop teaching and everything. And I know how that sale developed, but I still don't understand why it developed the way it did. There was a guy named Bob Tanner who was then president of New English Library, and Doubleday had the book in hand, and they agreed to publish it, and they didn't want to sell the paperback rights right off. They expected to have an auction on that, and they had hoped to realize $80,000 on the paperback.

And Tanner got hold of it because they were selling foreign rights, and he was in New York and was doing business with Doubleday. And Bob Banker, who is Doubleday's subsidiary rights guy, said, "Here's a book that we're publishing and we're high on"—which is standard; they say they're high on the dog book of the month and all this—he took it back and read it in his hotel room. In one night. And he did something that was terribly unethical: he called up his people at New American Library—the parent company in New York—and he slipped Elaine Koster a copy under the table. And she read it and *she* flipped for it, for whatever reasons of her own, and that's where the mystery is. But she called up Banker and said, "Look, we'll pay $400,000 for this book. We want it." And he said, "I would consider that a preemptive bid, and I would accept it. But—if you waited until the auction, you can get it cheaper." And she said, "I'm not convinced of that," and so they went ahead with the deal!

Q: Steve, before you made it, when your early novels were still being rejected and you were just starting to sell stories regularly, how was it that you kept going?

KING: Two reasons. Number one: you think you can do it. You think you have the talent to go over the top and earn your living that way. In a way, you feel that's what God meant you to do, you know? You don't feel satisfied with what you're doing because you know that's not what you were meant to do, you know? I won't say I've led a grim life, but it was—and still is—sort of a humdrum life. It isn't any big deal. I don't go out and ride around in a limousine, sniff cocaine with a babe on each arm. And neither does Peter—you've probably changed a few diapers and I know you get up at six o'clock every other day with the baby. But it's *fun*. You can go and get away from all that shit. And it's escapism. It's the same reason why people watch TV. But this is like "mind TV" or "mind movies."

STRAUB: That's right. There are really two aspects, and they're contradictory. One is the enormous fun, and anybody who is a writer does it because that's what he likes to do. You enjoy it. But there is also the unutterable tedium of it, and I don't think most people can take it.

KING: They can't, man.

STRAUB: When people say, "Gee, I wish I could do what you do..." You know? I wouldn't wish it on anyone, because you spend most of your life alone in a room. And that's hard to adjust to at first, but you *do* adjust to it.

KING: There was a guy who wanted me to look at a book he'd written when I was living in Bridgeton. He was a judge in Maine, but earlier in his life he'd spent time in jail for transporting stolen vehicles across state lines and forging checks, and along the way he'd gotten Jesus in prison, and he had homosexual experiences, and all this. He had a story to tell, but it wasn't told well. It was really sort of... flat. And to me, I thought this was an insult, but he said, "Boy, I wish I had some glue on the seat of my pants like you do. But I'm a kind of get-up-and-go-to-it sort of guy and I just can't sit down that long!"

STRAUB: He was too good to be a writer!

KING: He was too good to be a writer!

STRAUB: There really must be a love of just working the language. A delight in making sentences. There's a wonderful character in this Philip Roth novel that I enjoyed very much, *The Ghost Writer*, and there's this character who's an old writer and he says, "I get up in the morning and I write a sentence. And then I turn the sentence around. Then I turn it around the other way again, and then I turn it inside out." And you really have to like doing that! That's essential, that's the nuts and bolts. You really have to get a deep joy out of writing itself. And out of other people's writing, too.

KING: The other thing that was always in play with me was I was convinced—deeply convinced—that somewhere deep inside me was a money machine waiting to be turned on. And that when I found the dials and the combinations, the money would just pour out.

Q: But was there any motivation to write so as to say, "I told you so" to those early critics who didn't share that faith? Who thought you were never going to make it?

KING: Well... a little bit of that. But, really, not that much. It was never a question of I felt I had anything to prove to anybody else. But, in a way, with those early novels I felt like a guy who was plugging quarters in the machine with the big jackpot. And yanking it down. And at first they were coming up all wrong. Then with the book before *Carrie*, I felt I got two bars and a lemon; then with *Carrie*, bars across the board—and the money poured out. But the thing is, I was never convinced that I was going to run out of quarters to plug into the machine. My feeling was, I could stand there forever until it hit. There was never really any doubt in my own mind. A couple of times I felt like I was pursuing a fool's dream or something like that, but they were rare. They were moments of real depression. . . .

Q: We know that Doubleday was your first hardcover publisher, and now you're with Viking—why did you go with Doubleday originally?

KING: I went to Doubleday because they are a book *factory*. My feeling about that was, if I was going to get published, they would be the ones to do it because they publish *everything*. They publish across the board. Somebody was pointing out to me the other day—not a Doubleday person—that it's the only publisher in New York where the book enters at point A and exits at point Z and it never leaves the house. It isn't jobbed off to Brattleboro, Vermont, to be printed or anything. Doubleday has their own presses, they have a book club—the Literary Guild—they have *everything*.

And at the same time, they originally enforced this fifty-fifty paperback split, which is why I finally left. The idea is that if the paperback sale is $100,000, they get fifty and I get fifty. And I think that 50 percent, when it's cut right down the line on paperback royalties and everything else, is an awful lot to pay for what is essentially an agent's fee. I left them because of that. But also, when they get that paperback money, they've got a bird in the hand, and they don't want to spend it back and go for two in the bush.

I mean, with *Carrie*, even after Doubleday was assured of $200,000 income that was going to just pour in for essentially saying, "Yes, we will publish this book," they went to New American Library and said, "We're going to advertise this, and you're going to kick in on the advertising—aren't you?" And New American Library said yes, and so most of the advertising on *Carrie*—the hardcover—was financed by the paperback.

Q: There's no denying that NAL has bent over backward in getting you in the front of the stores instead of buried somewhere inside.

KING: You see, that may be the essential point: New American Library busted their asses on *Carrie*, and the reason they busted their asses is that they had a $400,000 investment in that book. You know how much Doubleday had put in for an initial investment in *Carrie?* Two thousand, five hundred dollars.

STRAUB: I was going to guess $1,500.

KING: That's the nature of that beast, you know, where you have to prime the pump with so much money before you get anywhere.

STRAUB: You bet.

Q: How do you feel about the current state of the horror film?

KING: The thing that's amazing about the films is that there are as many good ones as there are! You wouldn't think there would be; there's such a tendency to play safe, isn't there?

Q: But isn't that what Stanley Kubrick did with *The Shining?* He went with the bankable stars like Jack Nicholson rather than the right actors to interpret the characters you had created.

KING: That's the only place that Kubrick falls down, really, because he's not very good at casting.

Q: But doesn't it bother you that Hollywood is still turning out so many terrible films, à la *Prophecy?*

KING: What bothers me is that Paramount or whoever can give John Frankenheimer $12 million to make a picture that looks like it was made for $500,000. It was not just a turkey, Peter, it *looked* cheap. But I saw it three times. The reason I liked *Prophecy* was because it looked so cheap; there was something about that that appealed to me. If you love horror movies, you've got to have a love for pure shit!

This is not an aspersion on anybody that's in this company, but you turn into the kind of person who will watch *Attack of the Crab Monsters* four times. And you know how shitty it is, but there's something in that very shittiness that appeals to you. Which doesn't mean you don't want to do better. But that's why I liked *Prophecy*, because everything about it was wrong. And, boy, I loved that old monster—you knew it was just a guy in a grizzly bear suit with a big snout. My kids loved it!

Q: What horror novels have you two read lately that have worked for you?

KING: Actually, I've read a couple of good ones in the last year or so, which is rare. There's a book by Anne River Siddons called *The House Next Door*. It's a haunted house, but it's a *new* house—that's the gimmick. It's a house that's just been built. And Siddons is a Southerner, and she's got a way of getting really, really nasty about these things, like

Flannery O'Conner. There's this one guy who's very proud of his masculinity, and the house makes him sort of sexually hot for this other guy, and everybody's at this party, and open this door and these two people are making love! And the guy later—*pow!*—blows his brains out. Then there's a couple who've lost their teenage son in Vietnam and who buy the house after the first group vacate. And they start to see their son on the TV saying, "I'm still alive! I'm rotting in the jungle—why did you leave me?!" It's nasty; it's a nasty book. A *nasty book!!!*

STRAUB: I read a lot. I read when I brush my teeth. I'd read in the shower if I could.

KING: Listen, hey—you want to hear something really gross? You've heard of people who read when they go into the crapper—I read when I take a piss!

STRAUB: I do too! I do too!

KING: And I read when I brush my teeth, too.

Q: Well, I've got my headline for this interview! Seriously though, does it bother you when your fans seem to be upset at the way your novels have been adapted to the screen, as if in some way you were still responsible for the way they turned out cinematically?

KING: I'm getting to the point now where I'm starting to get actively pissed when somebody walks up to me and says, "You know, they ruined *Carrie*." And I say, "They did?" And they say, "Yeah—the town, it blows up in the novel, it goes up in flames." And I say, "Hey—Paul Monash was lucky to get that picture made at all." He went to United Artists—it was like the third or fourth place he had gone—they had told him no soap at Paramount, they told him no soap at Warner Bros. and a couple of other places that he went. And finally UA said yes, and we'll give you a shoestring budget—I think it was $2 million or something like that. And that director Brian De Palma got to make the picture at all—I mean, how can you blow up a whole town with a budget of $2 million?! These days it probably costs $50,000, $60,000 just to have somebody fall down a flight of stairs!

Q: Any particular horror films that have struck a nerve in your life? With *Dead of Night* perhaps as one example?

KING: I'm thinking about *Dead of Night*. I saw that at the World Fantasy Convention last year, and it just didn't affect me. I liked *Wait Until Dark*. It's not a horror movie at all, but....

1980 *World Fantasy Convention, Baltimore, Maryland*

Q: Steve, would it be fair to say you've been writing adaptations of your own works because you've been dissatisfied with the results of other screenwriters you've dealt with to date?

KING: No, that wouldn't be fair at all. It's done because sometimes it's fun, and because I want to see what that's like. And a lot of times I felt like a high school kid who is almost getting laid but not quite. Like when you're a high school kid, and you say to yourself—if you're a boy!—you say that one of the major factors working in wanting to get laid is that once you do it, you don't have to worry about *worrying* about it anymore.... And I sometimes think that if I could get a screenplay that was actually produced—whether it was good or bad or indifferent—then I could say, "Yes, I *am* capable of doing that. I don't have to worry about that anymore!" There are some other things I'd like to do, and ultimately I think I'd like to try to direct. At least once. I might make an awful mess of it, but....

Q: Could you tell us the origins behind your nonfiction book *Danse Macabre?*

KING: Sure. There was quite a bit of research involved in it, but I don't think it shows in the book a lot! That is to say, hopefully it shows in the sense that the facts are right, the facts are straight. Bill Thompson, who edited the first five novels that I did—*Carrie* through *The Stand*—went to Everest House. He called me up later and said, "Do you want to do a book about horror in movies and on TV and radio and all this stuff over the last thirty years or so?" and I said, "No." And he said, "How many times have you been asked, 'Why do you write that stuff?'" And I said, "Billions." He said, "How many times have you been asked, 'Why do people read that stuff?'" And I said, "Billions." He said, "Write this book. And whenever anybody asks you those questions, you can just say, 'I wrote this book.' And then you'll sell books and never have to answer those questions again!" So I said, "Okay, I'll write the book." I got into it in a very casual way and found it very difficult to write.

Q: Anything about yourself, any autobiographical material?

KING: It's got some autobiography in it, because in discussions like this, they always want to go back to Freud: they want to know what your childhood was like....

STRAUB: Yeah! In fact, sometimes they say, "Didn't you have a really rotten childhood? You *must* have had a rotten childhood!"

KING: I told a story—this is in the book—at a convention, a mystery convention. And we were on a panel about fear. There was myself, and there was Robert Morasco, who did *Burnt Offerings*, and there was Janet Jeppson, who is Isaac Asimov's wife and who is also a psychiatrist, a clinical psychiatrist. So you know why she was there. And that shows where they came from, when they set that panel up.

Somebody in the audience said, "Did anything ever happen to you in your childhood that was really horrible?" And I told a story that I thought would satisfy them. I mean, it isn't anything *I* remember, it's something my mother told me. She said I was out playing one day with this friend of mine. I was about four. I came home, deadly pale, and I'd peed in my pants. And I didn't want to talk. She asked me what happened, but I went upstairs and closed the door and stayed in my room all afternoon. She found out that night that this kid I had been playing with had been run over by a train, okay? I can remember her telling me that they picked up the pieces in a basket. A wicker basket.

I don't remember anything about it; the chances are very good that by that time he had wandered off on his own somewhere and that I wasn't anywhere around. There's a small chance that maybe I *did* see it happen, maybe the kid chased his ball onto the tracks or something. So I told this story and said, "I don't remember it at all," and immediately what Janet Jeppson said was, "And you've been writing about it ever since!" The whole audience applauded—(*claps hands together*)—because they want to believe that you're twisted!

Q: Well, supposedly Robert E. Howard was all messed up psychologically, and so was H. P. Lovecraft.

KING: Somebody almost hit me about that last night; some guy cornered me in the hall. He was drunk—

STRAUB: You defending Lovecraft!

Q: Well, my point is, are people still disappointed to find that you aren't a slobbering monster dressed always in black?

STRAUB: Oh, yes! Always! Then people say, "You look surprisingly normal. What's a guy who looks like you doing going around writing books like this?"

Q: But it would seem to me that you're slighted either way: first because you both don't appear to follow the cliché of what a horror writer should look like, and then because you appear too "normal" to be a genuine horror writer. It's as if the public really wants you to run around in a black cape acting crazy.

STRAUB: Yeah—absolutely nuts.

KING: But these things... it's odd that it should work that way. One of the things that psychiatry—the Freudian brand—is supposed to do is allow you to open lines of communication from your subconscious to the outside. So, on the one hand, we say that psychiatry allows us to talk about our innermost fears, and that's wonderful, it helps you to get "normal." But if you do what Peter and I do, you *must* be weird because those channels are open. If they were closed, people would say you're normal because you can't talk about your fears. You're all fucked up. Situation normal, all fucked up.

STRAUB: On the other hand, there's probably a great deal of truth to the proposition that books like this come out of conflicts which are imperfectly resolved. And I suppose these conflicts—if we presuppose their existence—are things that we actually are not aware of, but they seek their resolution in our books. I think it would be disastrous to be analyzed! I would never want to be analyzed! It would be like being taken apart and polished up, and I don't think the machine would work as well. You really want to protect those problems.

KING: That, for somebody like me, is what's so frightening about what's happened to somebody like Ray Bradbury. I read his new collection, *The Stories of Ray Bradbury*, because I reviewed it. And basically what happened is, you begin with someone who's totally—apparently—fucked up, if he had these imperfectly resolved conflicts, and I think he did. Little by little he works them out, and his fiction ultimately becomes very boring.

STRAUB: In general, I think one of the most satisfactory things of writing novels is that you do improve, and as you get older, you do tend to get better.

KING: Yeah.

STRAUB: And I can't see that kind of banality happening to Steve. And I can't see it happening to me, either.

KING: No, I don't believe so, either. One of the things that has comforted me about my own work is that, in almost all cases, I've begun with a premise that was really black. And a more pleasant resolution has forced itself upon that structure. Like in *'Salem's Lot*, I was convinced that everybody was going to die. That's what I wanted to happen in that book. But it didn't, I didn't try to monkey with the fact because I knew in the end that it was right that they not all die.

STRAUB: Oh, of course! It would have been disastrous if they all died.

KING: Yeah, I think so. So that's okay, I think. It works both ways.

STRAUB: However, I think part of what our work is trying to do is to celebrate aspects of humanity which are worth celebrating. Courage. Gallantry. Humor and steadfastness. These things ought to be celebrated.

KING: It's the only place you can write anymore, it seems to me, where you can still deal with romantic notions and not seem impossibly corny. You still have to be really careful, though, or people will laugh. At the end of *Ghost Story*, you know, there's a scene that's almost transcendental. When he goes into the ocean and everything becomes love, everything is bright. Everything is clear. It's wonderful! It gives you goosebumps. It's beautiful. And if it was in another book, you'd just go, "Ah, sure! Right!" But it works there. You never know.

Q: How important is it for you to really get under a reader's skin? To really get close to the actual fears someone may have?

STRAUB: That's an important part of the job. You are supposed to burrow under the reader's skin. And unsettle them. Steven sometimes uses the word "hurt," which is a wonderful word, in a way, because it sounds so violent! That you want to hurt these readers. But at the same time you don't want to hurt them too badly—I mean, you *do* want to hurt them very badly at a couple points, but I don't think you want to leave them that way.

KING: No, not really. Which is one of the things about *Pet Sematary* that I don't like.

Q: Critics are now reading all sorts of things into your work. Have there been some "underlying meanings" purposely placed in your work which readers might have missed along the way?

STRAUB: Well, especially in the case of reviewers. People sometimes construct meanings that I had never seen and never intended. In a way it's interesting, and I don't mind it at all. They can make elaborate structures, and when I come to meet them, I look like an absolute idiot because that stuff has never crossed my mind. But very rarely do people actually fasten on what I thought of as the center of a book.

KING: I got a letter from David Morrell, the guy who did *First Blood* and some other novels. I'm going to do a speaking engagement with him because that way we can drink across Iowa and all the rest, which is a small price to pay. But he was talking about *Firestarter,* and he said he enjoyed "the green motif" that ran through it. And I had not planned that, that wasn't anything that even crossed my mind. For instance, an editor at Viking enjoyed the thing with Charlie McGee and Rainbird that's kind of unstated—to me, at least, it was—an unstated erotic thing with her and Rainbird all through it. She has a dream where she's riding naked on a horse, and there's a fire, and Rainbird's up ahead and all the rest. And nobody's mentioned *that* to me at all! I loved it, and I didn't want to go any farther with it because there's no sex in the book except for that. And that seems to me to be very powerful sex because it *is* unstated. It's just there, and if nobody notices it, I don't care. I noticed it.

Q: That's true. It seemed to me that Rainbird was seeking some kind of "terminal orgasm" with Charlie. Anyway, it's obvious that the vast majority of your short stories deal with horror in supernatural, rather than psychological, terms. Any reason for this preference? "The Man Who Loved Flowers" is one of the very few stories that fall into the latter category.

KING: I like to make stuff up. There's a scene in *Shadowland*—it's my favorite single moment—where this guy looks up from an examination and there's this pencil floating in the air, and Delmar Nightingale sees it and snatches it away because he doesn't want anyone else to see it. But that's the essence of the attraction the supernatural story has for me: that pencil just floating there in the air. It's like those Magritte paintings where trains are coming out of the fireplaces, Dali paintings where clocks are lying over branches. In "The Mist," for instance, the great attraction in a story like that to me was I really don't *care* what causes it or anything else. It's the idea of that train coming out of the fireplace. The familiar juxtaposed with the unusual and the strange. That, to me, is the attraction. The psychological stories just seem…nastier, somehow.

In fact, I've got a crime story in the December 1980 *Ellery Queen's.* But it was a lot better crime story before they bowdlerized it! In some ways I wish I had just withdrawn it, there was no need of it. It's a story called "The Wedding Gig," and it's about a fat Irish girl who gets married to a very skinny Italian. The narrator of the story is the leader of a small jazz combo, and they play at the wedding reception. And the thing that made the story play was that the piano player in the jazz combo is Black, and everybody called him "boy," or they called him "spade" or "nigger."

But they cut all the pejoratives out of it! They wouldn't let anybody be called a "mick" or a "wop" or anything like that either. I let them do it, and I wish I hadn't now, I guess. But they *were* used in the time period. And the other thing about that kind of story is you get to talk like Cornell Woolrich, where somebody like that can talk about "hoods" or "gats" or "molls." There's a line in the story about these hoods staggering about the wedding reception hall "with Sweet Caporals pasted in their mugs." To be able to write a line like that is incredible.

Q: It seems that Charles Beaumont, one of my personal influences, has always been one of the great unsung horror and fantasy writers. What did you think of him?

KING: I think he was great. I think he was wonderful, and I think—if he had lived—he would have been just an amazing writer. I just wish I had gotten to meet him sometime. I think he was amazing, wonderful. *The Magic Man* and *Night Ride* and all that stuff. It was good.

Q: Since you must read horror as much as you write it, is there anyone out there who is still capable of giving you a chill or two?

STRAUB: There's only one place I can go. And that's my buddy here. But most of it isn't; most of it I find is so hamfisted and unsubtle and badly written that I really have a lot of trouble reading it. That's not the case with Stephen King, anyway.

KING: Well, I like Peter's books better than anyone else, so I guess I'm stuck with that. I read a lot of horror novels, but I don't get a *frisson* from too many of them. Every now and then I get a book that scares me, that is not supposed to be "in the genre"—at least it *says* it's not in the genre. But I usually just go to a movie. It's easier to get scared in a movie.

STRAUB: Yeah, it's easier to get scared in a movie. But I have a hunch that what I said was too harsh. Like Steve, I'm sent a lot of galleys, and I don't have time to read about half of them, but sometimes when you read those galleys, you find something that is very, very good by some young guy who is writing his first novel, probably. And I don't think I've ever been *scared* by one of those books, but I've certainly read a couple that I liked a lot. There's a guy named Jonathan Carroll who wrote this book called *Land of Laughs*, which I read in galleys and liked very, very much. And it seemed to me that he has a real talent that is going to grow. But the reason I'm not scared when I read these things is that I'm too conscious of the technique. Because I know what he's doing—I just want to see how well he can dance.

KING: Yeah!

STRAUB: Which is not to say I'm immune to shocks. But I think, really, that if you think about that kind of thing all day long, you're more open to fear, you're more open to shock.

KING: But good writing in itself is a pleasure, and it can seduce you into the story. I'm not very concerned with style or anything like that, but I *am* concerned with the balance. Language should have a balance, and it should be a balance the reader can feel and get into and feel a sort of rhythm to the language as it moves along. The language should be able to carry you into the story. And that's *it*. Because if the reader is seduced into the story, then it carries him away.

Q: Speaking of language, should the horror writer not only seduce the reader but terrorize or enrage him as well?

STRAUB: Not as far as I'm concerned. As far as I'm concerned, it does not. If you mean to fling an outrage in the public's face? No—I can't find any echoes there. That's not what I'm trying to do. It's not the same as scaring someone, because we definitely do want to scare. But gross-outs? I'm not interested in that.

KING: Oh, I am!

STRAUB: You are?

KING: I *like* gross-outs. But every time I've done it—and I have had that impulse to do it—unerringly, an editor has cut that from the book. Every time! There was a scene in *'Salem's Lot* with rats in the basement. And there have been rats in other things—one of the stories that was in *Cavalier*. And, by God, when they printed it in *Night Shift*, they cut that part right out! They cut that part right out of the story!

Q: There's a scene in the film version of *'Salem's Lot* where the young hero is shown to be "monster-crazy." At least in the sense that his room is filled with monster models, posters, and so forth. A lot of people, including myself, went through that phase as kids. Was your room anything like that when you were that character's age?

KING: No. I think maybe I had an Aurora model werewolf at one time that I put together, but that was all. I wanted to try to set up a situation where we would be able to believe in the kid dealing with this. I knew that there were kids who were—and are—big monster freaks. You know, about the only thing that still amazes me about Forry Ackerman's *Famous Monsters of Filmland* is the letters page. And they have something that says: "Wanted—More Readers Like Sean Beatty of Camden, New

Jersey!!" And there'll be a picture of some smiling, beautiful little boy. They always look beautiful, and you think to yourself, "Here's this kid, and he's wild about monsters. But he doesn't *look* like he should be wild about monsters."

I got a couple of Polaroids from a nine-year-old in the mail the other day. The kid had read *'Salem's Lot*, and he sent two Polaroids. One was of himself, this kind of chubby little blond kid with short hair. And the other one said, "Me as a Night Monster with a snake on my arm." It was the same chubby little kid—only he had a rubber snake on his arm. That's all.

STRAUB: That's wonderful!

KING: But in his head, he *was* the monster; he was really scary.

Q: Peter, did you go through any similar phases growing up?

STRAUB: I didn't surround myself with the accouterments of monsterdom, but as a kid I certainly read those horror comics, those E. C. Comics that were so awful that my parents really objected to these kind of things! But I thought there was some kind of marvelousness to them. But I didn't have stuff like that on the wall....

KING: You said on *The Dick Cavett Show* that your imagination was powerful enough that you had to put down *The Rats in the Walls* once or twice. It was in that big collection....

STRAUB: Did I? Oh...the *Great Tales of Horror and the Supernatural*. Yeah, it was very scary. That was a great one. And there was one that had something to do with cancer where these awful, wormy, white sluggy creatures flowed down a staircase and into a son's room, and two years later he died of cancer.

KING: *Holy Shit!* Isn't that awful! I don't remember that one—I've blocked that one out! Wow!

STRAUB: I remember the Arthur Machen story, "The Great God Pan," and that really affected me.

KING: Yeah, me too.

STRAUB: In fact, I cribbed from it unmercifully in *Ghost Story*.

KING: Oh, that's an amazing story. That's just a *good* one.

Q: How do either of you feel about the rash of recent slasher films in which seemingly only defenseless women are the victims? The media is making a lot of this, and since most of these slasher films are typically lumped in with all other horror films, the entire genre has been taking something of a bad rap lately.

KING: I think we have, but I don't think anybody points the finger at either one of us with any real authority. Because neither one of us have ever treated women in that stereotypical fashion. Peter, for instance, writes the most well-rounded female characters of just about anybody in popular fiction. But I think a lot of this has always been there and will continue to be there. Peter was talking about imperfectly resolved conflicts, and I think that a lot of what this comes from is imperfectly resolved sexual conflicts. And it's involved with sex as a power trip rather than sex as a manifestation of love, where a man and a woman stand on pretty much equal ground, and each has something to give to the other. It's some kind of imperfectly realized conception of where sex is in those relationships.

Q: David Cronenberg's films certainly like to deal with a primal fear of sex, especially *They Came From Within*.

KING: I liked *Rabid* better. I liked *Rabid* and *The Brood* better than *They Came From Within*. There's something about that idea, played off against Marilyn Chambers, who seemed very vulnerable and touching in that film... it was a good combination.

Q: I was wondering if we could just get a little into your work habits? What's a typical work day for you both?

STRAUB: Well, in my case it's what I do; it's my job. And I do it in a way people do jobs. I try and start in the morning. I suppose my usual writing day is from about eleven to about six. But if I am "warmed up," and it's getting toward the end of a book—and I'm writing in my head all the time—then I might write to very late at night. But in general, it's just like, "Daddy's going to the office," and then Daddy comes home.

KING: I start at about eight-thirty—I try and get out and walk two or three miles first—and start to "write" as I'm walking around.

STRAUB: Walking is so wonderful for that. I don't know why, but it's just magical.

KING: Yeah. And you see things. A lot of times I'll see things while I'm walking that will turn up later that day at some point in my work. Not as a major thing, but I'll come back and have a big glass of ice water, and then I'll write from, say, eight-thirty until eleven o'clock. Then I'll stop, and then for the rest of that day and that night I'll go in there with two quarts of beer and rewrite for about two and a half hours. So I work maybe five hours a day.

STRAUB: That's about what I do....

Q: But you don't let the work sit there—you go back at night and rewrite what you've just done in the morning?

KING: No. I always let it sit—the rewrite that I do is always on something else. What I'm working on in the morning is what I'm *working* on. The other material that I'm rewriting, that's a different function altogether for me. That's a very—"mechanical" is the wrong word—but it's a nuts-and-bolts kind of operation. You get down there...it's like adjusting the carburetor or something to make it right. That's what you do. But I always like to drink beer with that because it's fun, and it's not as demanding of something in me that says in the morning when I sit down, "I'm really working!"

STRAUB: "Invent!" Get in there and invent—work!

Q: Okay, so when the muse tells you to go "invent," do either of you need a special room or setting in which to get your creative gears turning?

KING: Both Peter and I have our special rooms.

STRAUB: Yes, we have our rooms, but that's not what triggers it off—because if we were stuck on a boat, we'd write on the boat.

KING: Maybe not as well!...

STRAUB: But it's internalized—there's an internal lightning bolt or something that one is very grateful for. It just comes up and slams on the brain!...You set up this little universe, and you order it just the way you want it, and then you get hot.

KING: Yeah.

Q: I'm sure you're aware that when it was published, more than one review of *Firestarter* compared it to an earlier novel by John Farris, *The Fury*. Would you care to respond?

KING: Sure. I did read that—but one of the things that happened before that was we had set a price tag on the movie rights for *Firestarter* for $1 million, and that was supercool. Then I heard that producer Zanuck and Brown were close to buying it, and then the next thing I heard was that Zanuck and Brown were in a screening room with 20th Century-Fox watching Brian De Palma's film version of *The Fury*. And I said, "Uh-oh, this is not going to happen." Well, basically, the telling of the tale is this: *Carrie* came, and then *The Fury* came, which is a lot like *Carrie*, and then *Firestarter* came. And to me, I saw a relationship between *Carrie* and *Firestarter*, but I never thought of *The Fury* in the course of writing my book, although I liked the original novel. I didn't care for the film *The Fury* very much at all.

Q: But the overall critical reaction to *Firestarter* was favorable?

KING: I don't know if *The Shining* legitimized me to a degree, but I thought the reaction to *Firestarter* in the critical press would be terrible. And it was quite good. I got a good review in *Time*, a bad review in *Newsweek*, a pretty good one in *The New York Times*. *The Washington Post* reviewed it under the headline, "Stricken à la King: You can't win 'em all, you know!"

With Stanley Wiater and Roger Anker

1984 World Fantasy Convention, Ottawa, Canada

Q: How did the idea of collaborating on *The Talisman* first come about? We've been hearing about it for years.

STRAUB: The first time we talked about it was at my house.

KING: Yeah, that's right! In Crouch End, England. The night that Bing Crosby died. It was a question mostly of talking about it and deciding that we'd like to try it—

STRAUB: —and when we could do it. We talked about *The Talisman* for a long time before we got started—for years, actually—and a couple of times we got together and talked about the events. We sort of had the basic notion from a dream that Steve had. Then we thought of the "Territories," and after a long, long time, we made up an outline. We had an *extremely* long outline. Someday, people ought to read this weird outline because it's not much like the book.

KING: No, it's really not.

STRAUB: And then one day Steve came to my house so we could actually start it. And we wrote, I think, about the first two chapters—more or less—together. And then we just sent them back and forth via modems of our word processors until the ending when I went to Steve's house and we wrote the last couple of chapters there.

KING: It isn't a horror novel per se—it's a fantasy. It's gross in places and it is horrifying in places. But on the whole it has a tone that is a little bit delirious and sort of crackbrained, and I think it's a lot of fun! And I think that coming off *Floating Dragon* and *Pet Sematary*, it's cheered our little buns up. It's got a very recognizable voice, but you just don't quite know which voice it is that's talking. Wouldn't you say that's true?

STRAUB: Yes. I think that in 99 percent of the cases of the people that will read it, that will be true. Steve or I can hardly tell who wrote what. I think that just sort of happened—we started off trying to write a kind of neutral style and then we just gave that up and let ourselves rip. But somehow it did make a kind of neutral style, here and there. There are certain things that Steve does that show up, and there are certain things I do. . . . Then readers might be able to pick up a part and say, "Ah, I know which one wrote this." But normally, it's mysterious—because the book did kind of find its own peculiar voice, which isn't the voice of either of us.

KING: I'll tell you what the thing is: Peter and I are both professional writers. We do this for a living, and a lot of times that gets overlooked, because there's a tendency to want to find art or try to find some kind of a holy divination or something like that. But I think in a lot of cases we realized that we're doing something like making a coat, and we were careful to try and dye all the pieces so they were pretty much the same. There are places where you can pick things out; on the other hand, I can point out a number of places in the book where it looks as though you might sense that I had written it, and yet I know damn well that Peter wrote it.

STRAUB: In fact, the book is full of little tricks between us where we're trying to fool the reader into thinking that the other guy wrote it. And if you come along something you think is a dead giveaway, the thing with a dead giveaway is a trick.

KING: *Kirkus Reviews* mentioned parts that were "typically King" and "typically Straub," but they very carefully did not provide any passages.

Q: Did you ever reach a point in the narrative where one of you would say to the other, "This is your kind of scene, your kind of setup. Why don't you handle it?"

STRAUB: I think that happened from time to time. If there was something that I knew that Steve was really trying to do.

KING: There are a couple of things in the book that I pretty consciously tried to arrange when we were parceling out the outlines so that Peter would write them, because I knew that he would do a better job.

Q: You were working on this collaboration through modems on your word processors while you were still doing separate novels?

STRAUB: Well, I wasn't doing anything—*he* was doing other things.

KING: I was doing a whole bunch of stuff....

Q: We know you worked a long time on this project.

STRAUB: A *long* time. I think almost two years. We had little vacations, every now and then, but not many.

KING: And in terms of actual hours and time spent on the book, I mean, it's just staggering. Nothing I ever did before touches it—and I hope nothing ever does again!

STRAUB: Amen! Yeah, it was a lot of work.

KING: And there were times when Peter would be working and I'd feel, "Well, there, I don't have to worry about *that* for a while," but I'd still be thinking about it.

Q: By actually writing together, do you feel you've learned from one another?

STRAUB: I feel I've learned a lot from Steve....

Q: Has working together affected your style of writing?

KING: Just my personality.

STRAUB: It wrecked my personality! But in a way, my instincts about storytelling were broadened up, as if some rough spots were knocked off of it because of the closeness I had to the way Steve works. Which is extremely narrative, extremely well-informed.

KING: And I learned a lot about style. I can't remember ever writing anything and being so conscious about what I was writing. I mean, it's a little bit like when you know you're going to dinner with somebody who's got manners and your mother says, "Look, if you eat like a barbarian, people are going to know it."

STRAUB: I think we're both supposed to be pretty barbarous now!

KING: No, no, I don't think so.

Q: To segue into the obvious, what are Hollywood's present plans for *The Talisman?*

STRAUB: Well now, this is a long story. But to tell you the short form: Universal has bought it—after intense and lengthy negotiations—for Steven Spielberg. Because Spielberg is apparently now going to direct it and has commissioned a script.

KING: One of the reasons the negotiations for the film with Universal were as long and arduous as they were—and I'm sure that even Steven Spielberg would agree it was true, so I don't have any problem with you printing it—is that Spielberg has expressed interest in things as diverse as Michael Jackson in *Peter Pan, Schindler's List,* remaking *A Guy Named Joe.* He's like a kid in a candy store at this point in his career. So he's got a number of different projects, and Universal's view is Steve is a money machine.

But at the same time, how much do we want to pile into development when, if he touches it, it may turn to gold, but if somebody else touches it, it may turn to shit? So, finally, the deal was made. And I guess one of the reasons it was made was because Spielberg is extremely determined. He was determined to have his own way about this, and I was delighted he got his own way—and Peter was delighted he got his own way. And he's involved in a production level, come what may, and what I hear now is that he will probably direct the picture. Which will be good. I think he wants to do something like this.

STRAUB: I think it would be great. We went to California, on that visit that left kind of a sour taste in both our mouths, but we sat down with Spielberg—unfortunately, other people were present—but Spielberg, every now and then, popped up with something that we actually should have thought of.

KING: Yeah—he's very bright.

STRAUB: So he's in tune. Once you do that, you've got the music of the book.

KING: One of the things that really impresses me about him—and I've met Steven three times now and I've talked with him on the phone a half a dozen times—is that he is not a jerk and it's not hype, you know? He is what he is. He is a tremendously talented and tremendously bright guy. And anybody who thinks it can be a fluke—three, four, or five great big movies in a row—it's not. So I'd love to see him direct it, and I think he'd be good.

STRAUB: Yeah.

Q: Would either of you like to have a hand in the screenplay?

KING: I think Peter and I were asked if we would like to be involved in that, and I don't know, Peter can answer for himself. . . .

STRAUB: In fact, I think we shook hands in a taxicab on the vow *not* to. . . .

KING: We did. Yeah. We came back from meeting with the studio executives with all that "Gremlin" shit all over us.

STRAUB: Exactly. On the other hand, I have a hunch that Spielberg is going to keep in touch, and it won't be the typical "hands off, don't bother us, now we know more than you know" attitude you usually get from the studios. That'll be nice, to be included a bit. Because what never occurs to directors or producers is that the writer occasionally can help. And occasionally he can say, "Now don't do this, because that's not going to work." Maybe this time they'll know that.

KING: Or sometimes a writer can suggest a quick way to do something that's bothering the director.

Q: Could you tell us briefly about another long awaited project: Romero's film of *The Stand?*

KING: The screenplay's done. So, we'll see.

Q: The scope of the book would seem to make a four-hour movie version inevitable.

KING: It's down to around two and a half hours. Something like that. It's okay. In terms of budget and time, it's all right. And everything's in there.

Q: Is there a difference in writing fear for film as opposed to writing fear for a book?

KING: It's *worse*. When I'm writing for film I get really nervous. I get all wired up when I'm trying to write a story because I can see everything and I know if I can narrate it, it will ease my mind. But when you write it in a film script, it's like you're playing this game with an audience that you can't even see and can't get to, though you can set it up and everything. I think that it would be fun to direct a horror film, and I'd feel that sense of narration that I don't get when I'm writing a film script, because I feel now like I'm doing a blueprint instead of a picture.

Q: Considering the millions of words you two have published over the past ten years, are you still—

KING: Friends?

Q: —bubbling over with new ideas? And are you still at the stage that the more you do, the better it gets, and so you want to do still more?

STRAUB: Certainly I think Steve and I both have many, many ideas yet. I'm conscious now that I'm in a different stage in my own approach, and maybe working on *The Talisman* had something to do with this. That is, I'm much more level-headed about it and I rewrite and revise much, much more than I ever did before.

KING: It's the word processor, I think.

STRAUB: I don't think so...

KING: I revise—I mean, it's insane how much I revise.

STRAUB: But I think it's also that I've become more conscious of my errors than I used to be, and I can see them much better. Maybe this means I just grew up a little bit as a writer. When I read over a page or four or five pages I wrote during the day, I can see right away the goofy spots and the errors and the dumb passages and the unnecessary parts. And I didn't used to be able to see it that well. The only other changes I feel, right now, is that I'm not very interested in supernatural horror anymore, and I'm not going to write it for a while because I figure that I pretty much did it. I did what I could with that.

Q: But aren't your publishers saying, "Look, you're doing just fine writing chillers. Don't risk it all by changing"?

STRAUB: No. I felt that particular pressure much more strongly several years in the past. And I understand that I have a duty, if I'm going to get large advances like that, to be entertaining and to interject in these books a lot of narrative tension. To tie the reader to the book. So I'm going to continue to do that. But I just don't want to have dead bodies lurching around. I'm a little tired of that.

Q: We hope not too tired. Steve, are your publishers ever afraid that you might someday not want to frighten your readers anymore as well?

KING: No. No, I don't really think so. I do think that it's true that "if we give you enough rope you'll hang yourself." I think now I have enough rope so I can hang myself in Times Square at high noon with three-network coverage. If I told somebody I wanted to rewrite the Bible in common prose, I could probably get six figures for it at this point. And that's the problem—I'm not saying that to be a hot shit or conceited or anything else. But for me, that's the problem.

As far as I'm concerned *It* is my final exam. I can't say anymore about monsters. I don't *have* anything else to say about monsters: I put all the monsters in that book.

But then I never had any interest in horror to begin with. *I never did!* I just wrote all these "horror novels" because that's what came out. I mean, I didn't write it to make money, because, Jesus, when I started and when Peter wrote *Julia*, you couldn't make any money writing this stuff. It's ridiculous—the money came to us, we didn't go to the money! Like *Pet Sematary*—I didn't know what that was going to be, I thought it would be so much fun to write that book, because I didn't know what it was going to be. You just follow it along, and I think that a lot of times my mind goes down this path. . . . The people who like my stuff and the people who like Peter's stuff will come along unless you shortchange them.

STRAUB: Yeah! If I wrote a nice polite little comedy of manners without any narrative tension in it, I'd be asking for trouble, because I would lose a lot of readers. But I have no interest in doing *that*. I wouldn't mind at all writing a big, inventive comedy of manners with tons of narrative tensions in it. Boy, that would be something.

Q: Okay, so you both realize you could sell your laundry lists to the publishers at this point. Don't you ever get tempted to try and get away by selling something that you secretly, personally consider just a "laundry list"? Don't you ever worry about oversaturating the market?

KING: Well, I was worried about it. I guess it was when there were three films in a row and all those tie-in editions. . . .

Q: Some critics were calling it the "King Movie of the Month."

KING: Yeah. And at the same time it was hilarious! I felt like such a fucking star! Then when *Pet Sematary* came out, the result was like the book sold 600,000 copies hardcover trade. There was this huge jump in sales.

STRAUB: Some backlash!

KING: None of the films are real howlers and none of them are real terrible. Some of them come close—I thought that *Firestarter* could have been *Myra Breckinridge* with a push in just the other direction, if there would've been just something else a little bit grotesque added to it. But the thing is, none of them have been really great, either. So I don't think it's had an effect one way or another on our careers.

Q: You have both already achieved an incredible degree of success in your careers—

KING: And I have enjoyed it!

Q: —but do you have any other goals beyond writing? Has this success opened other doors for you?

KING: To be a good husband and a good father. . . to try and stay alive. . . try not to get too fat, try not to drink too much beer. . . I'd love to hit the inside fast ball. . .

STRAUB: Sounds like me!

Q: Peter, what about you?

STRAUB: I don't know. I couldn't tell you. I'd love to be able to play "Cherokee" on the tenor saxophone at a real fast tempo. I'd like to be able to do that!

KING: Guys like me, you know, and I won't say guys like us because I won't presume for Peter, but guys like me, we were duds in high school. . . . Writing has always been it for me. I was just sort of this nerdy kid. I didn't get beat up too much because I was big, played a little football and stuff like that. So mostly I just got this, "King—he's weird. Big glasses. Reads a lot. Big teeth." I've thought about stopping—sometimes it seems to me I could save my life by stopping. Because I'm really compulsive about it. I drive that baby....

STRAUB: I don't want to be a school teacher. I've escaped being a school teacher. I don't want to be an IBM manager, because that's boring. One advantage to this position that we have, is that we can meet people we like, whose work we admire. Steve can hang around with rock and rollers and I can hang out with jazz musicians that I just cherish. Somehow we've got a mysterious access, and they sort of believe in us.

KING: I don't know exactly what it is, but they treat you like maybe you were...smart.

Q: Didn't you purchase a radio station, Steve?

KING: I got a radio station, yeah. We rock a lot. We brought Twisted Sister up to Bangor. Man, did we get hit with an act. Dee Snyder got all the kids to say, "I am one sick motherfucker!" After a while they're all screaming at one another...oh, boy, that Dee Snyder....He's read all my books....

Q: Now if that isn't a dream come true. I read an AP clip on it. It seemed to me that you wanted to make sure that station would always be on the dial, so to make sure, you bought it.

KING: Well, it would have been on the dial, but they were going to go to a different format and play a lot of elevator music. And now we still have rock and roll. It's fun.

Q: Steve, we're always under the impression that writers are supposed to lead some kind of private and sedated lifestyle. Of course, we realize that when you became a best-selling author, you're obviously going to become a little more accessible to the public. Yet you acted in *Creepshow*, and now you've done a television commercial for American Express....

KING: "Do you know me? Instead of saying, 'I wrote *Carrie*,' I carry the American Express card."

Q: Isn't it coming to a point where you'll be recognized whenever you walk down the street? Was this a conscious decision to get your face known as well as your name?...

KING: No, it wasn't. I mean, if only people know—this idea that somehow you have a career planned. But we were sitting around the living room and George said to me, "Do you want to play Jordy Verrill?" Because I did this redneck in *Knightriders*. George has got a certain sense of humor and it tickled him. He thought it would be funny—and so I did Jordy.

I did the American Express commercial...because I thought, "Jesus Christ, that's really flattering. I must have arrived." So I did the commercial. I also did it because I thought it was a chance to do something amusing that was diametrically opposite to Jordy Verrill—sort of a late seventies gay Hugh Hefner! Then, you have to draw a line someplace. The other day these people called me up from some other agency: "Saw your American Express ad. Loved it! You wanna do a Miller Lite ad?"

And I went, "Jesus, Yeah, I *do* want to do a Miller Lite ad—those are really cool!" Then I thought to myself: "You know, you're a *writer*. You do about three more of these things and you can go on Hollywood Squares, for all the reputation that you've got." Not that I've got much of a reputation anyway. But there has to be a point when, before you sell, you say, "I'm not a huckster, a commercial object." So I did the American Express spot and I can't explain why any better than that. But it was not for the money, and it wasn't specifically for the fame so much as it was, I guess, because we get to be such commercial creatures of our time that I started to feel like, in some perverse way, that it was an *honor* to sell their product.

STRAUB: They want you to feel that way.

KING: Well, I *did!*

Q: That's one of the most elaborate setups we've ever seen for a commercial.

KING: They did take after take after take! Boy, I got slammed a couple of good ones by that sliding bookcase—and I had diarrhea that night, so I got slammed in the knee and simultaneously thought I was going to shit in my pants.

STRAUB: Oh, jeez.

Q: Have you two reached a point where you still can stop and say, "No, it's not good enough," and start over, or do you just say, "Yeah, that's good enough to make the grade because my name is on it."

STRAUB: I'm less satisfied than I used to be. I think I work harder to get it right. And I see it as a part of the obligation.

KING: I'll tell you what: it's getting later and I want to get better, because you only get about so many chances to do good work. There's no justification not to at least try to do good work when you make the money. I mean, there are guys who are starving, just about. And they're trying to do good work. Some of them are.

STRAUB: Some of them—some of them don't know what it is.

KING: And that's why they're starving, in some cases.

Q: Do you two feel any responsibility for "double-handedly" raising the public awareness of the horror genre so that it's now far more acceptable—and respectable—than it ever was before?

STRAUB: I think the reason that is, is because we wrote novels that were "horror," but were actually novels and were different from previous horror novels that had been written. And, in a way, kind of redefined what it was. Then others came in and started pushing away at the idea of what a horror novel was, too. And then commercial success gave what we were doing acceptability. Part of it is that we obtained the commercial success because we gave people the horror in a flavor in which they could take it and *believe* in it.

KING: And they were not expected to say, "Well, this is a horror novel so I have to expect all of this junky characterization and unbelievable developments and everything." I think that's what Peter means when he says we ask them to accept it as a novel first. I'm not sure how much we raised the awareness of horror or gave it any kind of a cultural cachet. I'm sure that we allowed a lot of contracts to be signed by a lot of writers, put a lot of money in a lot of pockets, that otherwise wouldn't have gone there. And I think that's a wonderful thing and I'm delighted, because most of the people who are doing it aren't in it for a free ride. They're really serious about it. I think now—and I didn't use to think this way—but I think now that we might actually have a serious place in American literature in a hundred years or so. . . .

STRAUB: In a kind of queer way, yeah. . .

KING: Well, I think that we might first look to people like "Monk" Lewis or Anne Radcliffe, or neogothic revival, or something like that! But maybe we'll still do a lot of good work and people will say, "Hey—they weren't so bad."

STRAUB: And the answer to the other question is, "Yes, every word is autobiographical!"

KING: Peter gave me this manuscript to read, and I brought it down so that I would have something to read on the elevator.

Q: We're surprised you don't read while taking a shower!

KING: My son does that.

STRAUB: Really? That's pretty good. But then you always have one dirty arm!

KING: Yeah, but you just rotate the arm you read with!

CHAPTER SIX

❖

DANCING IN THE DARK

❖

Bugs are bad. Bugs are real bad. Sometimes I think about taking a bite into a big hoagie, you know, and...full of bugs. Imagine that. Isn't that awful? Elevators...airplanes...the dark is a big one. I don't like the dark.

With Bob Spitz (*Penthouse Magazine*)

Q: Considering your reputation as the number one purveyor of horror fiction, how do you feel when you glance at newspaper headlines like "Baby Frozen in Refrigerator" or "Mom Nails Kid to Door"?

KING: Love it, love it! Listen, I can say, "No, I hate that shit. I hate those papers"—and part of me does. But tabloids appeal to everything that is just sleazy in my nature. There must be a lot of it, too, 'cause, man, I open that paper and something jumps out at me on every fucking page. The headlines! Jesus! I mean, "Nun Raped in Brooklyn" and "Mob Puts Out Contract on Killer." Tabloids have gone directly to whatever it is in people that needs to go the worst things in life.

Q: Do you think there's a dark side in our personalities that relates to that kind of horror?

KING: Take the headline, "Baby Nailed to Wall." You say, "I never did that to my kids, although I had the impulse a couple of times." And that's where the horror is born. Not in the fact that somebody nailed a baby to the wall, but that you can remember times when you felt like knocking your kid's head right off his shoulders because he wouldn't shut up. *The Shining* came from my own really aggressive impulses toward my kids. It's a very sorry thing to discover, as a father, that it is possible, for bursts of time, to literally hate your kids and feel that you could kill them. And that's where, on one level, tabloids help us say, "Thank God it isn't me." They're helping people explore the dark limits of human behavior.

Q: Is there anywhere you draw the line about how graphic violent horror should be?

KING: Anything that you can see on the street, at any time, should be in a book. If the situation comes up, you point the reader right at it. That is to say, you shouldn't walk away.

Q: Even if it means leaving too profound an effect on impressionable minds?

KING: In 1957 Arthur Penn made a film called *The Left-Handed Gun*, with Paul Newman. And in that movie Billy the Kid shot a guy who flew backward right out of his boots, and you're left with this image of the western street with one cowboy boot standing there. People started saying, "This is gratuitous violence, this is too much." Whenever anyone says "gratuitous violence," what they mean is that someone showed us what it was really like, what those foot-pounds mean when they translate out of a fucking physics book and into the real world.

For years, in western movies, someone would get shot with a .44 and the gun would go *bam*, and the guy would fall down. Kids went off to World War II who, son of a bitch, thought that was going to happen to them if they got shot. They didn't know that maybe they could get one of their balls shot off or get shot in the guts and never eat anything but poached eggs again. So if you're going to do it, tell the truth, because otherwise you're telling a very dangerous lie.

Q: Even so, you've drawn stiff criticism for the irreverent portrayals of violence in your books.

KING: A lot of critics see blood and say we're turning the country into a bunch of mongrel dogs that are running for blood. What a pile of bullshit that is! As a matter of fact, when you shoot yourself in the mouth, blood and brains and hair splatter all over the place. If that's going to happen, I want to see it. I'm going to wince, it's not going to make me feel good, but I want to see what's there.

Q: Then how do you answer those people who claim that violence begets violence?

KING: You show me the person who says, "King, that stuff you write is just full of gratuitous violence, you're pandering to people's lower tastes, you've got a tabloid mind," and I'll show you someone who doesn't wear a seat belt in their car, because they don't want to think about their fucking teeth going down their throat and aspirating into their lungs. They're the people who, sooner or later, will be like Ronald Reagan; they're going to push that button because they have no conception of what they're doing or that it can really be the end.

Q: Is "the end"—oblivion—something you've personally come to terms with?

KING: I think that this idea about the end of the world is very liberating. It was for me, and I think most people feel the same way. It's the end of all the shit, and you don't have to be afraid anymore, because the worst has already happened.

Q: That makes horror an escape mechanism to sublimate our primal fear.

KING: I think that's very true.

Q: Then why does this generation seem obsessed with terrifying itself?

KING: We're the first generation to have grown up completely in the shadow of the atomic bomb. It seems to me that we are the first generation forced to live almost entirely without romance and forced to find some kind of supernatural outlet for the romantic impulses that are in all of us. This is really sad in a way. Everybody goes out to horror movies, reads horror novels—and it's almost as though we're trying to preview the end.

Q: You're saying our ultimate attraction to horror stems from a creeping paranoia?

KING: I think we are more paranoid, but I don't think that's necessarily an outgrowth of the bomb. I think we have a pretty good reason to be paranoid because of the information flow. More information washes over us than washed over any other generation in history—except for the generation we're raising. In college I became aware that a lot of people are paranoid, and I used to think: "Jesus Christ—*they're all crazy!*" And then the thing about Nixon came out; the man was making tapes in his god-damned office. We find out that Agnew was apparently taking bribes right in the vice-presidential mansion—money being passed across the desk. Jimmy Hoffa is inhabiting a bridge pylon somewhere in New Jersey. And then you say, "Well, we really do need to be paranoid." This flow of information—it makes you very nervous about everything.

Q: Is there a fine line where horror and reality become indistinguishable?

KING: Yes. It's when I'm sitting there with the TV on, reading a book or putting something together, and this voice will say, "We interrupt this program to bring you a special bulletin from CBS News." My pulse rate immediately doubles or triples. Whatever I'm doing is completely forgotten, and I wait to see if Walter Cronkite is going to come on and say, "Well, DEW line reports nuclear ICBMs over the North Pole. Put your head between your legs and kiss your ass goodbye."

Q: Isn't that carrying it to extremes?

KING: Yes, it is. But even so, you think of the times that didn't happen, when you got some other piece of news: when that bulletin came on that Robert Kennedy had been killed in Los Angeles, Martin Luther King had been assassinated, the president shot in Dallas. It changed everything.

Q: So there is a very fine line where horror and reality cross.

KING: Sure there is. And one of the reasons I think I've had some problems with *Cujo* is because people get a little bit worried when they read a book about this woman and kid trapped in a car by a Saint Bernard, and they say, "This could really happen." Then they write me a letter that says, "Gee, I liked your vampire novel ['*Salem's Lot*] better, I liked *The Shining* better, because we know in our hearts that there are no vampires, and we are sure in our hearts that there are no hotels haunted by ghosts that come to life. But a Saint Bernard with a woman and boy in the car, that's something else."

Q: It's almost too realistic a horror to endure, the quintessential nightmare. Is that something you've had problems with in the past?

KING: The review in *The New York Times* about *The Stand* was very downbeat. The [reviewer] didn't like the book at all; he called it *Rosemary's Baby Goes to the Devil* and slammed it off in five paragraphs. One of the things he said was that too many people pee in their pants in this book. Well, when something happens to someone that's really scary and is very startling—that kind of "boo," but it's not "boo," it's something genuinely frightening—most people piss in their pants. I'm sorry if that becomes tiresome after a while. That doesn't change the fact that it happens.

Q: Don't we get enough of that kind of horror on the six o'clock news?

KING: I think the reason we do, and that this stuff is popular and successful, is because we get too much of it. If there is a utilitarian purpose, it's to understand an essentially irrational act. With a lot of horror fiction, it's an effort to observe irrational acts, or terrifying actions, or just to experience that feeling of being out of control.

To be totally out of control is what the best horror movies, in particular, can do to you. And that doesn't imply any conscious flow—to say, "Oh, well, I'm going to see *Friday the 13th* because I'll understand what happened to Sadat"—because it wouldn't work on that level. But on a subconscious level, or even a psychic level, you may be able to say, "Well, here's what I was feeling when I heard that Sadat was shot"—that same kind of helpless revulsion, terror, whatever it is. It's on the screen, and it's controllable—and it's not real. It's an effort to get around those feelings; sometimes it's an effort to want them, and to say, "I can let you out. You can't hurt me."

Q: Considering the influence that works of art wield over the public, are there any people who shouldn't read your books?

KING: I don't think so.

Q: No one ever borrowed a plot point or two to play out their own fantasy?

KING: Well...there's this thing that happened in Boston, where the police and papers called [the murderer] the Carrie Killer. He killed his mother—stuck her to the door with all these kitchen instruments. Obviously he had gotten the idea from Brian De Palma's film; the kitchen implements weren't in my book. But sooner or later there may come a time when some guy will do something and say, "I got the idea from a Stephen King novel." I could say that people like that shouldn't read my books. But if they didn't get an idea from something that I wrote, they would get it from something somebody else wrote.

Q: So there's a chance that terror could, indeed, have a negative influence on someone teetering on the edge.

KING: If he hadn't been the Carrie Killer, he might have stabbed her to death in the shower and then he would have been the Psycho Killer.

Q: What about the kid who blamed *The Catcher in the Rye* for driving him to murder John Lennon?

KING: Same thing there. But I don't feel any responsibility for the nuts and dingdongs of the world any more than any of us can live our lives on the basis of what some crazy person might do. For instance, I can get a bodyguard to walk around with me everywhere—which is not to say that at an autographing session someday, someone might not decide that I'm doing the devil's work and shoot me in the head. We all live with that possibility; that's a part of life.

Q: Do you think people should be allowed to get away with blaming their violent acts on what they read or see?

KING: No, I don't. But the classic case of this is when the kids burned a woman to death with gasoline and then said, "Well, we got the idea from the ABC Movie of the Week"—which was *Fuzz*. It really put the kibosh on TV violence. It was the end of all those series like *Peter Gunn* and *The Untouchables*. But it's still really killing the messenger for the message. If you are telling the truth, then it seems to me that if somebody— some nut—does something based on what you wrote, all you can say is that this nut was too unoriginal to think up his own method of killing somebody, so he had to use what was in the book.

Q: Speaking of TV, how do you feel about the current state of the art?

KING: I think we're seeing the death of established television. It's happening right now. You know, network TV is like this big dinosaur stumbling around. When I was growing up, TV was a dominating factor, at least in my life. Ed Sullivan on Sunday night, *Maverick*, *Sugarfoot*.

Q: Pure entertainment.

KING: Yes. You know, *Route 66* raised the consciousness of every white kid in America. You found out there was a different way to live than taking college courses and getting out and going nine to five. And what have my kids got? *B.J. and the Bear*.

Q: What about television's use as a political instrument?

KING: It can be argued that Kennedy was the last president to be elected pretty much without TV being the overmastering factor. So that once TV began, there were no more good presidents. And every time we elect a new president, we get farther away from real politics and real people and more into the world of guest-of-the-week on *Three's Company*. (*mimics*) "Oh, guess what, Suzanne—the president's coming for dinner. We've got to clean the place up!" And then the president comes in, and he's somebody from Central Casting that you've seen on soap operas, with silver hair. Till, finally, we come to Reagan, where the TV image and the politician meet, and we've got an ex–movie star in the White House who, when he speaks... God! he looks so good, he looks like he's trustworthy. But you look into his eyes for a long time, and (*hums theme from The Twilight Zone*).

Q: Politics runs through your novels almost as much as another King favorite, religion. Is that a particularly horrifying part of your life?

KING: It scared me to death as a kid. I was raised Methodist, and I was scared that I was going to hell. The horror stories that I grew up on were biblical stories. "Lo, the false prophets shall be thrown into the lake of fire!" and "Lo, he shall burn there forever!"—and this kind of thing. They were the best horror stories ever written.

Q: If you had to single out the scariest one of them all...

KING: Lot's wife turns back to look at Sodom and Gomorrah after she was told not to, and she turns into a pillar of salt. I used to pretend I was one of these guys running away and could hear the city burning behind me and the screams from the bolts of fire coming down from heaven—I could feel my head go "Booooom!" Scared the shit out of me. So maybe it's an obvious connection between what I'm trying to do now and what it did to me as a kid. But it's also an effort for me to get around this whole business about religion and death and what comes after death and all the rest of it—and to try to make some decisions for myself.

Q: Have you become more of a skeptic in the process?

KING: No, I'd say I'm probably more religious now than ever in my life. I don't go to church or anything like that. Organized religion is always the same thing: sooner or later, somebody drives a sword through your heart. They cut you up. They put spikes in your eyes. It's always the same; it's never really altered very much.

Q: Is there any aspect of it you find more tolerable?

KING: Everything that I see about organized religion appalls me. Jerry Falwell appalls me on the tube. He amuses me as well, but he mostly just appalls me, because there is a kind of an intransigence there that's almost beyond my ability to comprehend. That is to say, there's no way to engage in a dialogue with Jerry Falwell. Anything that he is doing is right simply because he says it's right—and he's standing there in the middle of the church. I don't see any difference between him and the Reverend Moon. Falwell says that sex books like *Penthouse* should be taken off the lower racks, where little children can look at depravity and barnyard sex acts and words and all this other stuff. Of course, he's standing up there on TV saying this, and never in my life have I ever seen a *Penthouse* magazine down there where three- or four- or five-year-olds could grab it off the shelf. They don't do that. It's a lie. The guy is lying.

Q: Are you on their hit list?

KING: No. I'm well liked by Fundamentalists, and I should be, because my own views are pretty fundamental. But when I see Jerry Falwell get up there on that TV in that $300 suit, I say, "Fuck you! Get off!" I don't know where their money comes from, but I think that if their books could be opened, you might find they top the Mafia as far as the money that comes in is concerned. It's all money, it's all imperialism, it's all America Firsters, it's all a bunch of fascism. They're living off people's fears.

Q: And yet there are people who say you do the same thing.

KING: I don't think that I really prey on people's fears, because people who are fearful don't want to have anything to do with what I write. They don't go to horror movies either. It's like the roller coaster rides at the amusement park. People who ride the roller coaster aren't the people who are afraid of it. They may relish the drop in their stomach or may scream because they are afraid when they are on the ride, but that's a kind of courage in itself. The people who are really afraid are the ones who walk up to me and say, "Gee, I don't read your books. I watch the *Praise The Lord Club*." In other words, the reason that people like Jerry Falwell can afford to say, "I don't listen to my critics" is because the people who are watching him don't listen to his critics. They love him, he loves them—there is basically a religious circle jerk going on here.

Q: How do you feel about the influence organized religion exerts on topics like abortion and gun control?

KING: And the electric chair. They *like* the electric chair.

Q: Where do you stand on capital punishment?

KING: I don't feel very good about it. I can think of isolated cases where I wouldn't feel bad if a person was executed.

Q: Anyone in particular?

KING: Although I'm not a New York State resident, I would feel infinitesimally easier in my mind if Son of Sam were fried, if David Berkowitz were fried. I feel both for and against capital punishment. The same way that I am very much against abortion. I hate the idea. I *do* think it is murder. I think when you kill potential, it's murder. At the same time, what Falwell and some of the others are saying is that we have to legislate this. And the Bible—the supposed word of God—is based very firmly on one thing: free will. And, basically, what these people are saying when they say we've got to outlaw abortion on demand is that we have to outlaw free will. It's an anti-God statement.

Q: They're also very firm on the issue of gun control.

KING: I think that I would like to see permits needed to get any kind of a handgun. You'd have to have your picture taken. You couldn't have any kind of a criminal record or a record of mental illness, beyond having seen a psychiatrist, in the last six years.

Q: Does that mean you favor gun control?

KING: No. I want people to be able to go out and get a shotgun or a rifle if they want to go hunting. I can't see Mark Chapman walking up to John Lennon on the street with a .410 shoved down his pant leg and managing to pull it out, cock it, and shoot the guy. I mean, Jesus Christ! I don't think that we should have a tight, nonbending gun control law in this country, but I think it's time to put some curbs on handguns. You see all those bumper stickers that say: "If guns are outlawed, only outlaws will have guns." Well, that's fine with me.

Q: While we're on the subject of control: why is there very little graphic sex in your books?

KING: Well, there has been some... in *The Stand*, and I think there is some in *Carrie*. But Peter Straub [author of *Ghost Story*] says I never wrote a sex scene because "Stephen hasn't discovered sex yet." Actually, there's sort of an unpleasant sex scene in *Cujo* which shows that Joe Camber fucks the way he eats, the way he deals with everything else: almost machinelike. But one of the reasons that I shy away from sex is that it's such an elemental act, and the physics of it are so familiar to everyone that it is hard to do in a novel way.

Q: But isn't sex a repressed horror for a lot of people?

KING: Yeah. There are all sorts of possibilities there.

Q: If you had to write a horror novel that dealt with your greatest sexual fear, what would it be?

KING: A couple of things. The vagina dentata, the vagina with teeth. A story where you were making love to a woman and it just slammed shut and cut your penis off. That'd do it. I've just completed a book called *Different Seasons*, and one horror story in it is about a pregnancy and is called "The Breather Method."

Q: You've mentioned *Penthouse Forum* in two of your books—*Firestarter, Danse Macabre*...

KING: Along with everyone else, I believed the letters were staff-written. And finally I changed my mind. But I don't think that most of the things happen. I think they are fantasies.

Q: Healthy fantasies?

KING: Sure. I would say that 90 percent of them are healthy. And some of them are tremendously clever. I'm kind of glad that *Forum* got away from the amputees and all that stuff.

No, I love *Forum* for one reason. It's because, sexually, I'm not terribly adventurous—which is to say that there are no orgies in my life.

I'm faithful to my wife. I don't go out when I'm in a strange city and get four dollies off the street and say, "Let's have a ménage à trois or Dom Perignon in your snatch"—or something like that. I like sex very much, and I'm highly sexed. I'd just as soon screw a lot, but compared with *Forum*, that's a little bit like saying I like steak and potatoes. And then you go into a fucking delicatessen and see people do *that!* I probably would never do it, because I would be embarrassed, or that Republican thing in me would come out, and I'd say, "Well, you're not going to get me into that rubber diaper."

Q: I think a lot of people might say they read Stephen King novels for the same thing.

KING: They can identify with it; they probably would never go out and do it.

Q: What about all the Stephen King imitators that are suddenly jumping on the bandwagon?

KING: There are quite a few. I don't know—most of them aren't any good. They have a hard time taking the material seriously. Maybe they're too bright. You get the feeling that they are stooping to the material. Maybe they are not having enough fun. Maybe they do it for the money.

Q: Several critics have accused you of the same misdemeanor.

KING: When people say that, they are so wrong—they are wrong across the board. That's the elitism that's inherent in more of the reviews. You can always tell a bad review coming, because it will be a review of my checkbook and my contractual agreements. A review like that will start out saying, "This is the third book in Stephen King's multi-million-dollar contract for New American Library," and then you know, well...the trouble's going to start.

Q: Care to mention any of the bankable rip-off artists we should stay away from?

KING: I won't mention any by name. But I see a lot of books that must have been inspired by some of the stuff I'm doing. For one thing, those "horror" novels that have gerund endings are just everywhere: *The Piercing, The Burning, The Searing*—the this-ing and the that-ing. It's a little embarrassing in a way, because *The Shining* was a title that I originally turned down. When I turned the manuscript in, it was *The Shine*. The contract had been issued that way. And one day we were sitting around talking about it, and the sub rights guy at Doubleday said, "Are you sure you want this book to go out under this title, with a Black cook in it?"

And I said, "What do you mean?" He told me that in World War II, a "shine" was another pejorative that meant the same thing as "nigger" or "coon." He said it was short for "shoeshine boy." I didn't know that, and the others in the conference room dismissed it.

I wasn't afraid that people would think that I was a racist; I was afraid that people would laugh at my not knowing. And, so, at that point, I said, "Let's change the name of the book." It was very late. They were getting ready to go to press and were setting the plates. And I said, "Suppose we call it *The Shining?*" And I just changed a few of the references in the book, changed the heads on the pages. And they said, "Okay."

Q: Do you usually encounter problems in coming up with the right title for a new book?

KING: Well, I've finished a book about five kids who are mostly rejects. They were kids in 1957, and the idea of the book is that they've grown up and have to come back to this town where they grew up and discover, as a result of phone calls that are made to them, that they have completely forgotten a whole year out of their childhood. They realize that something awful happened and that they have to go back and face it again. I got everything in this book. I got Frankenstein, Jaws, the Creature from the Black Lagoon—fucking King Kong is in this book. I mean, it's like the monster rally. Everybody is there. I thought it would be a good one to go out with. Called *It*. I should call it *Shit*.

With Randi Henderson

KING: There are times when I feel a little bit irritated at the publishers, who seem to think that the tour is a necessary adjunct to bestsellerdom. Or who have somehow got the idea, that publishers didn't used to have, that if your books sell well you ought to be some kind of celebrity, that that's yours by right, that you must want it. Or that you're writing books that are accessible and popular only because you want to be a celebrity.

That isn't the case for me at all. I can take it or leave it. But if I have to take it, I can only use it in small doses. I think it's poison anyway, if you take too much of it, it kills you.

I didn't go to the market. The market came to me. I write about ordinary people in extraordinary situations. I don't think I'll ever be re-membered as a literary giant. You can't help wanting to have the whole ball of wax. And besides, anybody who doesn't go for the whole ball of wax is stupid. I don't understand why somebody who writes decent good prose, who's able to tell a story, who's able to think, would want to turn up his nose at popular success, any more than I can understand why a good popular writer would not want to do the best work that he or she is capable of.

The ideas start out like dreams or something. You know the way you have a dream and a lot of disconnected elements make perfect sense, and when you wake up you say, gee, these things don't fit. And suddenly elements will kind of click together.

Writing itself, creative writing, just sitting down and getting your hooks into a story, sort of flying along with it, is like automatic writing or writing on a Ouija board. You just replace the Ouija board with an IBM Selectric. . . . [With *Carrie*], the movie made the book and the book made me. People have a vision of a Brinks truck pulling up at your house, Wells Fargo guards unloading great big sacks of currency. It doesn't work like that. The money is paid in increments.

Q: With real-life horrors abundant, why are manufactured terrors so popular?

KING: When you've got a lot of free-floating anxieties, the horror story or movie helps to sort of conceptualize them, shrink them down to size, make them concrete so they're manipulable. When you can do that, and then it's over at the end and it just sort of blows away, there's probably some minor catharsis involved.

I think it's a rehearsal for our own deaths. It's a way of trying to grasp all the various elements of what that means. I also think that there's a real element of, thank God it isn't me, in the situation. And there's sort of a childish fascination with death and disfigurement and torture and a lot of things that maybe isn't even morbid so much as it is childish curiosity.

CHAPTER SEVEN

THE BAD SEED

Why don't we all just go crazy when we know we're going to croak? Because the mind's a monkey. You put things in departments and you go ahead. You go on and plan for the future and assume that the future's going to work out okay. Yet we know that sooner or later we're all going to be eating worms, whether it's fifty years or sixty. It might be tomorrow. It might happen today.

With Joel Denver (R&R)

Q: From the music in the background to the mentions of radio stations in just about every book to your purchase of WZON, it's obvious you have a love for music and radio.

KING: Yeah, I've somehow worked a radio station into just about everything I've written. In *Christine* I mention "Rock 'n' Roll Heaven" and quote lines from many of my favorite rock songs, but in others I have made a lot of mentions of WLAM/Lewiston, which is near to where I grew up. In my books I created the fictional town of Castle Rock, which is served by WLAM.

Q: Why the constant mention of radio and music?

KING: Well, for me, radio, and in particular music, made me real as a kid. It's where I discovered my identity. You reach out and find something that belongs to you and it's yours. It's difficult to explain, but it's like a pair of shoes that fit you. My first record was a 78 rpm version of Elvis Presley's "Hound Dog." From that moment on I knew it's what I wanted, and I wanted all I could get.

I grew up listening to Joey Reynolds, Arnie Ginsberg, Cousin Brucie, Murray The K, all those guys. The essence of it for me was always AM rock. To me, FM rock—or as it's called now, AOR—was never exciting. The jocks generally sounded like they just dropped a 'lude and mumbled through their set. To me, this is contrary to the type of music they play and is still an outgrowth of the sixties. A sort of stoned outlook on the world.

Q: When did you buy WACZ, and why the call letter change to WZON?

KING: I actually assumed control right around Halloween, oddly enough. The station belonged to a corporation called Acton, hence the "AC" part of the calls. I figured since I was paying a lot of money for this station, why did I want to keep their calls? Since it's my station, I thought I'd put my own identity on it. Because of my book *The Dead Zone* and my love for *The Twilight Zone*, it seemed pretty natural.

The phrase "You're in the Rock Zone" fit in nicely, and people have picked up on it as well. Our bumper stickers and T-shirts have creepy logos and lettering to match. The idea for the skeleton with earphones wasn't my idea, but it sure works fine.

Q: The station has always had a "Z" in the calls, right?

KING: Years ago, it was WLBZ, then WACZ, now WZON, so it's always been known as Z62. My program director, Jim Marshall, wanted to keep a "Z" in the calls because of the identification factor. He may be blowing smoke, but I pay him to make these decisions. I'd be a fool not to listen to him.

Q: So you put a lot of trust in your people?

KING: The same can be said for people who say, "I know nothing about art, but I know what I like." In fact, *anyone* who owns a station should trust in his people. Over the last few months I've begun to learn about ratings, sales, day parts, and such. Jim knows what he's doing, and so does my general manager, Chris Bruce. They're both smart and aggressive, and so am I, but in my own line of specialization. In radio, I'm a babe in the woods and would be foolish to monkey around with something I know very little about.

Q: What are your thoughts on AM radio today?

KING: AM radio has turned into this hemophiliac that's bleeding to death in front of everyone's eyes. I hate to see it happen. These stations have turned into garden club interviews playing oleomargarine and such.

Q: Why did you buy this radio station, knowing the problems of AM?

KING: I bought it because I could, for the first reason. I also bought it because it's in my hometown, for another, and because it was rocking on AM. This is important to me, since it's a part of my past. To rock on AM is such a brave and unusual thing, especially to rock as hard as we do. This station rocks as hard as, if not harder than, some FM stations. Had I not bought it, I feared Acton would have sold it to another outside group, who would have programmed it with some AOR or country format.

This was also the chance to plow money into the community where I live. It's easy to buy things all over the country for tax purposes, but I bought this station to make money and see it grow. When you own things long-distance, you can't deal with the problems directly. Here, if there's a major problem I'm available to act if the station's hot water heater leaks and is going to short out the transmitter and electrocute everyone. It's also served as a bonus to my salespeople, who've been able to introduce me to clients. That's a bit tough for me, because I'm a bit on the shy side.

Q: Obviously you're not shy about putting your thoughts on paper. Will WZON become another form of your self-expression?

KING: Yes, it will become that. There are things we're going to do with WZON to make it an interesting station, and I've got to be able to harness some of my own talents to it. This is like the dry-run period, where I'm studying how everything runs. It's like I'm on my student driver's permit.

Eventually, we want to do some radio drama, or theater-of-the-mind programming. I used to listen to that stuff when I was a kid and have also been listening to the *CBS Mystery Theaters*. I don't think they're very good, and now I understand why. You've got to learn to image a story for a blind person, since radio is only an aural medium. Even worse is the point of view. A camera can define that for you as a viewer, where all you have is the microphone in radio, so you've got to be very specific about the setting.

I've been working on the screenplay of *The Stand* with long-time friend George Romero. Actually, it would make an incredible serial for a radio drama. We've tried to hang on to the radio rights for all of my books, so this may be something to work on down the road.

Q: Is WZON broadcasting in AM stereo yet?

KING: No, but it's going to as soon as possible, probably by fall. I think AM is going to have a tough struggle going into the eighties, so I've not chosen an easy road for my first venture into broadcasting.

Q: Do you have thoughts on purchasing an FM sister station or other FM properties outside of the market?

KING: Yes, these are things I've been thinking about all along, but for the near future they aren't in the picture. One step at a time. If I can buy an FM in Bangor, then fine. Eventually a TV station too. I'm interested in all phases of communication, but I don't want to interfere with my writing career.

Q: Aside from interviews, have you ever spent any time as a disk jockey?

KING: No, I can't do it. In fact I've got to do a stint for WHSN, a college station, very soon. I'm not able to carry it off. I stumble around and am not able to put that sunshine in my voice that's necessary. I have an extreme admiration for those folks who do, including my own at WZON. They work very hard, and I think they're the best.

Q: Your music director, Michael O'Hara, told me the first thing you wanted WZON to do was rock harder.

KING: True. Little by little I've learned they're right about not playing AC/DC in the morning. I'd love to wake people up to that because it just seems natural to hear something lively and loud at that time of day. I love AC/DC, Motley Crüe, Twisted Sister, and such. I'm just not into classy rock music.

Q: Do you think there are other closet rockers out there in your generation?

KING: I sure do. WZON rocks hard and it sets us apart. When the ratings come out, I think we'll be on top as always. Over at WGUY, they play a lot more Black music than we do. It's a carryover from the fifties and the sixties when Dow Air Force Base (now Bangor International) was in existence; the population of the base was about 75 percent Black. As a result the area became accustomed to a lot of R&B, so we play it as well.

Q: Other than suggestions to rock harder, have you made any other contributions to the programming of WZON?

KING: Just a few. I don't even maintain an office at the station because I don't want to make them think I'm looking over their shoulders. First of all, my writing sucks up so much of my time I don't have the time or desire to meddle in the programming. Second, I've got a tremendous manager in Chris Bruce. Third, these guys were totally on their own for a long time when Acton didn't take much of an interest in the station and they did fabulous. If I was in there every day they might ask themselves, "Doesn't that son of a bitch ever go home?" They know I listen and that I'm in control, but I've got to let the radio professionals run the station.

Q: But you have left your mark on the station by airing a couple of humorous editorials.

KING: Yeah, and we've gotten our share of responses from them. We did one on the "Napkin Barrens," which is an area in Maine where they grow linen napkins for restaurants. We also did one on the missing three miles of the turnpike. There was one on a new fast-food franchise called "Corpus Delicious," featuring fast food served by the dead. I delivered most of them in a flat Paul Harvey type of voice. They were more for entertainment than anything. The editorials ran for six weeks and were stopped for fear of beating them into the ground.

My wife Tabitha also did one, calling herself Ruta Magowan, using a real Maine down-easter accent. She talked about Santa being a commie because of his red suit, and how NORAD was powerless to stop him. It really got a lot of laughs. This one was day-parted so it wouldn't upset children, which is something I wouldn't have considered before coming into this business.

Q: What kind of reaction have you evoked from other Bangor broadcasters?

KING: I'm sure some of them think this is just Stephen King's new little play toy. But WZON is very important to me. While I'm not optimistic about the future of AM overall, I've got a good situation here in terms of audience, marketing, and the number of AM-only cars and homes. We're holding our breath and hoping everything will be cool.

Q: From your experience as an author, you realize the value of promotion. How do you feel about spending promotional dollars when they come out of your pockets?

KING: When WZON comes to me for money for a good purpose, I simply sign the check. If I put $60,000 into a contest in a market this size, I'd be using a "money club" to win listeners. Sure, we give away money tying in with our bumper stickers, but we do it in smaller, easy-to-handle doses. They only win if ours is the only radio bumper sticker. We tell the audience we don't want to share you with anyone. In addition, we have "Z-cards" which are good for discounts all over the area.

Q: What about salaries? Are your wages comparable to bigger markets?

KING: Nah, slave wages; most of them are on food stamps! Actually, I think I pay them very well when matched against the standards of the market, and by comparison to what they made under Acton. You've got to pay for good people, and I believe in making my people happy.

With Martha Thomases and John Robert Tebbel (*High Times*)

Q: Why do you think that parapsychological investigation is not well-regarded among mainstream scientists and medical researchers?

KING: Because they can't see it. They can't wear it. It's as simple as that. You're dealing with empirical results from something that can't be seen or weighed or felt or hefted or split in a cyclotron. You're talking about people that might have 20 hits out of 25 on those Rhine cards at Duke, and what scientists are reduced to saying is, "Well, hey, he did it. But it was coincidence." Even if the odds may be millions and millions to 1.

They can't say, "Well, we'll investigate it" because, for instance with telepathy, it's a capricious phenomenon. People can hit 20 out of 25, come back a week later, and hit 12 out of 25.

Q: Where do you think that research is going to go in the future?

KING: Unless there's some kind of significant breakthrough, I don't think it's going to go anywhere. It will stay pretty much where it's been. One of the things that *Firestarter* tried to say is it's gotten to the point where people are saying, "Don't think about it, just do it. If it works let's use it and let's never mind what causes it or anything else." Which is a military and scientific philosophy this country has always pursued.

When we blew the first atomic bomb at White Sands near the end of the war, nobody knew what was going to happen. There was a theory that the chain reaction would continue forever. And we would have created a little tiny sun out there in the desert that would burn until the end of the universe. It wasn't a widely held theory, but it was a theory that nobody had a way of disproving. There were people who thought it wouldn't go off at all, that it would simply sit out there and melt and produce a great big dirty cloud of radioactivity. Nobody knew.

We've got appropriations in this country right now for psychic research. But when they say "psychic research," they're not really interested in psychic research. They're interested in producing experts who can read thoughts so they can chuck this guy over to Czechoslovakia or somewhere, where he can tell us where the silos are and that sort of thing, simply by reading thoughts.

The Russians are spending more than we are. They have an installation in Siberia where they test these guys. And it's a matter of "We don't know what makes it work, but then we didn't really know what made the atomic bomb work, either."

Q: Do you believe organizations like The Shop really exist?

KING: I don't think that they exist as one corporate entity under one roof. But I think elements of The Shop exist in the CIA and probably in the DSA [Department of Scientific Activities] in this country. And I think that a lot of that stuff has gone on.

It comes and goes. Right now, there's probably more sunlight than there's been in ten years. I think there are a lot of projects like the one that's described in *Firestarter* that go through the Senate with things that say, "This is for a study of the mating call of tsetse flies." In reality, the money is being shunted aside, either to study telepathy or to study new and better ways of improving the neutron bomb, or chemical and biological warfare, or anything at all.

Q: Do you think that drug research similar to what's described in *Firestarter* is going on, too?

KING: I think what they've done with it primarily is to use it as a sort of arm lock on somebody when you need information, a kind of brainwashing technique.

I don't know if there's ever been any testing in the files to find out whether or not LSD or mescaline or any of those things can pop psychic talents. D. H. Lawrence claimed they did. He claimed he could communicate back and forth with friends when he was high.

I got a letter from a guy last week. I would have taken it to have been just another crazy letter except that the guy was very well spoken and very low key. He had known, supposedly, this guy who had visions. This fellow had predicted back in 1948 the end of the world in a cataclysm. Just this year he realized that what he'd actually seen was a scene from *The Empire Strikes Back*. Maybe that's what Edgar Cayce saw all those years ago, just a piece of *Star Wars*. "That's okay. Don't worry, folks."

Q: Your books describe parenting very effectively. Do you spend a lot of time at it?

KING: I spend a lot of time parenting because I'm home. A friend of mine told me that the average father sees each kid an average of twenty-two minutes a week, which I found almost unbelievable. Mine are in my hip pocket all the time. And I like it that way.

When I knew I was going to be able to write full-time, I wondered,

"What's going to happen to the relationships within my family? Are they going to change? Is it going to be the kind of deal where you say, 'I can't take this! Get me out of here! I can't stand these screaming kids!'" The way it turned out was, I was able to change the diapers okay after I stuck the pin through my fingers a few times. I had a dawning realization that children are not particularly hard to deal with. I think a lot of people say to themselves, "If I'm going to be a parent, I've got to be a perfect parent. It's just too much responsibility. It's too hard." They've got an image that it's going to be a twenty-four-hour-a-day security-service kind of deal. And it's not.

It's a trip. It's like being in a time machine, too. You go back. If you don't have kids, a lot of things they experience, you never have a chance to reexperience: taking kids to Disney pictures and watching *Bambi* and saying, "Jeez, what schlocky shit this is." And then you start to cry, 'cause it pushes the old buttons.

Q: Disney is known for his scary material.

KING: Those cartoons are all rated G. It's really funny. There are kids all over the world who still have complexes over Bambi's father getting shot by the hunter and Bambi's mother getting crisped. But that's the way it's always been. This is the sort of material that appeals to kids. Kids understand it instinctively. They grip it.

We live in a society now where the sexual taboo for children has really passed by the wayside. Any nine-year-old can go into a 7-Eleven and check out the Playmate of the Month, but you don't want your kids to know about death. You don't want your kids to know about disfigurement. You don't want 'em to know about creepy things because it might warp their little minds.

Little kids' minds are very, very strong. They bend. There's a lot of tensile strength and they don't break. We start kids off on things like "Hansel and Gretel," which features child abandonment, kidnapping, attempted murder, forcible detention, cannibalism, and finally murder by cremation. And the kids love it.

Q: Do you agree that scary tales are an important socializing force?

KING: A lot of fairy tales are thinly disguised hostility raps against parents. Kids know that they can't make it on their own, that if they were left alone, they would die.

I've always thought it would be fun to update "Hansel and Gretel." I'd have these white parents in the suburbs with an income of $50,000 or

$60,000. Daddy loses his job, and the wicked stepmother says, "We could get along, we could keep our Master-Card, if you'd just get rid of those shitty kids." Finally the father hires a limo and tells the driver, "Drop 'em off on Lenox Avenue in Harlem at two in the morning." These two little white kids land there. They're menaced. And this supposedly nice Black lady says, "Would you like some candy?"

Kids know they can't make it alone, yet at the same time, built into each one of us, is a survival ethic. It says, "Nobody cares, and you have to look out for yourself and if you don't, you'll die." These two things work against each other. I think most kids are very frightened of their parents, and that's what all fairy tales reflect: Parents will fail you and you'll be left on your own. But, of course, everything comes out right in the end and the parents take you back.

Q: In *Firestarter* the parents are the ones who are apprehensive about their child's psychic powers. Do you feel that? Are you ever a little wary of your own children?

KING: Well—not yet. The one thing about kids is that you never really know exactly what they're thinking or how they're seeing. Kids are bent. After writing about kids, which is a little bit like putting the experience under a magnifying glass, you realize you have no idea how you thought as a kid. You can remember things about your childhood, but I've come to the conclusion that most of the things that we remember about our childhood are lies. We can have dreams where we redream things that are truer than what we remember waking. We all have memories that stand out from when we were kids, but they're really just snapshots. You can't remember how you reacted because your whole head is different when you stand aside.

Q: The experience of childhood is much more benevolent in *The Shining* than in *Firestarter*.

KING: Well, Charlie McGee's a good kid, you know. It isn't that Charlie McGee wants to hurt anybody. After *Carrie*, people would say, "Why do you want to write about evil children?"

Everybody wants to psychoanalyze horror. They don't want to psychoanalyze a book like Gay Talese's *Thy Neighbor's Wife* or something like that. It's pretty much accepted that Americans should be interested in who they're diddling and how they're doing it.

But this is a *Popular Mechanics* country. What's really going on here is that they're discussing the rocketry of sex and they're saying, "You can do it, too." The Talese book is a kind of *Popular Mechanics* guide. Instead of "How to Put on a New Garage Door," it's "How You Can Get a Swingers' Club in Your Town."

But when it comes to horror there's this need to analyze. When this "evil children" fad happened, there was *The Exorcist* and *The Other* and *The Omen*. People would say, "What this really means is that Americans don't want to have kids anymore. They feel hostility toward their own children. They feel they're being tied down and dragged down." In fact, in most cases, what those books are about is nice children who are beset by forces beyond their control.

Certainly Regan in *The Exorcist* was not to blame for what happened to her. In *Carrie*, it's not really Carrie's fault anything happens to her. She's driven to it. And when she perpetuates destruction on her hometown, it's because she's crazy. She doesn't want to make fires any more than she wants to wet her pants. That image is made in the book, that correlative. And she's kind of driven to it after a while.

Q: The person who makes that connection in *Firestarter* is the assassin, Rainbird. He is an authority figure and seems to be pretty nasty. A lot of authoritarians in your books are pretty nasty. Do you think authority is a malignant force?

KING: I do. I think that the curse of civilization is its chumminess.

When we get together we have to have authority, or so we say. But it's like a cancer. Of course, if we just had chaos, nobody would have air conditioning and nobody would have Touch-Tone phones. So you have to say to yourself, "Do you want to be out there planting your crops with a stick and then shitting on your corn to make it grow? Or do you want to have the sort of society that we have?" Believe me, we bought it.

A lot of authority figures want to be good. I sense that, and yet at the same time I sense that authority, after a while, always leads to some kind of oppression. When the minority report comes in, what you do is run the minority out of town with a flaming cross. It's just the way things are.

But then again, that's what we fought Vietnam for. I think we fought Vietnam for the benefits of civilization, and certainly we fought it to oppose authority. To show our authority, to show we weren't weak. Isn't that what Nixon kept saying? "We have to show the world that we're not weak." So of course we ended up showing the world that we were, yep, weak. 'Cause we couldn't beat these kids in black pajamas.

Q: Are you saying that you can't have good without evil, that you can't perceive anything without its opposite?

KING: I'm not sure that it has so much to do with good and evil as it has to do with the question of chaos versus order. We all have this tendency to want order in our lives. I got such a kick out of watching my wife pack for me. She didn't want me to pack because I don't know what goes with what. And I have the same need in my life. I had to be on national TV twice this morning and this is really the rattiest jacket I own. But it's my *lucky* jacket. It brings order into my life.

All horror stories are really about this incursion of disorder on order. That moment in *The Exorcist*, the movie, where it starts in Georgetown, is total order. It's civilization. It's where people know what wine to order. Ellen Burstyn is upstairs in bed, and she wakes up and she hears a noise that sounds like a lion.

You say, "Oh, dear, something's getting out of order here." Order presupposes authority, and authority presupposes, sooner or later, that we'll all need hooves. It's going to happen sooner or later, isn't it? You know it is.

Q: Do we know? Why then do people carry on?

KING: Why don't we all just go crazy when we know we're going to croak? Because the mind's a monkey. You put things in departments and you go ahead. You go on and plan for the future and assume that the future's going to work out okay. Yet we know that sooner or later we're all going to be eating worms, whether it's fifty years or sixty. It might be tomorrow. It might happen today.

I always think about this when I go on a talk show, particularly when it's live. When J. R. Rodale was on *The Dick Cavett Show*, and Cavett said, "You eat all these health foods. How do you feel?" And Rodale said, "I never felt better in my life." A little while later, he keeled over.

This is the sort of thing that should drive anybody crazy. Yet we're sane. We go on. We have our little neuroses but we continue.

And that's why we can continue in the face of knowing that by 1985 there will be terrorist groups with homemade atomic weapons and sooner or later somebody will use one to impose their own idea of order on the West Bank or on Northern Ireland or wherever it happens to be. It's going to happen. I don't think there's any question about it. But what can you do, except compartmentalize and hope that things will go on a little while longer?

What do you do about the fact that Reagan's president? What do you do about that? Do you go crazy? The man strikes me as extremely dangerous. But I can't go hide under my bed.

I've got a boy who's eight, Joe Hill, and he puked during the Iranian crisis. We used to watch the news at dinnertime, and he started to vomit about the news. I mean literally. He grew pale and left the table and then vomited. Finally I said, "It's the news. It's bumming you out, isn't it?" He said, "Yeah. Every time I hear it my stomach's like a fist." So what we did was watch the news late at night. I don't know what else to do.

He hasn't learned to compartmentalize. When you're eight, the tunnel vision isn't developed yet and you have a tendency to see everything. If we saw the consequences of where we are now, if we raised our heads more often from the job we have to do and the next thing that's going on, it would be very, very frightening.

Q: Is the repression of drugs a good idea? Gore Vidal has been quoted to the effect that no drugs need be illegal because, after all, no one eats Drano.

KING: That can't happen because that's the antithesis of order, to say we don't have the authority to regulate these things. There's a constant struggle going on about how much will be illegal and how much you will be free to take. Can we open the pharmacies? Can we put Valium and Percodan and those sorts of things out on the shelves? I wouldn't take it. I don't know.

I thought it was very funny when McDonald's discontinued the very tiny coffee spoons that people could snort coke with. The last time I went to McDonald's I got a great big spoon, and you could snort a *lot* with that!

For some reason California's always been where the struggle is about how much authority you can impose on people's private lives. It seems to show up there most clearly. They had a helmet law for motorcycles in California and the bikies were saying things like, "It restricts my vision. I can't hear what my bike's doing. If it was on fire I wouldn't know it until my ass caught." And at the bottom line what the bikies were saying was, "Look, it's *my* goddamn head and if I want to splatter my brains all over the guardrails on the Coast Highway, super for me."

They kept the helmet law, and then the dentists decided that they ought to have a mouth-guard law. Because they were repairing all these shattered jaws and teeth. They said, "Football players wear mouth guards, and prizefighters wear mouth guards. We'll make the bikies wear mouth guards." It was the final straw, and the bikies came into Sacramento asking, "What happens next? Will I have to wear a jock when I get on my bike?" And they repealed the helmet law.

This is a dreadful thing to say, but I have wondered in my darker hours that, if everything were legal, wouldn't it be kind of a Darwinian solution to a lot of problems? Who are the bikies that you see who are cruisin' around with no helmet or with a hat turned around like that yoyo in Cheap Trick? They're dummies, and if they splatter their brains all over the sidewalk, they're not going to be collecting food stamps.

The one thing I could never swallow in the sixties was this idea that Nixon and the Republicans of that time were totalitarian, fascistic, faceless things who wanted to take over and destroy the resistance movement and everything else. Yet they were saying, "Don't stone out your head with drugs. You can't do this. You can't do that. You can't do the other thing."

If you were a *really* fascistic society and you had a vocal minority that was shouting, "Stop this, stop that, stop the other thing," what you would say is, "Let's give them all the drugs they want."

In a lot of states, something very much like that happened. They lowered the drinking age to eighteen and said, "Get juiced."

Q: There's a theory that the reason marijuana is now so popular is that it's the perfect drug to keep the young people quiet. And you have to say, "Don't do it," so they'll do it.

KING: "Don't throw me in that briar patch!" That's kind of interesting. I've never really thought of that.

Q: Maine is a decriminalized state. Do you think that's a good idea?

KING: I do approve of that. I think that marijuana should not only be legal, it should be a cottage industry. It would be wonderful for the state of Maine. There's some pretty good homegrown dope. I'm sure it would be even better if you could grow it with fertilizers and have greenhouses.

What we've got up there are lobsters and potatoes. And a lot of poor people. My wife says, and I agree with her, that what would be really great for Maine would be to legalize dope completely and set up dope stores the way that there are state-run liquor stores. You could get your Acapulco gold or your whatever it happened to be—your Augusta gold or your Bangor gold. And people would come from all the other states to buy it, and there could be a state tax on it. Then everybody in Maine could have a Cadillac.

I don't smoke very much marijuana at all anymore because I'm afraid of additives, which come from decontrol and deregulation. Anybody can squirt anything into it that they want to. And that scares me. I don't like the idea.

My idea of what dope is supposed to be is to just get mellow. And what I do, if I smoke it anymore, is when I'm driving to the movies, to smoke a couple real quick so I can sit there in the first row. It's kind of interesting and they have all that good munchie food, too, you don't have to make yourself.

Q: Randy Newman once told an interviewer that wanting to be mellow is like wanting to be senile.

KING: I've known people who were so laid back that they just weren't there. They might as well be dead.

I drink a lot of beer, and that's the drug of choice. You find the drug that works for you. I know, for instance, this guy named Harlan Ellison—and he's not alone—who's very proud of the fact that he doesn't put dope into his body. He tries not to put additives into his body, or anything like that. But he can afford to do that because Harlan's drug of choice is Harlan.

Q: When you wrote about the horror genre in *Danse Macabre*, why did you start in the fifties?

KING: There were no horror movies or horror books to speak of in the forties. I picked the fifties because that pretty well spans my life as an appreciator—as somebody who's been involved with this mass cult of horror, from radio and movies and Saturday matinees and books.

In the forties there really wasn't that much. People don't want to read about horrible things in horrible times. So, in the forties there was Val Lewton with *The Cat People* and *The Curse of the Cat People* and there wasn't much else.

Q: What do you think is the difference between a scary book and a scary movie?

KING: A scary movie puts a lot of people, a mob, in one place. There are advantages to that because the panic runs through the audience. If it's a good movie, the fear jumps from one person to the next. You can find yourself screaming just because everybody around you is screaming. There's a real atmosphere of terror.

It's also visual, which means that you can't look away from this thing—it's *happening*. You're in the dark. It's like a nightmare. It's like a dream. It's very, very visual. It works on all those levels.

The advantage to books is to take the reader and cut him out of the pack and work on him one on one. It has its advantages because the people that are there in the movie theater really *are* a mob. If you get one guy alone you can do a more efficient job of scaring him.

Q: One review said you use the technique of cataloging—setting up a complete, mundane, comfortable world with name-brand products and familiar language.

KING: That's my world. On a larger scale, any world will do as long as the reader can touch it. The reader is like a guy in space. You create this world and the ideas must get him down there. Then, if you're writing this kind of novel, you take his spaceship away so he can't get out. Then you stick it to him as well as you can.

But the first thing you have to do is create any kind of environment that the reader can identify with totally. That doesn't mean that it has to be something that everybody knows about, or that you have to say Triscuit or Colgate in every book. There are certain things that run through society. Anywhere in New York, anywhere in the country, somewhere there's going to be a Coke sign. People identify with Coke. You can write a novel about New York and people from the country will read it if they feel that you've made them familiar with New York.

That's why I've never written a book using the city as a setting, because I don't know it well enough yet. God knows there are opportunities. Somewhere in Central Park there's a deserted subway tunnel that's just sort of sitting there.

Q: Hitchcock has said he was performing a service, that there was too much order and he injected some needed chaos into our lives.

KING: Part of us really responds to that. By writing a horror novel where this inexplicable disorder takes over in our ordered lives, you make order look better by comparison. But below that, there's a part of us that responds to the Who bashing their instruments to pieces on the stage. There's a very primitive part that says, "Do it some more."

There was a game on TV a while ago called *Supermarket Sweep*. You ran around and got everything. I never really wanted to win that show. This was when I was much younger. I never wanted to go and grab things. What I wanted was for them to let me loose in there for an hour with a sledgehammer. Or imagine it in Tiffany's. With a sledgehammer. They would say, "For an hour, do what you want." If I got the chance to do that—I wouldn't do it, but I would *want* to do it.

At a lot of county fairs you see this. Somebody will get a moderately good used car and put it up on a pedestal. Then, for a quarter or 50 cents you can have three whacks at it, with a sledgehammer. They always make money.

Q: In *Firestarter* you set up The Shop as a model of diabolical authority, and then it's revealed to be less powerful than we thought.

KING: The thing about The Shop is that you see it first as a monolithic authority, and when you get down to the bottom you just see a bunch of hairy bureaucrats doing their job. The thing that worries me more than monolithic authority is that there may be no such thing, and that if you could meet Hitler, at the end you would just find this hairy little bureaucrat saying, "Where are my maps? Where are my armies? Gee whiz, gang, what happened?"

A lot of people were disappointed in Flagg at the end of *The Stand* because he turns out to be a straw man. But that's always been my view. I have a friend who claims that the devil was in Lyndon Johnson. "The devil entered Lyndon Johnson when he became president and forced him to do all those awful things in Vietnam." And this guy says that when Johnson went on TV after the New Hampshire primary and wouldn't stand for reelection, that he actually saw the devil *leave* Johnson's face. I wonder if there isn't a lot of truth in that.

David Berkowitz, for instance—Son of Sam—if they fried him in the chair, strapped him in and threw the switch, would they be getting whatever did it? That's the question. Because he's just sort of a guy that's getting a little bit fat now, who sits around and writes letters to the papers and that sort of thing.

Manson is a bald gardener in California in a sort of middle-security prison. He doesn't want to get out. He's afraid somebody will kill him if he gets out.

Q: In lieu of punishing the criminal, what could society do? Regulate television more closely? Take the billboards off the highways?

KING: I don't think any of that stuff will work. I think that these things are inbred and you can't get them out, any more than you can get an egg out of a shell without making some kind of hole in it. We're stuck with it.

Human beings have got a lot of good, noble impulses inside them, and most people want to be good and do more good than they do evil. Hell, we've had nuclear weapons now for thirty or thirty-five years and nothing's happened yet. That in itself seems to be a miracle. If Reagan pushes the button or somebody pushes the button in Russia or somebody pushes it in Costa Rica, they can put a big tombstone in outer space that says, "We gave it a good try." Because we have.

There's two kinds of evil that horror fiction always deals with. One kind is the sort of evil that comes from inside people, like in *Dr. Jekyll and Mr. Hyde,* where Jekyll makes this potion because he wants to go out and rampage at night and doesn't want anybody to know.

The other kind of evil is predestined evil. It falls on you like a stroke of lightning. That's the scary stuff, but, in a way, it's the stuff you don't have to worry about. I mean, if we went out and worried about getting hit by lightning, that's too much. I have to worry about whether or not I'm getting cavities. I have to worry about whether these cigarettes are giving me cancer. Those are things I can change. Don't give me lightning out of a clear sky. If that hits me, I just say, "That's probably the way God meant it to be."

But that's the thing in *Dracula,* too. There are a lot of people in *Dracula* who are wiped out who are good people, and you ask, "What did they do to deserve this?" In most cases, they didn't do anything.

Q: How did you hook up with George Romero?

KING: He came by one day. He was on his way through Maine and he was going to speak at a college in New Hampshire. He called and said, "How about if I drop by?" He said, "Can we do anything together?" At the end of the afternoon, because I admired his work and everything, I ended up saying, "These are the things that are not optioned." I just sort of put everything out and said, "Take what you want." And he said, "Let's do *The Stand.*"

Q: Is there a relationship between humor and fear?

KING: You bet there is. Think of all the gags you ever heard that have to do with dismemberment, or something that's horrible in one way or another, even if it's just horrible in the sense that somebody's being embarrassed.

What do kids laugh at? Kids laugh if your fly's down. That's hilarious. For the kid whose fly is down, it's a horrible situation.

The funniest cartoon I ever saw has this little schmo in a French restaurant with this waiter bearing down on him with this maniacal expression on his face. He's got a tray in one hand, with this awful smoking charred thing on it, and he's screaming at the poor customer, "It's a fried telephone book, and *you* ordered it."

With Jack Matthews

KING: Horror is one of the ways we walk our imagination. It's a way to relieve bad feelings rather than something that causes them.... It does have a bad effect on some people, makes them scared, they can't sleep, they have nightmares. But those people, after one or two experiences like that, will avoid horror the same way a person who vomits after a roller coaster ride will avoid roller coasters.

Nightmares are another way we exorcise our emotions, our feelings of insecurity, and they come right out of our own imaginations.... That's a wonderful thing.

My mom hated those gruesome E. C. Comics of the fifties, but she let me read them... until the nightmares started. Nightmares where people were on baseball teams disemboweling the bad guys and lining the base paths with their intestines. That was one of my favorites. They used his head for the ball, and this one eye was bulging out as the bat hits it.

That's when she said, "OK, that's enough," and started taking them away. And that's when I started buying them and putting them under my bed.... She'd catch me and say, "Why are you filling your head with that junk?" I said, "Someday, I'm going to write that junk."

I love the irony in the E. C. Comics. I remember one story about a fat man married to a thin woman. Both of them were plotting to kill the other. Finally, the fat man stuffed an air compressor hose down his wife's throat and blew her up like a dirigible until she burst all over everything.

After committing the murder, he's walking upstairs where she'd rigged this safe to fall on him. Splat! It flattens him out. So, the thin one gets fat, the fat one gets thin. Ho, ho, ho. A little irony is good for the heart.

*　　　*　　　*

I don't think I ever will be taken seriously. People write to me and say how much they enjoy my books, but when someone walks by with a book by John Barth in their hands, they hide me so they won't get caught.

That goes with the genre but I think you can do serious work in horror and fantasy. You can reach people of all ages, provide a catharsis, and give them a way to get rid of some of their bad feelings.

In some ways, I feel like those Welsh sin eaters who took on the sins of the dying so they could go to heaven. Of course, the sin eater would go to hell at the end of his life, because by then his soul would be black with the sins he'd eaten.

My soul must be very black, indeed.